To Lucille

BARBARA F. VUCANOVICH

From Nevada to Congress, and Back Again

BARBARA F. VUCANOVICH
AND PATRICIA D. CAFFERATA

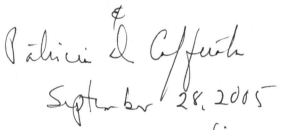

So glad you have returned to Nevada.

Barbara F Vucanovich

& Patricia D Cafferata

September 28, 2005

Winnemucca

UNIVERSITY OF NEVADA PRESS

Reno & Las Vegas

University of Nevada Press, Reno, Nevada 89557 USA
Copyright © 2005 by University of Nevada Press
Manufactured in the United States of America
Design by Barbara Jellow

Library of Congress Cataloging-in-Publication Data
Vucanovich, Barbara F., 1921–
Barbara F. Vucanovich: from Nevada to Congress, and back again / Barbara F. Vucanovich
and Patricia D. Cafferata.
p. cm.
Includes index.
ISBN 0-87417-623-9 (hardcover : alk. paper)
1. Vucanovich, Barbara F., 1921– 2. Legislators—United States—Biography. 3. Women legislators—United States—Biography. 4. United States. Congress. House—Biography. 5. Nevada—Politics and government—20th century. 6. Politicians—Nevada—Biography. 7. United
States—Politics and government—1945–1989. 8. United States—Politics and government—
1989– 9. Republican Party (U.S. : 1854–)—Biography. 10. Politicians—United States—Biography—Miscellanea. I. Cafferata, Patricia D., 1940– II. Title.
E840.8.V83A3 2005
328.73'092—dc22   2005006543

The paper used in this book meets the requirements of American
National Standard for Information Sciences—Permanence of Paper
for Printed Library Materials, ANSI Z.48-1984. Binding
materials were selected for strength and durability.

First Printing
14   13   12   11   10   09   08   07   06   05   5   4   3   2   1

Frontispiece: Barbara F. Vucanovich. Photograph by Bret Hofmann.
Collection of Barbara F. Vucanovich

For my grandchildren—Elisa, Farrell, Reynolds, Mike Jr., Trevor,
Jennifer, Casey, Heather, Nora, Maggie, Patrick, Katie, Scott
and David, and my grandchildren by marriage—Robb, D.J.,
and Janaya—and for my great-grandchildren—Brendan, Morgan,
Kenton, Philomena, Elizabeth, Patrick, Madelein, and Amelia,
my great-grandchildren by marriage—Monica and Kelley,
my great-grandsons by adoption—Dean and Quinn—and for any new
children that join my family in the future

CONTENTS

LIST OF ILLUSTRATIONS

PREFACE

Barbara F. Vucanovich: From Nevada to Congress, and Back Again would not have been possible without the assistance of family and friends. I was reluctant to even write about my life because the idea seemed so self-serving. I was persuaded, however, that my grandchildren and perhaps others would be interested in learning about my life experiences.

I told my story to my older daughter, Patty Cafferata, for an hour at a time over a five-year period. She wrote it down, and I polished it up after careful review. Bill Martin, Mike Pieper, Dale Erquiaga, and my granddaughter Elisa Maser spent untold hours reviewing, editing, and making suggestions. Their help has made this story much more readable, and I am grateful to them.

Dick Horton, one of my dearest friends and chairman of all my campaigns, was willing to assist me again by offering comments on this book. His insights are as valuable as they have always been. Mike Pieper, my former administrative assistant, helped with some research on my time in the House. I thank them all for their help.

This book is a first for Nevada. Of the thirty-two Nevada members of the House of Representatives, none of them wrote a formal autobiography. Thomas Fitch reminisced about his life in some newspaper articles that were later compiled into a book by Eric Moody. I am the first woman to be elected to federal office from Nevada and the first person—male or female—to represent the Second Congressional District of Nevada.

The book is divided into four parts. Part I, "Far from the House," is about my parents, my family, and my early involvement in Nevada politics before I ran for office. Part II, "A Flamingo in the Barnyard of Politics," covers my campaigns and fourteen years in the House. In Part III, "Not Your Average Congressman," I talk about my breast cancer, my views on the issues, and my thoughts on those people with whom I served in Congress. Part IV, "Back in the Great State of Nebraska," discusses my activities outside the House, including the presidents I have known and the world beyond America's borders. The story closes with my retirement and return to Nevada in Part V, "Home Means Nevada."

There is no greater honor than to represent Nevada in the House of Representatives. But politics was only a small part of my life. I have enjoyed some wonderfully high moments and some painfully low ones, ranging from the births of my children, grandchildren, and great-grandchildren to the deaths of two husbands and my oldest son. Parts of this story have not been easy to tell, but the difficulties in my life have been outweighed by the joy I found in my family and my friends. Being a tough grandmother has been a wonderful experience.

PART I

Far from the House

CHAPTER ONE

Grandmothers and Grandfathers— Tough and Not So Tough

The arrival of Elisa Piper Cafferata, my first "grandbaby," in May 1962, was as apolitical as it gets. I had no idea that one day I would be campaigning for Congress and calling myself a "tough grandmother" in television commercials. In fact, when Elisa joined our family, I still felt much more like a mother than a grandmother. My youngest child, Susie, was two and a half years old. Elisa's birth was a defining moment, although I didn't see it that way at the time. Little did I know that her birth, and those of her two siblings, Farrell and Reynolds, and fourteen cousins, would come to define my political persona twenty years later.

I was an "army brat." After World War I, my parents were stationed in Louisville, Kentucky, where my oldest brother, Thomas Francis Farrell Jr., was born, in April 1920 at Camp Zachary Taylor. Another move brought the family to Camp Dix, New Jersey, where I was born on June 22, 1921.

I have no idea why my parents picked my name, Barbara. When I was growing up, my family called me "Bobby." Later, I chose "Joan" as my confirmation name at age eleven or twelve. From then on, I was Barbara Joan Farrell until I married.

Shortly after my birth, the family moved to Camp Humphreys, now known as Fort Belvoir, Virginia, where the engineering school was located. We later moved to West Point, New York, where Dad taught engineering to the cadets at the United States Military Academy.

In 1926 we moved to Albany, and I started school at Vincentian, a

Catholic school run by the Sisters of Mercy. They were tough women, and I didn't like them very much. I was a maverick—always fighting with them over religion. I lasted there two years before my mother, deciding that I was a nonconformist, moved me to Miss Quinn's Academy, a small Catholic school. Classes consisted of six to eight students in each grade. There were eight grades taught in four classrooms, and I skipped the fifth grade because I was the only student in it. From then on I was the youngest in all my classes.

My father had resigned from the regular army, entered the reserves and was appointed commissioner of canals and waterways for the State of New York by Governor Alfred E. Smith. He was subsequently chief engineer for the New York State Department of Public Works, with appointments from New York governors Franklin Delano Roosevelt and Herbert H. Lehman.

A registered Democrat, my father served in the New York State Democrat administrations, except when he was on active duty in the army, but he and my mother were never involved in regular party politics. In their day, Albany, the state capital, was controlled by the Democrat machine, so Democrats were appointed to state positions. Most everyone in town was a Democrat, including most of my parents' friends. Dad was a Catholic, family-oriented, and fiscally conservative. He identified with the Democratic Party's concern about the "little guy," with compassion for the less fortunate. In later years, my father felt that the Democratic Party no longer represented his values and views, but he saw no reason to change parties.

I had no idea how well connected my father was politically, but I got an idea of his contacts in 1928, when I was seven years old and he took me to New York City to the Waldorf Astoria. Dad and I were dancing together when Governor Smith cut in to dance with me. Smith, a Democrat, was running against Republican Herbert Hoover for president. Of course, since my dad worked for Governor Smith, my parents were against Hoover, the first president I remember. Not long after Hoover was elected, the newspaper printed an insert about him with his picture on the front. I remember taking a pencil and poking holes in it, then gleefully showing it to my parents.

One morning in January of 1929, I was at home with the chicken pox. My mother was away from the house, so I was the first to learn that my grandfather Farrell had died of a stroke. I remember feeling totally devastated because I thought he was great, a wonderful man. I'll always remember how hard it was to pick up our black candlestick-type telephone to call my dad at his office to tell him about his father. My father was always calm in the face of a crisis and always matter-of-fact. True to form, he reacted no differently to the news of my grandfather's death than he would have to any other crisis. I never saw Dad give in to his grief; I think our family still carries on this tradition of stoicism even today.

I have many wonderful memories of my parents and grandparents while I was growing up. Every summer my mother would take my brother, Tommy, and me by train from Albany to Denver to spend a month visiting her mother and Granddaddy Buck. He was the commanding officer at Fitzsimmons Hospital in Denver, so they led a formal life. As the commandant's wife, my grandmother was "at home" every Wednesday for ladies to come calling. On the front hall table rested a tray where the ladies left their calling cards, a tradition that today has been lost.

Mealtimes were formal, too, often consisting of several courses. Meals were announced with a round Chinese gong. Lunch and dinner always included a hot homemade soup. Granddaddy was a great tease with a wonderful sense of humor. He started many meals by asking who had stuck their gum under the table, and we were always surprised to be caught!

Granddaddy Buck had a driver for most of his career, and as a result he was not a good driver when he was on his own. Nonetheless, one summer in the 1930s Granddaddy drove his dark green Packard on a tour of the West with my father, Tommy, and me. I remember that he attached a swamp cooler to the car window, and we carried water for it in a canvas bag that we hung on the front of the car. We visited Yellowstone, Yosemite, the new Hoover Dam, and Las Vegas, my first trip to Nevada. What I remember most about the trip, aside from the swamp cooler, was how hot and dusty it was in Las Vegas. The town's population was much less than ten thousand, and very few streets were even paved.

Often during the summer, too, we would drive to Rehoboth Beach, Delaware, from our home in Albany. Mother liked to swim in the ocean, so we would spend a month at the beach, at Mrs. Downs's boardinghouse.

Our rooms were on the second floor, and Tommy and I often got into a lot of trouble for staying up late listening to radio shows like *The Goldbergs, Amos 'n Andy,* and *The Great Gildersleeve.* During the day, slapping vinegar all over ourselves in hopes of getting a tan, we sometimes spied on the Catholic nuns at the local convent, who used a neighboring beach. We loved to watch them in their black swimming outfits and bloomers. I also remember watching Mrs. Downs wring the neck of a chicken she was preparing for dinner, an experience that ruined chicken for me for the rest of the summer.

After I graduated from Miss Quinn's, I attended high school at the Episcopalian Albany Academy for Girls, graduating at age sixteen. I was a B student, but I hated Latin and geometry. I flunked or barely passed both subjects and had to take them over again in college. At the academy, I learned to ride horseback and spent most Saturdays competing in horse shows. Gym class was problematic since I was too short for basketball and hated baseball—but I did love field hockey. The one class I'll never forget was public speaking. We were not allowed to prepare. The teacher just called on us in class. The first time that happened I was paralyzed; I couldn't and didn't say a word—quite a start for a future politician.

I had just turned seventeen years old when Mother and Dad took me to Manhattanville College of the Sacred Heart in New York City. Manhattanville's beautiful campus was located in Harlem, and we were not allowed to go out alone at night. During the day we walked from building to building to attend classes. Every afternoon the nuns joined us for tea served with cookies. The nuns were bright and interested in us. They were Madames of the Sacred Heart, so we called them "Mother" rather than "Sister."

The first night I was there, a hurricane hit the city. There I was, in this old, old building, and my parents had just left. I was in the shower when the lights went out, and I couldn't find my way to my room. I was terrified. All I wanted was to go home. My parents wisely did not let me come home every weekend. Ultimately, I survived the year and dealt with my homesickness. In the end, I actually liked the school.

I missed my family so much that I lasted at Manhattanville for only about one school year. When I returned to Albany, I attended St. Rose College for six months and a business college for a while. At the time,

Horseback riding was one of my preferred activities during high school. I am pictured here in an *Albany Times-Union* photograph. The caption states: "Lassie appears to be the favorite mount of Miss Barbara Farrell, daughter of Major and Mrs. Thomas Farrell. Miss Farrell, who is a student at the Albany Academy for Girls, is entering her senior year there this fall. Miss Farrell is among those who will participate in the Troop B horse show, which will be held at the Troop B armory in October."

school wasn't a love of mine. My interests ran to boys, dating, horses, and bridge.

Looking back, it's no surprise that I married quite young. After getting through so many scrapes, I guess I felt like I could handle anything life sent my way. But marrying young helped shape me as a woman and, eventually, as a member of Congress. The person I became later in life was greatly influenced by my family heritage, my parents, my brothers and sister, my children, and my husbands.

Family Heritage

My mother's family was Spanish through my grandmother, Maria Ynez Shorb White, and English through my grandfather, Stephen Stuart White, who died long before I was born. My mother, Maria Ynez White, was born in Southern California and when she was a girl they called her Ynezita (Little Ynez) to distinguish her from her mother, although for most of her life her name was shortened to simply Cita.

My mother was five feet four inches tall and never overweight in my memory. She kept her naturally curly hair short, but she hated gray hair. As she grew older, she dyed her hair almost black. Later, Mother let the natural gray show. Her eyes were like shoe buttons, so black you could not see the edges of her pupils. She was even-tempered and always calm, yet I do not remember her ever sitting still. She loved her garden and her yard, which was planted with peonies, roses, and hollyhocks.

My grandmother was a lovely woman, taller and slightly heavier than my mother. She wore her dark hair in the style of the day, and I enjoyed watching her comb it in a pompadour puffed up with a "rat." Her eyebrows were thick and bushy (and perhaps that is why my mother plucked her own eyebrows down to a thin line).

Shopping with Grandmother was quite an expedition. She kept her money in a buttoned pocket in the leg of her bloomers, under a midcalf skirt or dress. I can still see her when she needed to make a purchase, modestly turning around and bending over to unbutton the secret pocket and retrieve her money.

Grandmother's first ancestor to arrive in California was José Antonio Yorba, who came via Mexico from Villafranca, Spain, in 1769. José Antonio was a sergeant in the Gaspar de Portola expedition that escorted Father Junipero Serra when he established missions up and down the California coast. The family was later awarded a 65,512-acre land grant, Rancho Santiago de Santa Ana, along the banks of the Santa Ana River, by the king of Spain, in what is now Orange County. José Antonio's third

My mother, Ynez White Farrell, was a descendent of one of the Spanish land grant families who developed Southern California. Mother was a gracious, charming woman who devoted her life to her family and to church. She was a lifelong Red Cross volunteer. I've patterned my life after her example of how to be a lady, wife, and mother.
Collection of Barbara F. Vucanovich

son, Don Bernardo Yorba, my mother's great-great-grandfather, was given an additional 13,000 acres, known as Rancho Canon de Santa Ana, by the government of Mexico in 1834. The Yorba family was known throughout California for its hospitality. Don Bernardo build a hundred-room hacienda, called San Antonio, with a small church and a school, which remains today. The Yorba name is still prominent in Southern California, thanks to the Yorba Regional Park and other landmarks.

On another branch of my California family tree, my great-great-grandfather, Benjamin D. "Don Benito" Wilson, was the first county clerk of Los Angeles and the first mayor of Los Angeles, elected in 1851. He later served in the California State Senate. My great-grandfather, James de

Barth Shorb, was elected Los Angeles County treasurer in 1892. They are the earliest recorded politicians in our family.

My grandmother Maria Ynez Shorb's first husband, my grandfather Stephen White, was born in Maryland. He was descended from an old, established American family who once held land grants directly from Lord Baltimore. Some of my grandfather's family members served in the American Revolution. Stephen, after graduating from Columbia University in 1885, was commissioned an assistant surgeon in the navy. He and Grandmother were married in 1894 at the Old Mission Church in San Gabriel, California.

Coincidentally, more than fifty years before I would live on Newlands Circle in Reno, my grandparents' wedding presents included two silver dishes from Congressman Francis G. Newlands of Nevada and a crystal dish and fork from Congressman Newlands's niece, Jessie. On my grandmother's list of gifts, she wrote that the address for the Newlandses was in San Francisco, California. I was surprised to read that, since Newlands represented Nevada in Congress at the time of the wedding.

In her old age, Jessie Newlands lived in Reno, where the Newlands Mansion still stands today. When I moved to Reno in the 1940s, my mother gave me a letter of introduction to her—the way to be properly introduced to someone in polite society in those days. She was cordial, but I sensed that she wasn't pleased that I was in Reno to get a divorce. A little more than a decade later, I moved into my house at 2 Newlands Circle in Reno.

Unfortunately, my grandparents' marriage was not a long one. In 1899 Stephen White died of ptomaine poisoning while he was stationed in Alaska. His death left my grandmother with two small children: my mother, Cita, born in 1896, and my Aunt Ruth, born in 1898.

Grandmother and my great-grandmother, Sue Wilson Shorb, lived in Southern California with my mother and Ruth until about 1907, when they moved to San Francisco. A year later, my grandmother married Colonel Carroll Buck, an army physician. He actually raised my mother and her sister, and he was the only grandfather I knew. Granddaddy Buck's military service took him to Washington, D.C., which is where my mother met my father, Thomas Francis Farrell, and where they were married, on July 23, 1917, at St. Dominic's Catholic Church.

My father's family was of strong Irish stock. My great-grandfather, Michael Farrell, was a schoolteacher who immigrated to America from Ireland around 1848 and became a farmer. My great-grandmother was Catherine Danahy, who was also Irish. Their only child was my grandfather, John J. Farrell.

Grandfather John Farrell was born and lived his entire life on the 200-acre family farm in Brunswick, New York, not far from Albany. I remember him as a tall, slender man who was kind and patient with me, leading me around the farm on a horse so I could ride, taking time to talk with me about the animals, and taking me down into the farm's root cellar and explaining the vegetables and fruits stored there. Grandfather's farm had an apple orchard and pigs, cows, and horses, in addition to the crops he grew. They must have had a lot of dairy cows, because Grandfather delivered milk for more than forty years.

He and his wife, Margaret Connolly Farrell, who died before I was born, had nine children. My dad was the fourth child in this sprawling Irish Catholic family. While growing up, all nine of the children worked on the farm and helped deliver milk, but none of them stayed on the farm as adults.

My father, Thomas Francis Farrell, was born in 1891 in Brunswick. Dad was almost six feet tall, with wonderful military posture, always straight and strong. Physically fit, he took a walk every night after dinner. His Irish complexion was ruddy, and he had freckles all over his arms and legs. He had a square Irish face with twinkling blue eyes and sandy-colored hair. His hands and feet were long and slender.

Tom, as he was called, graduated from Rensselaer Polytechnic Institute in 1912 with a degree in civil engineering. He worked on the Panama Canal from 1913 to 1916, then entered the army as a second lieutenant in November 1916. He and Mother were married just before he sailed for France in 1917. Dad came back from the war as a major and continued his military career from then off and on until the 1950s.

In February 1941 my father was recalled to active duty in preparation for World War II. He served in several different capacities during the war. In November 1943 he became the chief engineer in the China-Burma-India theater, supervising construction of the Lido Road, B-29 airfields, and

From my father, Major General Thomas Francis Farrell, my brothers, sister, and I
learned, among other values, integrity, honor, loyalty, and love of country. Dad had
a marvelous Irish sense of humor. He had a brilliant army career in serving our nation.
He also held other important public service jobs. Before World War I, Dad first worked
as a civil engineer on the Panama Canal, and one of his last military positions was
during World War II, when he served as deputy to Major General Leslie Groves on
the Manhattan Project. Official U.S. Army Signal Corps photograph

the oil pipelines from Calcutta to China. He was promoted to brigadier
general in January 1944. When Dad finally retired, his rank was major
general.

In January 1945 Dad was given his biggest job in World War II—
perhaps the most important assignment of his life—when he became
Major General Leslie Groves's deputy on the atomic bomb project, code-
named "the Manhattan Project." General Groves apparently selected my
father as his deputy after careful consideration. According to letters I
received after Dad's death, Secretary of War Henry Stimson had grown
increasingly nervous as the Manhattan Project progressed because only
General Groves understood all aspects of the testing program.

Stimson feared what would happen if Groves suddenly died or couldn't continue to manage the project for some reason, so he urged the general to appoint a deputy with whom he could share his knowledge. After my father joined Groves's team, he and Groves made it a point never to be in the same place at the same time if there was any hint of danger present.

The Army Corps of Engineers was in charge of the Manhattan Project, with scientific direction provided by Dr. Robert Oppenheimer and his team. Work had been going on in secret for several years. The rush was on to end the war in the Pacific without an expensive and time-consuming full-scale invasion of mainland Japan—an invasion that would have cost tens of thousands of American lives.

In my father's obituary in the *New York Times* on April 12, 1967, it was reported that when Dad arrived at Los Alamos National Laboratory in New Mexico, he walked into a classroom where Oppenheimer was lecturing to a group of highly trained atomic physicists. Oppenheimer dismissed the group, erased a tremendously complex formula on the blackboard—and taught Dad nuclear physics in thirty-six hours.

Dad was there with Oppenheimer in the control shelter at Alamogordo, New Mexico, when the first experimental explosion took place on July 16, 1945. It is clear from my father's notes that they really had little idea what to expect, although they knew history was about to be made. Dad wrote: "Everyone in that room knew the awful potentialities of the thing that they thought was about to happen. The scientists felt that their figuring must be right and that the bomb had to go off, but there was in everyone's mind a strong measure of doubt."

None of the witnesses, including Dad, could quite grasp the magnitude of the explosion: "In that brief instant in the remote New Mexico desert the tremendous effort of the brains and brawn of all these people came suddenly and startlingly to the fullest fruition." The world suddenly changed forever, and Dad witnessed it. His feeling was expressed in his notes: "'Lord, I believe; help Thou mine unbelief.' We were reaching into the unknown and did not know what might come of it."

Later, Dad was given the "honor" of briefing General Douglas MacArthur, the commander of the Allied Forces in the South Pacific, on the bombs. In an editorial about my father and General MacArthur in the *New York World Journal Tribune* on April 26, 1967, writer/columnist

Bob Considine described the meeting. He said that when Dad arrived in Manila, MacArthur's officers were sick of unknown generals from Washington with ideas on how to fight the war, so they gave Dad a scant fifteen minutes to brief MacArthur.

According to Dad, MacArthur spent thirteen minutes pacing up and down in his office telling Dad about his plan to invade Japan. With two minutes left, MacArthur looked at his watch and asked why Dad wanted to see him. Dad quickly told MacArthur about the atomic bomb, the test on July 16, that the bomb was the equivalent of 20,000 tons of TNT, and that the United States possessed two bombs ready to be dropped on Japan. MacArthur was asked to issue orders to keep the Japanese skies clear of routine bombing raids over certain cities during the first clear daytime weather around the first week of August. MacArthur agreed, dismissed Dad, and went back to his invasion plans. The rest is history, as they say.

Dad traveled to the Mariana Islands to supervise the field operations for assembling the atomic bombs for delivery against Japan. Here again, his notes show that they did not fully understand the magnitude of what they were doing. My father personally took delivery of the plutonium charge that provided the fissionable material for one of the bombs. He later talked about how hot the metal casing was in his bare hands.

On August 6, 1945, the first atomic bomb was dropped on Hiroshima, Japan—twenty-one days after the Alamogordo test. An improved-design bomb was dropped on Nagasaki three days later. Immediately after Japan's surrender, Dad headed a scientific and engineering mission to Japan to investigate the effects of the bombs. More than anything, the deaths of countless civilians left an indelible impression on my father.

Dad often spoke to groups about the bomb and its aftermath. He described the tension of those developing the bomb, the dedication of the men involved, and the awesome responsibility of what he and others so quickly labeled "the Age of Atomic Science." He fully understood that atomic energy was a new force that could be used for good or evil. He described the effects as unprecedented, magnificent, beautiful, stupendous, and terrifying. Although a lifelong military man, Dad agreed that atomic energy should be controlled by civilians, not the military.

After the war, Dad returned to New York State to his chief engineer position and then in 1947 became the chairman of the New York City

Housing Authority for Robert Moses. Dad was called up by the army again during the Korean War and served until 1957, when he returned to New York City. He was a consulting engineer for various state agencies and for the New York World's Fair Corporation from 1960 until 1964.

While I didn't get my political leanings from my parents, something I definitely inherited from my mother was her involvement in community organizations. She volunteered during her whole life for the Red Cross. In fact, on the day she had the stroke that ultimately killed her in April 1966, she was dressed in her volunteer uniform. Like many Red Cross volunteers, she performed any odd job that needed to be done, driving people to medical appointments, assisting in the office, and working on the blood drives. She volunteered to raise money for the Community Chest and knitted items for "Bundles for Britain" before America entered World War II.

My mother was from a different social background than my father. Her family was a little more well-to-do than his and led a formal, gracious life, with household help and linen tablecloths and napkins on the table every night for dinner. When they married, my parents hired live-in help to babysit, cook, clean, do laundry, and iron. Even though she had household staff, my mother never drew distinctions between people. She treated everyone courteously, and everyone liked her.

Mother took things in her stride. She was always supportive of her children and expected us to behave and to "do the right thing." She never became cross or raised her voice when we didn't behave; she acted disappointed, which made us want to be better.

When my mother died in 1966, Dad moved to Reno to be closer to me. Shortly thereafter, the doctors discovered he had inoperable colon cancer. He was seventy-five years old when he died in April 1967. He is buried at Arlington National Cemetery, next to my mother and my brother Richard, who died shortly after his birth. A full military funeral, complete with twenty-one-gun salute, was held at Fort Myers, Virginia.

My mother and grandmother were traditional women devoted to their husbands, children, families, and communities, old-fashioned by today's standards. They attended church on Sundays and Holy Days, supported Catholic education, and abstained from eating meat on Fridays. Being Catholic was a way of life for them. They felt that people should contribute something to society and to their communities because we are put on this earth to make it a better place. They acted on this belief by living graciously and volunteering selflessly, a legacy I have tried to match.

Although the Farrell family background was in agriculture, my father, uncles, and aunts were all educated professionals or businesspeople. Like Mother, Dad believed in contributing to society. If there was a job to be done and you were asked, you responded. As a kid, I volunteered to help other children in recreation and park programs. The Farrell family had an abiding belief in hard work, patriotism, education, and individual responsibility. I wasn't the only one who learned from my parents; so did my brothers and sister.

My brother Tommy and I were only fourteen months apart in age, so we were extremely close as children. Tommy grew up to be about six feet tall, with a slender, athletic build. His hair was curly and red, and he had brown eyes and lots of freckles. Fair-complexioned, he was always getting a sunburn.

We had our moments, like all brothers and sisters. I often chased after my big brother and whined when he wouldn't let me play with him. Once when we were stationed at West Point, Tommy and two of his friends decided to ditch me—the little five-year-old girl tagging along behind them. Our mothers were playing bridge, and Tommy was supposed to be taking care of me. Tommy went into the house and told our mother, "Bobby has gone for a little ride." When Mother asked where I had gone, he said, "Oh, she's gone down the river." It turned out the boys had put me on an ice floe and pushed me out into the Hudson River. They panicked when they realized how serious this could be, so fortunately they decided to tell our mother. I think it was the Coast Guard that rescued me.

Tommy graduated from Christian Brothers Academy in Albany, New York, and then from West Point in June 1942. During the war, he earned a Distinguished Service Cross for extraordinary heroism. In July 1943, in Sicily, he destroyed three machine-gun nests with hand grenades, saving the lives of the Americans landing on the beach during the Allied invasion of Italy. He was promoted to captain, but his military career—and life—was cut short when he was killed by a land mine at Anzio, Italy, on February 25, 1944.

A family photograph of my brothers, sister, mother, and me in our living room in Albany, New York. The *Albany Times-Union* ran this photograph in May 1938 to celebrate Mother's Day. *Left to right:* me, Patsy, Steve, Mother, Peter, and Tommy.

I was at my parents' home the day the military chaplain visited Mother to tell her the news of Tommy's death. Dad was away in the China-Burma-India theater. It was the first truly traumatic event in my life, although I was already twenty-two. I never expected my brother Tommy to die so young.

On July 22, 1944, I watched at Fort Mifflin, Pennsylvania, as my mother christened an engineer port repair ship the *Thomas F. Farrell, Jr.* in Tommy's honor. Tommy is buried at West Point.

There was a big gap between Tommy and me and our younger brothers and sister. Although we were all part of the same family, living in one house, sharing family activities and meals, I spent most of my time with Tommy when I was growing up. To us, Peter, Patsy, and Steve were the "younger kids" or the "babies."

I was six in 1927 when my brother Peter Buck Farrell was born and almost nine when my sister Patricia Anne "Patsy" Farrell was born nearly three years later. When the baby of the family, Stephen Stuart Farrell, was born in 1937, I was sixteen years old. Another brother, Richard, had been born in 1934 but died within a few months.

Peter grew up to graduate from the United States Military Academy at West Point in 1950. He joined the field artillery and served a tour of duty in Vietnam in the 1960s. He met his wife, Joan Lang, while she was my sister Patsy's roommate at Manhattanville College of the Sacred Heart. After his retirement from a military career, Peter graduated from George Mason University School of Law and taught law in Virginia.

In 1949 Patsy married Jerry Naleid, an air force fighter pilot and West Point graduate. They lived all over the world while Jerry was in the service. He recently passed away, and Patsy now lives in Florida.

The baby of the family, Steve, is only three years older than my daughter Patty. I was pretty embarrassed that my mother was having a baby when I was in high school, so I know how Patty felt in college when her sister, Susie, was born. I was already married and not around the house when Steve was a child. The one thing Tommy, Peter, Patsy, and I all agreed on was that Steve was a spoiled child. Mother and Dad doted on him, so he did what he wanted. Steve came to live with us in Reno shortly after Dad died and stayed until I retired from Congress. It was a blessing because he took care of the house when we were in Washington; Steve also kept my campaign books. He is now retired and lives in Mexico.

In my day, big families were common, so it wasn't unusual for kids and grandkids to grow up together. They certainly did around my house. When my oldest child, Patty, began her family in 1962, with the birth of Elisa, my husband, Ken Dillon, and I had our own hands full with our daughter, Susie, who was only two and a half years old, and with our sons Kenny and Tommy, who were eleven and nine, respectively. Son Mike, twenty that year, was practically grown up, although he still lived at home in a room over our garage. Patty, just twenty-one, was married and, of course, away from the house. But we spent a lot of time together as a family, and that would continue as the years passed.

When Elisa was born, our clan of Dillons lived in a big, comfortable house at 2 Newlands Circle in Reno. This house and the one where I grew up, which my parents built at 10 Holmes Dale in Albany, New York—a house with a framed invitation to Franklin Delano Roosevelt's first inauguration prominently on display—are the houses I loved best.

The house on Newlands Circle was an oasis of calm to me, set back from the street and encircled by tall shade trees. Just off California Avenue and not far from the Truckee River, the two-story white stucco house with a basement and a steep black roof reminded me of my childhood and the houses I had known on the East Coast. Ken and I had added to the house several times over the years, so by the time Elisa was born there were five bedrooms, a nursery, and five and a half bathrooms in the main house, with one more bedroom and bath over the two-car garage. There was also a family room and a play area in the basement. Even though the house was large, it still felt cozy. Ken and I had purchased some of the furniture, and there were pieces from my parents' home and some antiques from Ken's family in Topeka, Kansas. Like many families, we hung pictures along the staircase of our children at different ages.

This was the home where my children grew up, and my home when I became a grandmother. Many of my grandchildren took some of their first steps there. I will always treasure the memories of the times our family shared there, whether it was hanging mistletoe in the front hall, listening to each child and grandchild learn to say grace, or remembering tiny Elisa's fascination with the smell of the cedar-lined storage closet on the stairway landing.

This home was far from the House of Representatives and farther still from the Southern California ranchero where my mother's family had its deepest roots and the northeastern states where my father's family had lived for generations.

CHAPTER TWO

A Family of My Own

I didn't begin a full-time political life until I was sixty-one years old. Before then, I was more focused on my growing family. Patty Dillon (Cafferata) and Mike Dillon were born during my first marriage, while my other children— Kenneth Price Dillon Jr., Thomas Brown Dillon, and Susan Brown Dillon (Anderson)—were born during my second marriage. My family has always been close-knit, so it was no surprise that my children and many of my older grandchildren worked or volunteered on my congressional campaigns.

At eighteen, without my parents' permission, I married James Henry "Jimmy" Bugden, a blue-eyed blond plumbing supply salesman, at St. Vincent de Paul's Catholic Church in Albany, New York. The marriage gave me my children Patty and Mike, so I have no regrets, but it was not a happy marriage. We were very young. Being Catholic, with two small children, we both made an effort to work on the marriage. In the end, we had little in common and, simply put, were incompatible.

Right after we were married, we lived in a third-floor flat on Lake Street in Albany, which meant I had to carry our groceries up three flights of stairs. The flat was small, with a living room, kitchen, bedroom, and bathroom. Through an open window in the kitchen, I hung the laundry outside on a two-way pulley. In the winter the clothes would freeze on the line and would be wetter when I pulled them in than when I put them out. After Patty was born, my father gave us a washing machine for Christmas. With a baby, that was a real blessing.

At the start of World War II, Jimmy went into the service as an army officer trainee. During his training, we moved around a lot. In Muskogee, Oklahoma, we lived in an off-base apartment, which became "infamous" in our family for its "milk delivery door," a common feature in those days. Every morning, from the hallway, the milkman would put milk and eggs inside on the kitchen floor. If I wasn't up right away, little Patty and her brother, Mike, would get into them and make an awful mess. Scrambled eggs and spilled milk are definitely a rotten way to start the day.

When Jimmy was sent overseas to New Guinea, the kids and I moved into my parents' home in Albany. Later we moved to a new two-story apartment complex, set back off the street with play areas in front. The complex contained a nursery school where I worked part-time in the office, so I could afford to have Patty and Mike attend the school. After the war, when Jimmy and I decided to separate, the kids and I moved to Forest Hills, New York, to live with my parents again. It would not be until I moved to Reno in 1949 that I would finally leave their home.

The house in Forest Hills was a big, two-story Tudor house, with a very formal living room that had a fireplace, a black grand piano, a long couch, and several comfortable overstuffed chairs. Even though I was home with my parents, I was miserable.

I knew the separation from Jimmy would be permanent, but contemplating the New York divorce laws was agonizing. In those days, a divorce took five years in New York, and the only legal ground was adultery; incompatibility wasn't adequate. In most cases, people didn't want to wait that long for a divorce. For many people, Nevada was an attractive alternative.

While the idea of divorce was difficult for my Catholic parents, they understood the problems in my marriage. They had not been thrilled about the marriage in the first place. They supported my decision to get a divorce, believing that I was entitled to a better life. In 1949 I reluctantly left Patty and Mike with my parents and took a cross-country train trip to Reno.

I stepped off the train at the station on Commercial Row in downtown Reno into what I fully expected would be the Wild, Wild West. Instead, I found a pretty little town of about 25,000 people, nestled on the eastern edge of the Sierra Nevada. Reno in the late 1940s was just starting to get its reputation as "the Biggest Little City in the World." In the 1960 Census it would surrender its position as the biggest town in Nevada to Las Vegas.

When I arrived, everything in Reno was centered in a four-to-five-block area just north and south of the Truckee River. Downtown was the social and business center of the city, and if you stood on the Virginia Street bridge, sooner or later you would see everyone in town. Everyone shopped downtown, at places like Hatton's Men's Store, Joseph Magnin's, Ginsburg's Jewelers, R. Herz Jewelers, Parker's Western Wear, Gotchy's Shoe Store, Conklin's Furs, Gray Reid's Department Store, and Woolworth's. For nightlife, the Riverside and the just-opened Mapes Hotel were popular, and the Golden Hotel, Harolds Club, and the Fortune Club (where Liberace played) were nearby. People went to the movies at the Majestic, the Crest, or the Tower theaters, and drank coffee and ate pie at Les Lerude's Wigwam Coffee Shop. The popular Big Hat restaurant was far out of town, at the corner of Virginia Street and Moana Lane.

Reno had a tendency to become isolated in the winter, since the only road over the Sierra was U.S. Highway 40, a steep and twisting two-lane highway with hairpin turns. Winter storms would block the road for days. Back then, the divorce industry was a booming business in Reno. The Truckee Meadows was dotted with "guest ranches" and boardinghouses for men and women who had come to town to establish a six-week residency in order to get what the society pages called "the Reno Cure." While I would later find the town to be warm and inviting, Reno was a little unfriendly to newcomers, especially those who came for a divorce. Since we usually lived in rooming houses, we mostly met the people who were in town for a divorce, as we were, so we didn't get involved much with the locals.

The first place I lived in Reno was a guesthouse at 427 Hill Street, a location that has long since become an office building. The guesthouse had five or six bedrooms and three baths upstairs and served three meals a day; everyone living there was in Reno for a divorce. The owner was a German woman named Charlotta Tsukalas. Her husband, Lee, was Greek and twenty years younger than she. I had a room on the second floor and shared a bath. Behind the house was a lovely old-fashioned backyard with lots of trees and places to sit and visit.

Also in the backyard was a little one-story cottage. Living in it when

I arrived was Kenneth Price Dillon, a native of Topeka, Kansas. Ken had graduated from Yale University and Yale School of Law and had also attended Harvard Graduate School of Business. At the time, he was an attorney with a New York law firm, and he, too, was in Reno for a divorce. Ken would take breakfast and dinner with the others living in the guesthouse, so we met over the dining room table.

I was immediately drawn to him. Ken was physically attractive, six feet two inches tall, an imposing, big man, broad-shouldered, dignified in both his looks and his demeanor, always proper and reserved. His hair was steel gray in color and quite curly, a fact he kept hidden. I learned later that his daily grooming ritual included slapping Vitalis on his hair to straighten it.

We shared a common eastern background, we understood each other, and we were interested in the same things. He was a Wall Street lawyer, but after arriving in Reno for his divorce, he saw a business opportunity, so he planned to stay and set up a law practice. After my divorce was final, I went back to New York, where I planned to live. But Ken and I had fallen in love, and it didn't take long for me to decide to come back to Reno. We were married by "old" Judge Clark Guild in his chambers in Carson City on an afternoon in March 1950.

Ken didn't meet my children until after we were married, but, as an example of the kind of man he was, he immediately accepted them. Although he wanted to, he never adopted them because my former husband would not agree to it. Ken and I petitioned the court to legally change Patty and Mike's last name to Dillon. Ken was really the only father Patty and Mike ever knew.

In 1949 Ken opened his law practice in Reno at 247½ N. Virginia Street, over Southworth's Tobacco Store. He was among the first legal tax experts in Reno. It was a much different practice from what he had done in New York because it was more personal, varied, and enjoyable.

A few years later, he went into partnership with George Vargas, whose main law practice was lobbying for well-known companies, mainly insurance firms. A strong Republican, Vargas was a flamboyant lobbyist who put on spectacular parties for the legislators. Later, John Bartlett joined the firm and Vargas, Dillon, and Bartlett became one of Nevada's most influential law firms.

Ken Dillon and me on our wedding day in 1950. We were married in Carson City, Nevada, by Judge Clark Guild in his chambers. Ladies usually wore gloves and hats in those days. The photograph doesn't show off the details of my hat, which was made of red feathers. At the time I was the mother of Patty and Mike. Subsequently, Ken and I were the parents of three children, Kenny, Tommy, and Susie. We had been married fourteen years when he died. Collection of Barbara F. Vucanovich

Ken and I rented our first home on a hill just off the Reno–Carson City highway (now U.S. 395) at the northern edge of Washoe Valley. Since we had only one car, if I needed to drive anywhere, I had to drive Ken into Reno to work. I remember the V&T train would pass our house as we were pulling out of the driveway, but we would arrive in Reno before it did.

Because the commute was crazy and Patty and Mike were attending St. Thomas Aquinas Elementary School in Reno, we soon moved into town and rented a house at 1725 Westfield Avenue, in relatively new Westfield Village, close to Reno High School. Some of our neighbors were Preston and Norma Hale, Mead and Jane Dixon, and Larry Struve and his parents, people who would become lifelong friends. I did all of the things a mother did in those days, including being a Cub Scout den mother for my son, Mike.

Around the time our son Kenny was born, we rented a larger house at 2200 Plumas Street in Reno. Before long we bought a two-story white house with a basement just down the street at 2400 Plumas Street. We splurged and bought all new furniture, paying for it over time. Son Tommy was born while we lived there, from 1952 to 1956. Then we bought the big house at 2 Newlands Circle in 1956. Susie was born while we lived there.

During those years of marriage, I played the traditional role of a wife helping to make her husband's law practice and his community projects successful, never realizing how much I was learning in the process. Our social and community life revolved around legal organizations, community groups, political activities, and our children's sports and schools. Ken loved to be with the kids, especially playing sports. He learned to ski, fish, and camp so he could spend more time with them; he had never done those things before we were married.

We had been married fourteen years when Ken suddenly died of a heart attack, on March 5, 1964. He was only fifty years old. Although he had suffered a heart attack a few years before, he was physically active and feeling good. He was in Las Vegas for a court hearing when his chest pains started, so he went to the hospital. In my initial phone calls to the hospital, I was told that he was resting comfortably and was going to be fine. In the middle of the night, I received a telephone call from a nurse at the hospital.

She said, without preamble, "Your husband just expired."

Then she hung up.

Memories of that telephone call are as painful today as they were then. I was forty-two years old and a widow. Kenny, Tommy, and Susie were twelve, ten, and four. I felt totally lost. I had never considered a future without my husband by my side. Now it was a reality.

I didn't have an opportunity to dwell on my grief for too long because Paul Laxalt asked me to manage his Washoe County campaign for the U.S. Senate. I'm still not sure why he asked me. I had helped on his campaign in 1962, when he was elected Nevada's lieutenant governor. Truthfully, managing a campaign, even at the county level, was something that women didn't do in those days. But I knew I needed something to keep me busy, and I agreed to take the job.

Ken had died in March and I went to work on the campaign in July, with the election looming in November. Throughout the campaign, my emotions were still raw. At times I would go into the back room at the headquarters and cry, then go back out to work. It was not easy, but in retrospect I think that it was good therapy for me. I didn't have time to feel sorry for the fact that I was a widow with three small children to raise. I was meeting the public and had to think of something besides myself.

During the campaign, while Dick Horton and I were organizing the precincts in Sparks, Dick suggested we call George Vucanovich to help. At that time George was a Democrat, but he was a friend of Paul's. (Later, George registered as a Republican.) As a result, George and I spent a lot of time together working on the campaign. When the campaign was over, we talked and sent notes to each other and eventually started dating. A year later, on June 19, 1965, we were married in my home at 2 Newlands Circle by district court judge Grant Bowen. My children, grandchildren Elisa and Farrell, and George's son, Craig, who is mentally disabled, were present. George's stepdaughter, Daryn (Potter), was not present, but later she lived with us for a while when she was in grammar school.

George was a very loving guy whose eyes would tear up at the least provocation. He took his role as a stepdad seriously and loved my kids, their kids (our grandchildren), and being part of the family. Elisa and Farrell started calling him "Popper George" because they called their Cafferata grandfather "Popper." Later grandchildren called him "Papa George." He could fix just about anything around the house and didn't mind doing it. I suppose it was because he grew up in a small Central Nevada mining town, where one either learned to fix things or they didn't get fixed.

George was a lanky six feet four inches. He was already bald on the top

George Vucanovich and me, in Reno, Nevada, during my time in Congress. George and I were married in 1965 at my home, 2 Newlands Circle in Reno. We had been married for thirty-three years when he died in 1998. Collection of Barbara F. Vucanovich

of his head with some dark hair when we met. Over the thirty-three years we were married he got balder and grayer. His hazel eyes were part of his Serbian features. He grew a moustache and was quite proud of it. When we lived in Washington, D.C., he wore the traditional navy blue suit, white shirt, and tie, and he happily wore a tuxedo when it was required. He wasn't fussy about clothes, but he looked best in his cowboy boots and jeans and was most comfortable in golf clothes.

George was born in Tonopah, grew up in Round Mountain, and was a graduate of the University of Nevada, Reno. He didn't make a big deal out of the fact that he was the first member of his family to graduate from college, but he was proud of it. George's brother, Johnny Susich, loved to tell the story about one of the first times George came home from the first grade and announced that he was too dumb to learn, so he wasn't going back. Apparently his mother and brother convinced him otherwise.

Professionally, George was an accountant. When we met, he was the controller at the Sparks Nugget, having started working for Dick Graves in the original Nugget across the street from its current location, then for John Ascuaga. Later, George was recruited by Nate Jacobson to go to the new King's Castle at Lake Tahoe, Nevada.

George was there only a couple of weeks when he realized it was the biggest mistake of his life. He had never been in a casino where the people in the pit carried guns. He was shocked. No other casino in Northern Nevada had armed employees, although that was the standard in Las Vegas. I never saw him as unhappy as he was after he went to work there. He lived at Tahoe during the week and came home on the weekends. That did not make him happy either. He decided to help them get the place open, then quit. He started there in March or April and quit in September. He was without a job for about a week.

He worked for Helms Construction for a few months, then went to work for Si Redd at Bally Distributing. After my second election in 1984, he retired, although in Washington he did some part-time accounting work for Congressman Mike Bilirakis—Bilirakis was Greek Orthodox, and George was Serbian Orthodox; they were soul mates—and for Congresswoman Helen Delich Bentley, a native of Ely and also a Serbian.

During the 1970s, with only Susie, the youngest, still at home, George thought the Newlands Circle home was too big and expensive to operate, so we sold it and purchased a condo in Riverbend, near the Truckee River. It was small, dark, covered with brown shingles and had "zero lot lines"—a big change from the huge house on Newlands Circle, to say the least. I was never crazy about this place, but it worked out because I was in Congress most of the time we lived there. It was home until 1994, when we bought a home in Hidden Valley, where I've lived ever since.

After I was elected to Congress, George and I bought another condominium in Alexandria, Virginia, on the second floor of a sixteen-story high-rise. Best of all, our condominium was just a few doors down the hall from my sister, Patsy, and her husband, Jerry. My brother Peter and his wife, Joan, also lived in Alexandria at the time. The six of us spent time together after church on Sundays, having brunch, playing golf, or attending Washington Redskins football games.

George's personal relationships around the state were invaluable to me when I decided to run for Congress. He grew up in Nye County and drove a truck from Ely to California for several years before the Korean War. Since he was Serbian, he was well known to the small but active community of Serbians in the state. The fact that he graduated from the University of Nevada meant that he knew people all over the state. We never pulled into a gas station in rural Nevada where George didn't know someone.

He was always supportive of me. Many people from the campaign trail remember George standing by while I gave a speech, holding my purse, with a name badge that identified him simply as THE HUSBAND. He was especially fond of George and Barbara Bush. He attended all of the Washington political events with me, until Bill Clinton was elected president. George balked at attending White House functions with the Clintons, so I took another family member with me when I went to the White House during those years.

George enjoyed our life during my years in Congress because of the things we were able to do and all the travel. He never resented the sacrifices we made while I served those fourteen years. He was proud of me and the job I did for Nevada.

When George died on December 19, 1998, at St. Mary's Hospital in Reno, we had been married thirty-three years. I was seventy-seven years old. During our marriage all but two of our grandchildren were born

(Elisa and Farrell were born before we were married). Most of our great-grandchildren were born then, too. George delighted in each and every member of our family, but to tell you the truth, I think he loved the babies best.

Ken Dillon and George Vucanovich were a major part of my personal life, wonderful husbands and fathers. They supported me financially and emotionally, and both of them supported my community and political activities. We had good lives together and contributed much volunteer time to make the Reno community a better place to live.

The encouragement that Ken and George gave me made my successes possible. I simply could not have done the things I did without their support. And all of that is pretty amazing when you consider the times they lived in and the way they were raised. These were the days before there was really much notion of equal rights for women. After all, women got the right to vote only the year before I was born. So it's quite incredible that women, for all practical purposes, have come from getting the right to vote all the way to serving in Congress during my lifetime. It's also a tribute to these two wonderful men in my life that I was able to grow so much myself.

But, of course, life would not have been complete without my children.

My children were born in the following order: Patricia Anne (1940), Michael Francis (1942), Kenneth Price Jr. (1951), Thomas Brown (1953), and Susan Brown (1959). They are known as Patty, Mike, Kenny, Tommy, and Susie, and each is unique and special in his or her own way. Like most mothers, I suppose, I have always been amazed how much they are alike and how much they are different.

Patty was named after my sister. A blue-eyed blonde, she is self-motivated and outspoken, as anyone who has known her will tell you. She has been successful in everything she has done, shares my love of politics, and played instrumental roles in all of my campaigns. Patty was elected to the Nevada Assembly—after winning her primary by one vote!—in 1980, and you can imagine my pride when she was elected Nevada's state treasurer in 1982. The same year I became the first woman elected to federal office from Nevada, she became the first woman elected to be state treasurer

My first campaign photograph, in 1982, of my children, George, and me. *Front row, left to right:* my younger daughter, Susie; my husband, George; me; my middle son, Kenny. *Back row, left to right:* my oldest son, Mike; my older daughter, Patty; my youngest son, Tommy. Collection of Barbara D. Vucanovich

in Nevada. In 1986 Patty was the Republican nominee for governor. She has also served as district attorney of Lincoln County, Lander County, and Esmeralda County, and she ran, unsuccessfully, to succeed me in Congress when I retired in 1996.

Patty has been extremely active in Republican Party politics in Nevada. She was our Republican national committeewoman from 1992 to 1996 and was the first woman ever to chair a state political party convention in Nevada.

Patty has been married to Dr. Treat Cafferata since 1961. Our entire family is important to her, and she works at including everyone in the family. She is generous, sharing, and interested in continuing and creating family traditions, though her siblings often tease her for attempting to overorganize and plan family activities and games for them.

Mike was born fourteen months after Patty, and they were always the closest of friends. Mike was compact and small in stature, but strong and wiry. He had a military carriage without being stiff, and he loved sports, especially baseball, golf, and wrestling. Even growing up, Mike was always self-sufficient and never seemed to need anyone to keep him entertained. I can still picture him outside by himself, throwing and catching a baseball.

Mike strongly identified with the military men in my family, especially my father and my brothers, and he really wanted to go to West Point. He didn't have the grades to be accepted, so he joined the army and became a Green Beret paratrooper, serving two tours in Vietnam. A mother's normal fears were compounded in part because of my brother Tommy's death during World War II, and I don't think I drew a calm breath until he returned home safely.

After he left the army, Mike opened a janitorial business in Reno, later winning the janitorial service contract for the ammunition depot in Hawthorne, Nevada. After that, Mike got his real estate license, a business in which he was successful until the bottom dropped out of the market in the late 1970s. Later, Mike worked for his brother Kenny in his roofing business in Reno and in Las Vegas and then became an independent roofing estimator.

Mike was an invaluable part of each of my congressional campaigns, especially in rural Nevada. He introduced me to his numerous friends, made appearances, gave speeches, and put up campaign signs all over the state for me.

Mike died on October 30, 1996. I had announced my retirement and was at a news conference with Jim Gibbons, who was running to succeed me. I was just walking to the podium to introduce and endorse Jim when someone told me my husband was waiting for me on the phone.

When I picked up the line, George said, "Come home immediately. It's about Mike."

I said, "What about Mike?"

He said, "He just died in Sacramento."

Mike had a heart attack and collapsed on a golf course and died before he reached the hospital. His death was a real blow to me; I never expected to bury one of my children.

My last three children were all born in Reno. Kenny, a towheaded child, was the first, arriving about two years after Ken and I had married. Kenny was very self-sufficient and highly competitive, with an outgoing personality. He always seemed to be a kid on a mission. He was active and innovative about keeping busy and has always made and kept friends. Kenny's father adored him, and the feeling was mutual.

Kenny, too, was an integral part of my campaigns, hosting fund-raising events for me at his home and donating plywood and rebar for those all-important campaign signs. Today he owns three roofing companies, including D&D Roofing in Reno. He married his second wife, Sandra, in 1980.

Tommy arrived a little less than two years after Kenny, and he and Kenny used to have fierce battles when they were growing up, as brothers do. Kenny was bigger, so he always got the best of Tommy, but today they are good friends (and Tommy is taller). When Tommy was a kid, his favorite activity was to fish on the Truckee River by himself all summer long.

Tommy's career has taken him the farthest away from home, and he is the only one of my children who didn't remain in Reno after getting married. He married Cathy DeTar, who grew up in a house around the corner from our Newlands Circle house. Tommy and his family lived for a while in Winnemucca and in North Las Vegas, where he played a major role in my campaigns by helping to organize those communities. Today he is an executive with Lowe's corporate office in North Carolina.

Susie was the baby, arriving six and a half years after Tommy. Susie was just five when George and I were married, and we took her with us all the time—no matter where we went. She has always been serious and hardworking. After becoming a CPA, she pursued a career in business. She is a self-confident woman, and everything she does, she does well. She and her husband, Butch Anderson, also a CPA, both served at different times as my campaign treasurers.

In a way, I grew up with my kids. I was the youngest mother in Patty's classes and the oldest in Susie's. When Patty was born, I was nineteen years old and frankly did not know a lot. I was thirty-eight years old when Susie was born—and still had more to learn. Since my children were born over an eighteen-year time span, I spent more than forty years of my life raising children. Because I came from a large family, I probably had a much better idea of what I was getting into than many other women did. I had to share a lot with my brothers and sister, so I didn't mind not having much time to myself when I became a parent.

As the years went by, I learned to be more flexible and understanding. I learned to look for solutions by getting consensus on issues that were difficult—although, when necessary, I put my foot down and let all of my children and grandchildren know what I expected of a family member. My values did not change, but my lifestyle was modified by my marital status, location, and financial affairs. My children, of course, shaped my life by exposing me to new experiences, thanks to their activities.

Because of my children, my life has been full, challenging, and exciting. All my children turned out to be bright, capable, hardworking, and successful, but there were many trying moments, too. None of them are saints. They are regular people, each with his or her own strengths and weaknesses.

We spent, and spend, most holidays together. When they were growing up we skied, golfed, camped, traveled, and did other things together. Some of our most memorable and laughable times were camping. Except for skiing, we still enjoy all those activities together. And, of course, my children all helped with my campaigns. Next to Ken and George, my husbands, they have been my greatest cheerleaders and supporters.

CHAPTER THREE

Outside the Home

My job as Paul Laxalt's Northern Nevada district director helped launch my own political career, but my family and earlier work experiences helped to shape and influence the person I would become in Congress. When I was busy managing Senator Laxalt's office in Reno, the office was close to our house. I could go home for lunch and was free to participate in Susie's activities until she graduated from Reno High School in 1977. All my other jobs also permitted me to be involved with my children's lives and projects.

I began working "outside the home," as they say now, right after I left college and was married. Before and during World War II, there simply weren't enough men to fill the available jobs. Everyone pitched in to help. With a family of two small children and my husband's small army salary, we needed the money.

My first paying job, before I got married, was as a telephone operator with AT&T in downtown Albany. In those days it was common for women without college degrees to be telephone operators, so most of the operators I worked with and our supervisors were women. I was paid a reasonable salary, for the times, with good benefits, including stock options. We had rest periods, and the company treated its employees well.

I sat with all the other operators in a big room, in front of a switchboard, connected to the board by way of a plug attached to my headset. I handled long-distance calls, known as the "long lines." The switchboard was like a big pegboard with little holes in it, and each hole was covered by a door.

The little door dropped open, indicating you needed to plug in at that spot. You used another plug at the end of the line to connect the call in a different hole.

Later, I moved to the statistics department, where I learned to use a "comptometer," which was like an adding machine, a forerunner of the computer, I think. My job was to trace telephone traffic to determine which hours needed more operators, and I worked a split shift from eight to noon in the morning and from four to eight in the evening.

After I was married, I left AT&T and sold insurance for Equitable Life Assurance Society of New York in downtown Albany, where most of the other employees were men. The company trained us, and we worked on commission, selling insurance to men who were homeowners. I learned about appraisals and real estate because I had to inspect the homes before I could sell the insurance. I also learned about home building, banking, and mortgages.

When I moved with Patty and Mike to live with my parents in Forest Hills, I worked for American Flange and Manufacturing Company in New York City. I was hired as the company's receptionist and switchboard operator, and I rode the subway to and from Rockefeller Center. It was a beautiful location, and I had an opportunity to take the kids to see Broadway plays and musicals.

The worst part of the job came in my introduction to the fact that some traveling salesmen cheated on their wives. I was expected to cover for them on the telephone, but I was never happy about it. So in addition to learning a great deal about business and manufacturing, I also learned some unsavory characteristics about people.

I left the company when I came to Reno for my divorce. After I married Ken, I answered a newspaper ad, and my past experience selling insurance helped me get a position with Ted Mattson in his real estate and insurance business. Originally, I worked for Ted as a part-time receptionist, but he encouraged me to take both the state insurance and the real estate exams, which I did. When I passed, I sold general life insurance and real estate part-time for Ted until Ken and I started a family. I didn't work outside the home again until after Ken died.

During those years as a "working girl," I learned skills that were useful both when I ran my own businesses and when I served in Congress. I got experience in setting priorities, organizing my time, and dealing with the public, bankers, and other businesspeople. I also learned about the difficulties of balancing work and family and understood the challenges of being a single mother.

Many of my feelings on women's rights and equality today are grounded in my experiences in business. I started out surrounded by women as a telephone operator, and I felt like a valued member of the business. From there, I moved to work experiences where I was surrounded by men—and again I felt like a valued part of the team. I didn't feel I needed rules to guarantee I'd be paid well or trained—those were things I felt I'd earned, just as every employee had, on the merits of my work. As an employee, I don't remember any sexual harassment or derogatory comments made in any of my jobs because I was a woman. When I tried to open my own businesses, however, it was a different story.

I decided to go into business for myself a couple of years after I was widowed, when my youngest child, Susie, started first grade. I thought a franchise would be a good way to start a business, because the franchise seller has a proven idea and a vested interest in the success of your business. I really had no business management experience, but I figured being part of a franchise would give me the help I needed to get started. I learned firsthand that being an employer is very different from being an employee.

In 1965 I answered an ad in the *Wall Street Journal* for an Evelyn Wood Reading Dynamics franchise. I drove to Oakland, California, for a demonstration of the speed-reading program and ended up buying a three-year franchise for Northern Nevada. Then I drove to Oakland once a week for eight weeks to take the course and learn the business, getting home to Reno around midnight each time.

I started teaching classes in a brand-new office building at 100 Washington Street in Reno. The tuition was $150 per student. I still think today that we were providing a great service to people, and certainly the response from the community was good. The classes were taught mostly at night because we were appealing to college students and businessmen. I started out teaching the classes myself, and then, as the business grew, I hired others to teach. I taught an eight-week class in Elko. Companies such as

Sierra Pacific Power and Nevada Bell paid for their employees to take the course. At the invitation of Governor Paul Laxalt, I even taught the course to interested legislators in Carson City.

At the end of the three years, although I'd taught about three thousand students, I hadn't made much money, so I decided not to renew my franchise. In many ways, though the business was time-consuming and demanding, I think I learned as much as the students did. I became much more comfortable speaking in public because of teaching classes and selling the course to those who attended the course demonstrations. I also met many people in the community, a number of whom would help me later in my congressional campaigns. In the long run, the experience helped me to relate to other people whose jobs or backgrounds might be different from my own. To this day, I still run into people who remind me that they took the course from me all those years ago. (And, of course, the speed-reading techniques I learned were enormously helpful when I was in Congress and confronted with a huge amount of reading material.)

Most important, perhaps, I learned how to operate a business. I had to meet the payroll, pay the rent and the taxes. I learned firsthand the problems so many small businesses face every day. While few women owned their own businesses then, I never felt discriminated against as a woman in that particular business—I suppose because being a teacher was viewed as "acceptable" for a woman.

Having decided to give up the Evelyn Wood Dynamics franchise, I looked for a new opportunity. Another ad in the *Wall Street Journal* led me to the travel business. George and I flew back to New York to meet with the owners of Welcome Aboard Travel. When I purchased this franchise, I was required to follow their business plan for a couple of years and to employ a person with travel agency experience. The company supplied the name, logo, printed forms, fare books, accounting procedures, and other information, systems, and materials.

The Welcome Aboard experience led me to the only gender-related discrimination I ever faced in business. Not wanting to spend my money to start up the business, I went to the bank to borrow the funds against my own credit. The bank informed me that in order to obtain a business loan I would have to have my husband's signature and use his credit. I was shocked. Finally, when I threatened to sue them, the bank relented and lent me the funds without George's signature.

When the business opened, I hired not only an experienced travel agent but also a couple of ticket agents and a bookkeeper. I took the training course to qualify as a travel agent. I learned about the tourism industry, including hotels, rental cars, airline schedules, fares, booking procedures, and cruise, steamship, and freighter lines. I started with a tiny temporary office, but my second office was in a nice little two-story building owned by Ralph Casazza and family in Shoppers' Square Mall on Plumb Lane in Reno.

In those days we wrote the tickets by hand on preprinted ticket stock. The stock was as good as money, almost like a signed blank check, so I kept the tickets locked up in a safe at the office and in a safe-deposit box at the bank. To book a reservation, we telephoned each airline using the *Official Airline Guide* to "construct" the routes and rates, something that takes only a few minutes on the Internet today but back then was extremely time-consuming. The goal was to get the best fares for our customers. There were very few direct flights from Reno to most destinations, so we really had to do our homework. For example, if someone was going to Washington, D.C., we had to consider whether it was less expensive to book a flight from Reno through Denver or through San Francisco, Chicago, or Dallas. We researched every fare and route about five different ways to find the cheapest one.

Cash flow was a constant struggle. Every twenty days, we filed our reports with the Airline Ticket Control Agency so we could get paid. The commissions were 7 percent on domestic flights, 10 percent on international flights, and 20 percent on cruises. The only common credit card in use then was American Express, which took a percentage off the top of the sale. That cut into our commissions, so we didn't like to accept it.

Of course, one of the fringe benefits of the travel business was that George and I were able to take several nice trips while I owned the agency. Cruises were free to travel agents, and for air travel we paid the tax, but not the fare. Just before I sold the business in 1974, we took a six-week trip around the world, flying first class and staying at deluxe hotels in Honolulu, Tokyo, Seoul, Beijing, Thailand, India, Athens, the Greek Islands, Italy, France, London, and Madrid. The hotel rooms, of course, were not free.

(It was on that trip, while flying from New Delhi to Athens, that we had a unscheduled middle-of-the-night stop in Iran or Iraq. Six gunmen dressed in military garb and brandishing Uzis boarded the plane and walked up and down the aisle, looking at each passenger but not speaking to any of us. Finally they got off the plane and let us go. Arriving in Athens was almost like being home.)

The travel business is labor-intensive, and it was not profitable for me. If anything went wrong on someone's trip—no matter what it was—it was our fault. That was always hard for me to accept. Ultimately, it was a relief to sell the agency. On the positive side, it was an important learning experience and even proved useful when I went to Congress. As cochair of the Travel and Tourism Caucus, I understood things like reciprocal trade and travel agreements with foreign countries, and I knew a little about other countries from having visited them.

As both employee and employer, I learned many things that were useful to me in Congress. For the lobbyists and the people from Nevada who came to see me—the insurance agents, the home builders, the telecommunications industry managers, the bankers, and the tourism-related businesspeople—I had a working knowledge of these heavily regulated businesses. I understood their issues and their frustration with government, and I tried to find solutions. Most important, when people pushed for more government control and regulation on these businesses, it was easy to be an advocate against their ideas. I'd been there.

Working in business was not the only part of my life outside of the house, of course. My mother and my father were always volunteering in one activity or another, and I think a lot of that rubbed off on me. It was never hard to keep busy.

When I first moved to Reno, I signed up as a volunteer with what was then known as the Community Chest, a forerunner of today's United Way. I picked that nonprofit organization partly because it was one that my mother had worked for in Albany, New York. Ken was involved, too, and he later chaired some of the committees, while I was happier making phone calls and stuffing envelopes. I wasn't looking for a leadership role and never aspired to be a chair of any of the activities.

At the time I joined, Community Chest was starting its annual fund-raising drive, raising money for agencies like the Boy Scouts, the Red Cross, and other service organizations. The group met with each of the different service organizations to discuss their budgets and also met with area businesses to raise money.

Nell Gerow headed up the door-to-door fund-raising activities, and I did my share of walking my neighborhood asking for contributions. I even called on some businesses. It was easy to ask for money because it wasn't for myself and Reno was still a small town. I'm not sure that I would walk door-to-door today. The one thing my volunteering did was introduce me to a number of people who really made the community successful, bankers Harold Gorman and Jordan C. Crouch, insurance agent Linn Hall, and other prominent businessmen.

At the same time, the people I worked with got to know me and learned I was a reliable person, willing to give of myself. I volunteered for Community Chest for several years, meeting many women as well as the businessmen who participated in its fund-raising drives. Volunteering allowed me to meet people in an informal and pleasant way, with husbands, wives, and families working together. Ultimately, these contacts helped me in many ways.

In addition, I was involved in all of my kids' school activities. If there had been such a thing as a "soccer mom" in the 1950s and 1960s, I would have been one. I felt like I was always driving kids somewhere. I belonged to the PTA or other parents' organizations in all the schools my kids attended, including St. Thomas, Our Lady of Snows, Mt. Rose, B. D. Billinghurst, Manogue, and Reno High Schools. Through these organizations I met a number of other parents, and we watched our children grow up together. I was a room mother for more than twenty-five years, baking cookies, supplying drinks, and driving kids to events, sporting activities, and field trips. The boys all participated in Little League and Pop Warner Football, and all the kids learned to ski through the Reno Junior Ski Program.

My husband, Ken, was active in the local and state bar associations. We attended the bar meetings and went to all the social functions, giving us a chance to meet most of the attorneys and their spouses not only in Northern Nevada but also the rest of the state. When Vivian Hammersmith started the Lawyers' Wives Auxiliary in Reno, I was involved in that, too, which led to a major community improvement project.

Looking for a worthwhile endeavor, we met with Dwight Nelson, the Washoe County juvenile probation officer, who told us the community needed to build a detention facility for juvenile offenders and runaways. At the time, juveniles who broke the law were housed in the Reno City Jail. When I became president of the Lawyers' Wives, we spearheaded the campaign to build what would become Wittenberg Hall. It was named after Helen Wittenberg, one of our Lawyers' Wives presidents, who had a leadership role in the effort.

My involvement taught me how to lobby and raise money, and also about juveniles, both offenders and those in need of protection. These lessons were also important after I went to Congress. It was through Lawyers' Wives that I first met Olive Hill. She was fairly new to Reno, and we became great friends. Many years later she managed my Northern Nevada congressional office in Reno. Her son, Rich, is one of Tommy's best friends. (We used to joke that we wanted to build Wittenberg Hall because we never knew if our own kids would wind up there.)

My first community leadership role came as a member of the St. Mary's Hospital Guild, when Katherine Quilici and I started the Pink Lady program. The hospital administration thought it was a great idea, but at first some of the employees felt that we might be a threat to their jobs. Of course, we weren't looking to replace anyone; we just wanted to help. We finally worked it out so we started delivering flowers and mail to the patients, helping with the discharge of the patients, and bringing the patients their food trays. We did tasks that the employees did not want to do. Still, we had a difficult time getting people to accept our wearing uniforms. Gradually, we took on other jobs, even in Admitting, as the employees became more comfortable with us.

I suppose I felt at ease in the hospital environment because of my Red Cross volunteer "nurse" training during World War II. I liked the idea of working in a hospital and volunteered two days a week. I was working at the volunteer desk one day when I was asked to serve as president of the guild. I had never thought about being president. It was a two-year term, and a bigger project than anything I'd ever done.

One of the things I did as president was to start the Mardi Gras Ball as a fund-raiser in 1963. The ball was modeled after the New Orleans Mardi Gras celebration and raised money for the guild, which in turn donated it to the hospital. Equipment was always a big need, so we had a different project every year. Sister Seraphine, the hospital administrator, let us know what the hospital needed, and we tried to raise the necessary money for that purchase. The ball was one of the hospital's most successful events for years.

I had a full life in the fifteen years I lived in Reno before Ken died in 1964. We were involved with our five children and their activities, supported many community projects, and were active in organizations committed to making Reno a better place to live.

But we still had time for politics.

CHAPTER FOUR

Politics, Nevada Style

I was no stranger to balancing my family life and working on various Nevada political campaigns from the 1950s to my own first election in 1982. George and I took Susie, my youngest child, everywhere with us until she went off to college, so she met a lot of Nevada politicians as we traveled around the state, and she learned early on the grueling realities of grassroots politics in Nevada. Jennifer Dillon joined the family in 1977, the same year Susie graduated from high school. Jennifer and her big brother, Trevor, were the children of my second son, Kenny, and his wife, Judi Moffett Dillon. After they divorced, Kenny married Sandra Ward in 1980. They are the parents of twin girls, Casey and Heather Dillon, born in August 1982, the last of my grandchildren to be born before I was elected to the United States House of Representatives.

Because I have so long been identified with the Republican Party in Nevada, people always find it hard to believe that I grew up voting Democrat, as my parents did. The first president I voted for was Franklin Roosevelt in 1944, and I am certain I voted for Harry Truman in 1948. I registered as a Republican for the 1950 elections in Nevada, mainly because my new husband, Ken, was active in the Republican Party, and I liked the party's position for limited government, lower taxes, and states' rights.

The first actual Nevada campaign—or really "non-campaign"—that I remember was when Ken ran for Washoe County public administrator in September 1950. I don't remember any campaign activity or ads; there probably weren't any. He spent no money on the campaign, merely putting his name up as a way to be involved. It was a job for which he felt qualified because the public administrator performs legal work settling estates of people who die without wills. Since Ken did not campaign, the result was exactly as expected: He came in third in the field of five candidates in the Republican primary. The primary winner, who went on to win the general election, was Cliff Young, who spent the grand sum of $80 on the primary. Cliff would later become a U.S. congressman, a state senator, and a Nevada Supreme Court justice.

Those early days were marked by battles within the Republican Party in Washoe County. Former assemblyman Les Gray and his wife, Aleta, organized a group of Republicans, including Marshall and Marvel Guisti, to challenge the party establishment. The Grays didn't like the fact that Noble Getchell, of the Republican National Committee, and William Woodburn Sr., of the Democratic National Committee, shared offices in the law firm of Woodburn and Forman.

Ken and I agreed, and we lined up with what the local newspaper dubbed the "Young Turks." I met many Republican women during this process, especially when we organized a grassroots campaign to register Republicans to vote. Several of us would meet each morning, usually at the home of Eleanor Holloway or Elsie Wycoff, and make random telephone calls to people asking if they were registered to vote. If they weren't registered and agreed to register Republican, we would send someone to register them.

("Tank" Smith, whom we later helped elect mayor of Reno, was part of the group. I remember he had all the alleys in downtown Reno paved when he was in office. Some skeptics suspected it was because he owned a ready-mix cement company.)

Another couple active in the Young Turks were Marvin and Lucy Humphrey. Marv served three terms in the Nevada Assembly, while Lucy earned the title of "Mrs. Republican" for her work in organizing Republican women. She was the first president of the Nevada Federation of Republican Women, and she also chaired the Study Club for the Republican Women's Club of Reno. She got me involved researching issues, and I reported monthly to the group. Lucy would serve for many years as Nevada's Republican National Committeewoman.

The story of the Washoe County Republicans in the 1950s and 1960s would not be complete without mentioning Hazel and Louie Gardella. Louie worked for the university as an extension agent, and when they moved to Reno from rural Nevada, Hazel became part of the heart and soul of the Republican women's volunteer force in Washoe County. She never looked for the limelight, but with Louie right next to her, she was involved in virtually every Republican campaign from the time they moved to town through the 1980s.

Also during the 1950s, Ken served as chairman of the Washoe County Republican Central Committee and, then, of the Nevada State Republican Party. His tenure helped restore calm to the party because he was organized and things ran smoothly. We held many events in the old State Building, which was where the Pioneer Auditorium stands today in downtown Reno. That building, which had no kitchen facilities, was a difficult place to hold events. The women had to cook all the food ahead of time and carry it up and down the stairs.

The Young Turks recruited and campaigned for candidates at all levels of public office. In 1952 we encouraged Cliff Young, then a young lawyer, to run for Congress against Walter Baring, the Democrat incumbent. Both Ken and I campaigned all over the state for him. Cliff probably would not be a conservative by today's definitions, but he advocated the traditional Republican philosophy. He was a diligent but not exuberant campaigner, more cerebral, pleasant, and laid-back. He had sandy-colored hair in those days, and he didn't dress like a typical lawyer; he liked the outdoors and dressed to reflect that preference. Many people ran against Walter Baring over the years. Cliff was one of the few who beat him, winning by 770 votes out of about 80,000 votes cast that year.

Interestingly enough, Pete Echeverria, a Democrat, later a state senator from Washoe County, and eventually chairman of the Gaming Control Board, was Cliff's law partner during those days. It was a good example of the bipartisan friendships and associations that exist in Nevada. Especially in the 1950s and 1960s, Nevada was such a small state population-wise that people were connected in countless ways, often related by blood, marriage, or school ties. I learned never to say anything bad about another politician, no matter what party he or she belonged to, because I might be talking to that person's relative or best friend and not know it.

In 1952 I also campaigned for the Republican nominees for president and vice president, Dwight Eisenhower and Richard Nixon, as well as for George "Molly" Malone in his successful U.S. Senate reelection effort. I first met Molly when Ken was chairman of the Nevada Republican Party. Malone was a big guy and looked kind of rumpled in his navy blue lightweight suits. He wore cowboy boots on occasion. A civil engineer, he stood up for Nevada issues, such as water and landownership.

Malone's big issue was "funny money"; he ridiculed Democrats in Washington who liked to spend more and more money on government programs. He was responsive to the Republican Party, but independent from the national party, especially if it took a stand against Nevada's interests. He put Nevada first and was more conservative than Cliff Young. Molly loved to campaign and traveled all over the state speaking at Lincoln Day dinners and county conventions. In those days before television, candidates had to campaign person to person. His daughter, also named Molly, campaigned with him, but his wife did not appear with them very often.

In 1954 I helped Cliff Young when he won reelection, beating Walter Baring by an even larger margin. I toured the "cow counties" with Cliff, did some advance work for him, walked door-to-door, held lunches and parties, and made stops at Republican women's clubs wherever they existed. In 1956 Cliff attempted to move up to the U.S. Senate but lost to Democrat Alan Bible by about 5,000 votes. Republican Dick Horton, a Reno attorney, ran for Cliff's congressional seat, losing to Walter Baring, who made a political comeback.

I worked hard for Dick Horton in 1956, doing advance work in the rural counties. In 1958 I campaigned for Dick's twin brother, Bob, when he ran for Congress, losing to Baring in a landslide. Both Bob and Dick ran person-to-person campaigns, using their connections all over the state. Their father and older brother were involved in mining, so they had lived in many Nevada communities when they were growing up. Committed to the Republican philosophy, they understood Nevada resource issues, but that wasn't enough to overcome the Baring name and the Democrats' overwhelming majority registration of voters. Both Bob and Dick became lifelong friends of mine. Today, Dick is a partner in Lionel, Sawyer, and Collins in Reno. He chaired all of my congressional campaigns and became one of my closest political advisors. Bob is a geologist and served as the director of the U.S. Bureau of Mines under Ronald Reagan.

Of course, I didn't realize it then, but the contacts I made throughout the state while helping Molly Malone, Cliff Young, and Dick and Bob Horton would prove invaluable during my own campaigns in the 1980s and 1990s. I was able to rely on people all over the state, both Republicans and Democrats, whom I had met while campaigning for these candidates. It was always helpful to have a few names of local residents to call for help. I also learned about the importance of grassroots politics and how incredibly valuable volunteers are to any campaign. They really make up the base upon which to built a candidacy, at any level. Of course, I had no inkling at the time that I'd be running for office as a tough grandmother almost thirty years later.

In 1956 I attended my first Republican National Convention, in San Francisco, where my husband was the chair of the Nevada delegation. One night during the convention, all the delegates and guests lined up to shake hands with President Eisenhower and Vice President Nixon at a reception at the San Francisco Civic Center. The president and vice president stood in the receiving line for hours. That doesn't happen today, of course; because of security concerns, delegates and guests no longer have such access to the candidates.

The convention was held at the Cow Palace, and I remember such a feeling of awe when Ike walked into the convention from the back of the room. I thought how exciting it was to be in the same room as the president, although I had met him on many occasions before he became president. He and my father were acquainted through the army, and even today, when I think about Ike, I think of him as much as a general as I do as the president. When I was just a little girl, he often spoke during commencement at West Point. My father and his friend General Lucius Clay, whom we called "Uncle Lucius," both knew Ike, and after the graduation ceremonies all three families would get together to visit.

Despite that family history, I was not exactly Ike's biggest supporter, nor was Ken. In 1952 Ken originally favored Robert Taft over Eisenhower for the Republican presidential nomination. A Kansas native, Ken preferred Taft because he was a midwestern conservative. Nonetheless, when Ike won the nomination, we worked hard for his success in the general elections of 1952 and 1956 against Adlai Stevenson. We even attended Ike's second inauguration.

Ken and I agreed on most political issues, but I recall that at one Republican state or county convention, I spoke up and supported a platform issue to which he was opposed. I can't remember the exact issue, except that it dealt with women, but I distinctly remember Ken was not pleased.

In the early 1950s, I was president of the Reno Republican Women's Club. As soon as I was elected, Mabel Havens started the Silver State Republican Women's Club, claiming that I wasn't conservative enough. I don't think her club lasted very long, but I went on to become the fourth president of the Nevada Federation of Republican Women in the mid-1950s.

In Nevada the road to a successful campaign is likely to include shaking hands and riding in parades in Tonopah and Hawthorne and advertising on television in Reno and Las Vegas. Although the demographics of the state have changed dramatically in the last fifty years, a candidate still must be willing to travel the state and to be seen at and participate in local events. Real participation is an important part of campaigning; it is not enough to dash into a town, ride in the parade, and leave.

Running for office means you have to know the dates of all the community celebrations—from Armed Forces Day in Hawthorne to Jim Butler Days in Tonopah, from Nevada Day in Carson City to Reno Rodeo Days in Reno, from the Ely and Elko Horse Races to the Jaycees State Fair in Las Vegas. Even today, in order to win, candidates would do well to attend as many of these activities as their schedule allows.

Even in the modern television and Internet age, Nevadans still expect to meet the candidates and shake their hands during a campaign. As a result, politicians meet hundreds and thousands of people. Since Nevada is still a small state, candidates must be friendly, not only to the people but also to opponents and members of the opposite political party. That goes for the campaign staff as well. If the candidate is friendly, word gets around, just as it does if he or she is not.

One of the keys to political success in Nevada has always been that the candidates must be natural, not phony. Nevadans are quite perceptive about the people they meet. After being a candidate myself, I have great respect for most officeholders and candidates. Campaigning "the Nevada way" is tiring, but also rewarding.

From the time I came to Nevada in 1949, I met just about all the U.S. senators, U.S. representatives, governors, members of the legislature, and other elected officials in the state, the lone exception being the legendary senator Pat McCarran, who died in 1954. Some of these officials I had extensive dealings with over the years, while others I merely saw on the campaign trail. Many of them are probably forgotten by most Nevadans today, but all were important to our state's development. All had strengths and weaknesses, and I didn't agree with all of them politically, but I do believe they all had Nevada's best interests at heart.

Charles Russell

One of the first Nevada politicians I met was Charlie Russell, a Republican from Ely who won the governor's race in 1950 by more than 9,000 votes. I helped him a little bit in his campaign, as I helped all the Republicans that year. A former congressman, he supported states' rights and the Republican philosophy.

Russell was tall and dark-haired, a nice family man with five children. I especially remember many Republican events that we attended at the governor's mansion in Carson City during his two terms as governor. His wife, Marge, was a gracious first lady who hosted luncheons at the mansion for Republican women. We shared a special connection because her father, Judge Guild, performed my wedding ceremony to Ken Dillon. One of their sons, David, worked in Washington, D.C., for Senator Bob Dole and later was chief of staff for Paul Laxalt after Paul was elected to the Senate. Another son, Clark, also worked for Paul, managing Ormsby House, the hotel-casino that the Laxalt family built in Carson City.

Walter Baring

Walter represented Nevada in the House of Representatives for ten terms over a twenty-four-year span from 1950 to 1974, in the days when Nevada had only one representative. He was a conservative Democrat, an affable guy who campaigned hard throughout the state. He was known for walking into the bars in the small communities and buying drinks for everyone. I don't think he drank much, but that was how campaigning was done then. He was friendly and actually listened to the people he talked to on the campaign trail. He knew Nevada and was well liked, a superb campaigner. Republicans were known to register as Democrats just so they could vote for him. A popular Nevada saying was, "No one likes Walter Baring but the voters." He wasn't a big man, just an average-looking Nevadan, and he always seemed rumpled. I'm sure that was because he spent hours driving around Nevada and always looked like he had just gotten out of a car.

Rex Bell Sr.

Lieutenant Governor Rex Bell Sr. was the front-running Republican candidate for governor in 1962 when he died of a heart attack on the Fourth of July while campaigning in Las Vegas. Because Ken was an active leader in the Republican Party, he was good friends with Rex. He was stunningly good-looking, often dressed in bright-colored cowboy shirts, cowboy boots, and western trousers. An urban cowboy, he owned at least one western clothing store. He wasn't much of a public speaker, but he was well liked, always smiling. He was married to Clara Bow, the movie star, who didn't campaign with him, and I never met her. Their son, Rex Bell Jr., went to the University of Nevada with my son Mike and later was elected district attorney of Clark County.

Alan Bible

One of the things I remember best about Senator Alan Bible was his distinctive speaking voice. He always projected his voice, and when he said, "Hello," it was almost as if he was giving a speech. I thought he looked like a lawyer, which he was. He dressed in a businesslike fashion, preferring dark suits. We were introduced at a State Bar of Nevada function when Ken was active in that organization. Bible was attorney general when I moved to Reno in 1949; he was elected to the U.S. Senate in 1954. He was a fairly conservative Democrat by most Nevadan standards, probably a moderate by Washington, D.C., standards. Bible focused on Nevada issues, especially in his role on the Senate Interior Committee. He also chaired the Senate's District of Columbia Committee before Washington was given the right to elect its own mayor. I can't think of a committee, however, that would have less of an impact on our state.

Shortly after he left office in 1974, I was managing new senator Paul Laxalt's office in Reno when Senator Bible came by one day. He politely asked if he could use the telephone to make some calls to Washington, D.C. He had Senate business that he needed to complete.

Howard Cannon

I first met Howard Cannon during his 1964 Senate campaign against Lieutenant Governor Paul Laxalt, but it was not until Paul was elected to the U.S. Senate in 1974 that I really got to know Cannon. He and Paul worked closely together in the Senate on Nevada issues. A Democrat, Cannon was a kind, nice person, always friendly to me, even though I was a Republican. A former jet pilot, he was interested in aviation issues and became chairman of the Senate Commerce, Science, and Transportation Committee.

He and Laxalt had a major disagreement over the Panama Canal issue when Laxalt was leading the effort to prevent the canal from being returned to Panama. The story told was that Cannon implied he would vote against the giveaway, but at the last minute he changed his mind. I think that vote partially contributed to his loss of his Senate seat to Republican Chic Hecht in 1982. Cannon stayed in Washington after he retired from the Senate, and I saw a lot of him at congressional golf tournaments.

Jim Santini

I got to know Jim Santini when he was a congressman and I was Paul Laxalt's Northern Nevada District representative. Then a Democrat, Jim was Nevada's only representative in the House, so his "district" was the entire state. Our offices were next door to each other in the federal building in Reno, and his excellent staff—Lynn Atcheson, Fritsi Ericson, and Kay Zunino—and ours worked together on Nevada issues. Jim was a moderate

Democrat, most frequently aligned with the "Boll Weevils," conservative southern Democrats. He worked with Senator Laxalt on many Nevada issues, such as tourism and natural resources, and was particularly interested in mining. He collected Indian artifacts, such as baskets, arrowheads, and cradle boards, which he displayed in his Washington office.

Jim gave up his House seat to run against incumbent senator Cannon in the Democrat primary in 1982, narrowly losing in a bitterly contested election. Resentment on the part of many Santini Democrats probably was a contributing factor in Cannon's general election loss to Chic Hecht. Four years later, Santini changed political parties to run as a Republican when Laxalt retired from the Senate, narrowly losing the race to Harry Reid. During that campaign I took several car and plane rides with Santini. No matter how he was traveling, he was writing hundreds of thank-you notes to his supporters and donors. Because of his moderate position on the issues, some have suggested that if Jim Santini had run against Howard Cannon as a Republican in 1982 he might have won. (An interesting theory! Those involved in politics often discuss campaigns for years afterward, offering different theories or strategies on how races could have been won or lost.) After he lost the Senate race, I saw a lot of him in Washington, at the Nevada State Society events and when he lobbied on tourism issues.

Mike O'Callaghan

Democrat Mike O'Callaghan was elected governor when Paul Laxalt retired in 1970. He is most remembered for not raising taxes and for improving state institutions. He took a personal interest and visited the state hospitals, prisons, schools, and other public institutions. A war hero, he was proud of being a veteran of the Korean War, where he lost part of a leg. Mike was the ultimate hands-on governor and was known to call state employees and politicians at three or four in the morning. More than one person told me of an early-morning phone call to the governor's office being answered by the governor himself. He truly believed in public service and was an enormously popular governor.

O'Callaghan was a big man with a burly and athletic build. He was pleasant, blunt-spoken, outgoing, and friendly, an informal, take-charge kind of guy. A partisan politician, he took an active role in advising Democrat officeholders when he was in office and afterward. He was active when the legislature was in session, calling legislators with his thoughts on bills under consideration. Once when I was in Congress, he telephoned me to ask me why I'd fired an intern from my congressional staff.

The young man in question had copied some confidential polling data from my campaign and sent it to the newspapers. After the intern admitted what he had done, I fired him. O'Callaghan demanded, "Didn't you know the intern came from a Democrat family?" He thought I should have checked the kid's voter registration before I hired him. I never inquired about my employees' political party when interviewing them for a job. I assumed if they worked for me they would be loyal. O'Callaghan thought I should have known better than to have a copy of a campaign poll in my congressional office. He was right.

We had a cordial but standoffish relationship. He never endorsed me, but on occasion he said halfway decent things about me. Throughout my career, whenever I was in Las Vegas, I called on O'Callaghan at the *Las Vegas Sun,* where he was the editor. When I was in Congress, I worked with the rest of the Nevada delegation to build the Mike O'Callaghan Federal Hospital for Veterans, named after O'Callaghan in recognition of his commitment to public service.

Bob List

I met Republican Bob List when he was the young district attorney of Ormsby County. He was elected attorney general in 1970 and reelected in 1974, defeating Richard Bryan. He was elected governor in 1978, but defeated for reelection in 1982 by Richard Bryan. Funny how that works, isn't it? Bob List's whole family participated in his campaigns. His first wife, Kathy, handed out her cookbook at parades and at events, and his parents, Frank and Alice, held the "List Round Up," a huge barbecue, every summer at their ranch in Washoe Valley. A few years after List was governor, his daughter, Suzanne, now a lawyer in California, interned for me in Washington.

One issue that Senator Laxalt's office and Governor List worked on together was the effort to keep the MX missile system out of Nevada.

Nevadans have always been willing to contribute their share to national defense, but that system would have put missiles on railroad cars and moved them around the state. It would not have been good for Nevada. Both Laxalt and List saved the state from that fate.

List got a lot of criticism for his "tax shift" proposal while he was governor, and I thought it was a bum rap. The shift moved the state from a reliance on property tax to an increased sales tax. The plan was later dubbed by opponents the "Tax Shaft," but it reduced the onerous burden of property taxes and was especially helpful to seniors and those on fixed incomes. The tax shift was a significant issue in his reelection campaign and was one of the reasons he lost that race. For all the criticism, though, his plan was a good one and has been successfully in place for nearly twenty years.

I can take some credit for postgubernatorial bliss for the former governor. In my 1990 campaign I hired Polly Minor, from Washington, to work on the campaign. It would be a truly life-changing experience for Polly; while in Reno she met former governor Bob List at an election-night party. (Bob was by then divorced from Kathy.) Polly and Bob eventually fell in love, and they were married in 1991. George and I attended their wedding in Alexandria, Virginia. Today they live in Las Vegas and are the parents of two children.

Bob Miller

I didn't know Democrat Bob Miller all that well. He was lieutenant governor when Governor Dick Bryan was elected to the U.S. Senate, so Miller became the acting governor in 1988. He was reelected twice more, becoming the longest-serving governor in state history. He and his wife, Sandy, also made history when their daughter, Megan, was born during his time as governor. There have not been many governors' wives to give birth during their time in office. George and I saw the Millers often at parades and community events around the state. He was an effective campaigner, friendly and laid-back.

Miller made frequent trips to Washington as governor to testify on Nevada concerns, and he usually met with the Nevada delegation before he testified. We even testified together before several committees on

Governor Bob List on the left, Secretary of the Interior James Watt, and me in Elko, Nevada, at a campaign event during my first congressional campaign in 1982. Collection of Barbara F. Vucanovich

Indian gaming and nuclear waste. He was well known and respected in Washington because of his work as president of the National District Attorneys Association (he was Clark County district attorney when he was elected lieutenant governor). One of my more embarrassing moments occurred in 1999 when I was interviewed by the press about Bob Miller's potential candidacy for the U.S. Senate. I dismissed his candidacy, saying, "He is really just a jock." It wasn't one of my better quotes.

Kenny Guinn

For years, Republican Kenny Guinn was mentioned as a potential candidate for governor. It happened just about every election year. And every time Guinn said something to the effect that he was interested, but it wasn't the right time for him and Dema, his wife. Then, in 1997, he announced he was running for governor in 1998. He was easily elected—

the first Republican governor in sixteen years—and reelected four years later with virtually no opposition.

I first met him when he was superintendent of schools in Clark County and Paul Laxalt was governor. Guinn was a loyal friend of Paul's. I would see Kenny and Dema over the years at functions in Las Vegas, as Guinn moved from the superintendent's position to president of Nevada Savings to chairman of the board of Southwest Gas. Later, he served briefly as president of the University of Nevada, Las Vegas, in almost a volunteer capacity since he was paid one dollar a year while a search for a new president was under way.

Kenny was and is memorable, handsome and distinguished. His hair was silver even when I first met him. He is a good family man with nice children, and he and Dema are closely involved with them. With his background in the public schools, it is not surprising that education has been his focus as governor. His Millennium Scholarships Program will have a dramatic impact on Nevada's future.

Nevada has been fortunate to be blessed with a long list of outstanding, truly committed state legislators. I've been privileged to know many of them, both in private life and in my official capacity as a member of Congress. There isn't space to talk about them as much as I would like, but here's a sampling of some of those with whom I had an opportunity to work.

Legislators

Virgil Getto—A Republican who served in the state assembly and the state senate, Virgil is an animated, interesting, plainspoken guy. Not too tall, with a ruddy complexion earned from a life of working outdoors— he owned a dairy farm—he looked and dressed like a cowboy. In the assembly, he represented mostly Churchill County, so his interests ran to issues such as agriculture, ranching, and the environment, and protecting the interests of the Fallon Naval Air Station. In the state senate, he had a geographically large district, including Churchill County, Nye County, and White Pine County. I remember that he would bring Fallon cantaloupes to the Cowbells Picnic during the Ely Horse Races. I watched

State senator Lawrence "Jake" Jacobsen (on my left) and me on the USS *Kitty Hawk* with
unidentified Nevada sailors in 1986. Jake had served on the "old" *Kitty Hawk* in 1986.
Wayne Arney, assistant secretary of the navy, invited me to visit the ship.
Official U.S. Navy photograph

him stand for hours slicing and serving those melons. He was well liked in
that mining community, too.

Lawrence Jacobsen—Better known as "Jake," he represented Douglas
County in the legislature and was a typical rural Nevada legislator—
candid, friendly, and proud of both his service in the legislature and in the
military. A navy veteran, Jake went with me on a trip to spend a day and
night on the aircraft carrier USS *Kitty Hawk.* Jake had served on the "old"
Kitty Hawk, and as we watched the planes take off and land on the deck,
I enjoyed hearing him talk about the differences between the past and the
present. He was so fascinated that he stayed up almost all night watching
those planes.

John Marvel—John was a low-key, loyal, outdoor guy, a strong representative for his Lander and Eureka counties district. I don't remember
ever seeing him in anything but cowboy hat, boots, western jacket, and
pants. John and his wife, Willie, attended the University of Nevada with

George, so they were old friends. John and Willie always campaigned together at every Republican event. He came from a big family with a couple of brothers, and his family's children were well-known competitors in rodeo events. His mother, Louise, was "Mrs. Republican" in Battle Mountain. We always stopped to see her when we were in town.

Bill Raggio—I've known Bill almost since I arrived in Reno. In 1970 Hazel Gardella and I ran his unsuccessful campaign for the U.S. Senate against Howard Cannon. When Raggio mentions that campaign, he jokingly tells people it was the only campaign he lost and I managed it. A man of great conservative principles, he has become an institution in Nevada politics and in the state senate and has helped countless Republican candidates to run for office.

There were others, of course, including those with whom I served in Congress—Richard Bryan, Harry Reid, Chic Hecht, Jim Bilbray, and John Ensign. But there will be more about them later. All of these people were important to Nevada and the Nevada political scene. But no one had the impact on the Nevada Republican Party—or gained the national prominence—of Paul Laxalt, the Basque sheepherder's son from Carson City. Certainly I would never have become a candidate myself without his encouragement and his example.

CHAPTER FIVE

My Mentor

My life has not been without trauma. As I previously mentioned, one of the most tragic events was the death of my husband, Ken Dillon, in March 1964. I was left alone to raise Kenny, who was twelve, Tommy, ten, and Susie, three and a half. Patty and Mike were grown and out of the house by then. In June of that year, Lieutenant Governor Paul Laxalt announced he would run for the U.S. Senate against Senator Howard Cannon and asked me to manage his Washoe County campaign. It turned out to be a blessing for two reasons. One, it helped me recover from the shock and grief of Ken's death; two, it introduced me to George Vucanovich.

I've been fortunate, as a Nevadan and in politics, to have met, known, and worked with many individuals whom I was able to look to as role models and as examples of how to put principle ahead of political expediency. One of the most important to me was the man I was most associated with during my political career, someone I'm proud to consider a friend and a mentor. Paul Laxalt was one of the most influential political figures Nevada has ever produced, and my association with him began long before I ever became a candidate myself.

Paul's upbringing as the son of Basque immigrants in Carson City is part of Nevada political lore. Almost as well known was the beginning of his statewide political career. As the young Carson City district attorney, he was handpicked by Nevada lieutenant governor Rex Bell to be his running mate when Bell ran for governor in 1962 against incumbent

Grant Sawyer. Rex and Paul were in Las Vegas on a hot Fourth of July to officially kick off their joint campaign. Following an afternoon rally, Bell dropped Paul off at his hotel, planning to pick him up later for an evening event. Shortly, Laxalt received a shocking phone call telling him that Rex Bell had suffered a heart attack and died.

Many people urged Paul to step up to the governor's race instead of running for lieutenant governor. But Paul, a virtual unknown outside of Carson City, wisely decided to stay where he was and went on to upset Democrat Berkeley Bunker by 9,000 votes. (After Bell's death, Las Vegas mayor Oran Gragson defeated newspaper publisher Hank Greenspun in the Republican primary for governor but was trounced by Grant Sawyer by a 2–1 margin in the general election.)

I got to know Laxalt during that 1962 campaign, as my husband, Ken, and I hosted parties for him in Reno and I attended Republican Women's Club events on his behalf. But it was two years later, when he decided to challenge incumbent senator Howard Cannon, that I truly became a part of the Laxalt team.

It was through my association with Paul Laxalt, more than anything else, that I learned how to run a political campaign. The unstoppable Hazel Gardella and I managed each of his Northern Nevada campaigns in 1964, 1966, 1974, and 1980. Dick Horton used to say, "Paul will be in deep trouble if his opponents figure out that the total of the 'Laxalt Machine' consists of Barbara and Hazel." We were a great team. Hazel ran the headquarters and managed the volunteer work. I planned Paul's schedule, performed the necessary advance work, and made the travel arrangements for all of his Northern Nevada activities. I met lots of airplanes, picking Paul up and driving him all over the state. I made presentations on his behalf, organized rallies, set up meetings, and made sure he got to and from the events on time.

The 1964 Senate campaign was the first time I was paid for my campaign work, although if you figure it on an hourly basis, it wasn't much. I agreed to work for $600 a month for twelve- to fourteen-hour days, seven days a week. Political campaigns have no fixed schedule. The old saying is that you can sleep after election day. As soon as I was hired, I shopped for a headquarters, selecting an old two-story house with big rooms, across from where Luciano's restaurant is now, on South Virginia Street in Reno.

My favorite photograph with Senator Paul Laxalt, taken in Washington, D.C., during the time we both represented Nevada. Collection of Barbara F. Vucanovich

It wasn't a bad place, but later we moved farther south on Virginia Street into the old Hansel and Gretel store, where parking was reasonable and we had more visibility. (We used this same building when Paul ran for the Senate in 1974; perhaps it is a sign of the changing times that the building is now an adult bookstore.)

Phone banks were always part of our Laxalt campaign efforts. We installed numerous black rotary dial phones (this was 1964, remember) in small cubicles for volunteers to use. Hazel and I worked together coordinating the phone bank operations while volunteers made thousands of calls to raise money and to get out the vote. During a typical day in the campaign headquarters, it was grassroots politics at its best. Volunteers updated the precinct lists by comparing the lists to the telephone book to find out if people were registered to vote. We called those who were not on the precinct lists to urge them to register to vote for Paul.

We had manual typewriters, of course, and copy machines that were nothing like the copiers of today. We poured gunky ink into a mimeograph machine, then we had to type on a wax form, roll that around the print drum, ink the machine, and crank the handle. The copies came out as fast as we could turn the handle.

The headquarters was a whirlwind of activity, even more so when Paul was in town. We held meetings all the time—breakfast, lunch, and evening—with voters and supporters. We tried to stagger the schedule for volunteers so we didn't wear them out. The first group showed up to help with breakfast. Another crew came in about 9:00 A.M. to stuff envelopes or to make calls. They would quit working at 11:30 A.M. when another group arrived with food for lunch if we had set up a luncheon event. At 1:30 P.M. we would clean up, and new volunteers would arrive to stuff envelopes or make calls. They worked until 5:00 P.M., then once again a new crew arrived with more food for another event in the evening.

I still have a few red berets, part of the French Basque native apparel, that our volunteers wore at events and while walking door-to-door for Paul. Most of the volunteers were women. We started "Ladies for Laxalt," but we had male volunteers too, including George Tavernia, Bob and Dick Horton, Fo Mentaberry, Buddy Jukich, Mike Lemich, Luther Mack, Richard Fulstone, Roger Trounday, and Woody Wilson, a Republican assemblyman from Clark County. Of course, one of the male volunteers became a very important man in my life. As I mentioned previously, I first met George Vucanovich when he volunteered during the 1964 campaign. Because he was concerned when I worked alone late at night at headquarters or when I was traveling the Nevada highways alone, he hung out at headquarters or escorted me on late trips to make sure I got home safely.

Mailings were a daily occurrence in the campaign. We constantly stuffed envelopes and mailed thousands of complimentary copies of the classic *Sweet Promised Land,* by Paul's brother Robert ("Frenchy" to his family and friends). The book told the story of their father, Dominique, and his Basque roots. This special edition, with a new foreword by Robert, was one of the most effective campaign pieces I've ever seen. We used it in every campaign, and many people still have copies in their homes.

Because of the Laxalts' Basque heritage, chorizo was the food of choice for events on the campaign trail. Hazel and I put together dozens of chorizo, bean, and salad functions all over the state. We worked on those events together, arranging for the food and making sure Paul's schedule allowed him to attend. People would line up for the food, and Paul would stand at the head of the line, greeting each person as he or she went through (sometimes they came back two or three times). Of course, the traditional Basque libation is the notoriously potent Amer Picon, and early in the campaign we served Picon Punch at some of the smaller events. One night in Tonopah, one of our "supporters" enjoyed the Picon a little too much and began crawling on the ground at the park, pulling on Paul's pant leg so he could talk to him. We decided it would be wise not to serve Picon Punch at other campaign events that year.

An important part of every campaign is arranging speaking opportunities. Of all the Nevada politicians I watched over the years, Paul was by far the best public speaker. He would jot down three or four words on a note card and then speak for an hour. He never used a script or a prepared text. He told wonderful stories to illustrate his point. He sounded like he was just talking to you over a cup of coffee; it wasn't "speechified." I suspect each person in the audience felt he was talking directly to him or her. I've always believed this ability was part of his success as a politician. He also was a good one-on-one campaigner. Believe me, meeting people and shaking hands and trying to be interested in everything someone says to you is hard work. Paul had an enormous amount of charisma, with both men and women, and he could make you feel like a friend even if he had just met you. That was true throughout his political career.

Visits from prominent officeholders usually boost a campaign's visibility in the media, although sometimes they can be a liability. In 1964, Republican senator Barry Goldwater was running an uphill battle against President Lyndon Johnson for president, and the Arizonan was not particularly popular in Nevada. Goldwater was scheduled to visit Las Vegas in October. Some Republicans felt it would not help the Laxalt campaign against Cannon for Paul to be seen as visibly supporting Goldwater. Paul was urged to stay away and not meet the senator. But Paul was always loyal to his friends and to his principles. He knew Barry and had worked with him in the past. As a result, he was there to meet Goldwater's plane when it arrived in Las Vegas. Many thought this public meeting coming late in the race, when undecided voters were making up their minds, made the difference in the election. Goldwater lost Nevada by 28,000 votes; Laxalt lost by fewer than 100. A few more ticket splitters might have made the difference, but turning his back on Goldwater would have been much more damaging, in my opinion. Paul did the right thing.

Hazel and I also worked with all of Paul's closest campaign advisors. He was open to ideas and involved all of his staff in reviewing his advertising campaigns and budgets. George Abbott was his political advisor, Alan Abner did early media, Ed Allison was his spokesman and handled public relations, Jerry Dondero was the overall campaign manager, Wayne Pearson did strategy and polling, Sig Rogich handled advertising, and Bill Sinnott was his gaming expert.

One week before the general election, I was walking into Paul's headquarters when I watched an open car drive by with Senator Howard Cannon and President Lyndon Johnson, waving as they passed, part of a parade put on by the Democrats. I was dismayed. Rarely does a president campaign for a candidate in Reno, Nevada. I remember walking into headquarters and announcing that we had just lost the election.

I was right, but just barely. That first campaign ended in disappointment, although it took a recount to decide it. The election-night returns were close, but favorable. Then, the Clark County clerk closeted herself in her office alone to finish counting the votes. By morning the report was that Paul lost by 48 votes. He demanded a recount. After it was over, the official tally showed he'd lost by 84 votes. Paul was undaunted and, in fact, would say later that losing was probably a good thing because he was not as ready to be a senator as he was ten years later, after serving as governor and working in the private sector. Still, the loss hurt.

In 1966, when Paul ran successfully for governor, his third statewide race in as many general elections, Hazel and I again handled his Northern Nevada campaign. Paul later said it was one of the best campaigns he was ever involved in, although in my mind we ran the same type of campaign operation as we did in 1964. By just fewer than 6,000 votes (out of more than 137,000 cast), Paul beat Democrat incumbent governor Grant Sawyer, who was seeking an unprecedented third term.

By all measures, Paul had a successful four years as governor. He opened the door to corporate ownership of Nevada casinos, which in turn led to an end of mob involvement in the industry and paved the way for today's modern casino environment. He successfully fought off federal government efforts to investigate the gaming industry. He also helped establish the community college system in Nevada and the medical school at the University of Nevada. One of the by-products of his time as governor was that it coincided with the second term of California governor Ronald Reagan, and the two developed a friendship that would pay dividends for both of them in later years.

There aren't many perks while working in a political campaign, but a politician who succeeds in getting elected is often able to make appointments, some paid and some not. After Paul's election as governor, I was honored when he named me to the Nevada Advisory Board for Higher Education, an unpaid position. He also nominated me to represent Nevada on a trip to Russia. Not only was that an unpaid perk, but I had to pay my own expenses. However, it was an honor for me to represent Nevada on this international tour. (More about that later.)

There's little doubt that Paul Laxalt could have been reelected to a second term as governor in 1970, but instead he announced that he was retiring from politics to spend more time with his family. He had a brood of lively youngsters who needed his time and attention. Not long after he left office, he and his wife, Jackie, divorced. Paul and his family started building a new hotel-casino in Carson City, named Ormsby House after the boardinghouse his mother had run when he was growing up.

But the political bug never really left him, and in 1974, when Senator Alan Bible announced he was retiring after three terms in office, Paul announced his candidacy for the Senate seat. He would be running against

Harry Reid, who at the time was the state's young lieutenant governor. And, naturally, before long Hazel and I were on board to manage his Northern Nevada campaign.

Our campaign activities followed the same pattern as in other races—a never-ending series of luncheons, phone calls, mailings, coffees, speaking engagements, rallies, and picnics. Because of our experiences in past campaigns, we had many more contacts across the state, and I set out to find at least one key person in every precinct in Northern Nevada who would be responsible for getting out the vote for Paul. These volunteers were to visit every person in their precincts, asking them for their support for Paul. (Little did I know that I would also be making valuable contacts for my own political campaign eight years later.)

Working against us was the fact that 1974 was not a good year for Republicans. It was the year of Watergate, and Republican candidates everywhere were trying to distance themselves from President Richard Nixon's troubles without being disloyal to the Republican Party. Democrats would make major gains in the House of Representatives that year, and one of the Republican casualties was Nevada's first-term congressman David Towell, defeated by the up-and-coming Democrat Jim Santini. Paul said, "Every day I wait for the next shoe to drop in Washington, D.C." We never knew what new problem would arise out of Watergate, and Democratic candidates everywhere were beating Republicans over the head with it. Even Nixon's resignation on August 9, 1974, in the wake of the impeachment process, didn't ease the pressure on Republican candidates. And President Gerald Ford's pardon of Richard Nixon compounded the problem.

The Republican National Committee assisted Paul by sending Vice President Gerald Ford to Reno to campaign for Paul on July 30. Ten days later he would be president, but no one knew that then. When Ford arrived at the Reno airport aboard *Air Force Two,* he was greeted by Reno mayor Sam Dibitonto and other Republican leaders. He was given a full escort with motorcycle police everywhere he went in town, apparently because of threats made against both the president and the vice president.

The media coverage was extensive, with front-page stories in the newspapers for several days in advance of the trip and afterward. Ford appeared at a rally at Park Lane Mall before attending a luncheon in the showroom at John Ascuaga's Nugget. The luncheon cost only $20 per person, and the Laxalt campaign and the Washoe County Republican Party sold tickets. Among those who purchased a ticket was former longtime Nevada congressman Walter Baring, who had been defeated for reelection in 1972. He was seated up front and received a standing ovation when introduced. I'm sure he attended the luncheon because he had served with Ford in the House of Representatives. In contrast, the press made much of the fact that Governor Mike O'Callaghan did not make an effort to publicly greet the vice president. I'm sure it was related to the fact that O'Callaghan was a Democrat and a strong supporter of Reid, whom he had taught in high school.

The media didn't let Ford get away without answering some tough questions on Watergate. Always loyal to the Republican Party—and loyal to his president—Ford stated that it was wrong to vote for impeachment. He believed that the president would be exonerated because he was innocent of an impeachable offense. Ford also said he wouldn't be a candidate for president in 1976. Events, of course, would change his future.

Ford told the media he supported Nixon's tightening of the belt in dealing with inflation and supported revenue sharing as a significant step in reducing the federal deficit. When he was questioned about gaming, he stated that he personally enjoyed gambling on occasion and he thought that it was a states' rights issue. The statement of his I liked the best was, "The government that is big enough to give you what you want is the government that is big enough to take what you have."

In mid-August, Senator Barry Goldwater campaigned in Reno on behalf of Paul's campaign. This was ten years after his campaign for president, and the unfairly negative public perception that once had been associated with him had significantly shifted. Goldwater was now popular with the growing conservative base in Nevada, regardless of party affiliation. The resulting publicity wasn't even a quarter of the coverage of the Ford visit, but I know the trip helped Paul's campaign.

The campaign was close and hard fought all the way. The turning point, I believe, may well have come when Reid was perceived as questioning the integrity of the Laxalt family, even going so far as to ask for financial statements from Paul's brothers and sisters (and one of his sisters was a Catholic nun). The attack on his family provided Paul an opportunity to respond in a way that was as much personal as it was political. The attack on the well-respected and well-liked Laxalt family made Reid appear petty.

On election day, initial results showed Paul ahead by 624 votes out of nearly 170,000 cast. A conservative Independent American Party candidate attracted nearly 11,000 votes, most of which probably would have gone into the Laxalt column. Reid demanded a recount. We spent some painful weeks holed up in the basement of the Washoe County Administration Building with both sides watching the ballots being recounted by hand. This process was repeated county by county. I saw some things I still barely believe. For instance, the labor unions, supporting Reid, brought in out-of-state workers to help with the recount. One of them was a guy who put pencil lead under his fingernails so he could mark ballots and have them declared void. (Election law stipulates that any ballot that contains identifying marks must be thrown out and not counted.) There was another guy we called "Specs" because he wore special magnifying glasses that allowed him to read papers and ballots from across the table. I was relieved when the recount showed that Paul had won by 611 votes.

It was a remarkable victory, both for the organization and for Paul Laxalt personally. In 1974 he became the only Republican in the country to pick up a Senate seat previously held by a Democrat. He would later jokingly remark that he had unusually bad political timing, running for the Senate the first time in 1964, the year of the Johnson landslide, and then in 1974, the year of Watergate. It also started him on the road to national prominence. Two years later he was one of the few established Republicans to support Ronald Reagan for president against Gerald Ford, support that Reagan never forgot. When Reagan ran for president in 1980, Laxalt was his campaign chairman, and after he was elected, Laxalt was known nationally as the "First Friend," the president's eyes and ears on Capitol Hill.

When Paul was elected to the U.S. Senate in 1974, he hired me as his Northern Nevada District representative. It was a paid position managing his office in Reno, which handled all Northern Nevada issues. I represented him at events throughout Northern Nevada when he wasn't able to attend, supervised all of the constituent casework in the office, and served as his political liaison in Northern Nevada. It allowed me to stay in touch with a lot of people who, as it turned out, would be important to me when I made my run for Congress in 1982.

In comparison to the campaigns in 1962, 1964, 1966, and 1974, his reelection campaign in 1980 was almost relaxed. It was the year of the Reagan landslide, Paul was enormously popular, and for the longest time it even appeared that the Democrats wouldn't have a serious candidate to run against him. In the end, former state senator Mary Gojack announced that she would run—she was the only Democrat who even dared to enter the race. The differences were stark. Paul was a respected conservative, with a strong pro-Nevada record in the Senate. Mary, who would run against me two years later for Congress, had a proven liberal voting record and got most of her support from out-of-state labor unions and feminist organizations. Paul defeated her by more than 50,000 votes, sweeping every county.

Paul was certainly a lock for reelection in 1986, but he chose not to run, announcing his decision to a packed crowd in the old senate chambers in the Nevada State Capitol in Carson City. It surprised many, but I know the decision was strictly a personal one. He had never felt that the job was his in perpetuity, and he felt that he had accomplished almost everything he wanted to accomplish in the United States Senate. It was time to move on. He established a highly successful consulting business in Washington, and he and his second wife, Carol, were finally able to carve out some time for themselves away from the public spotlight.

Paul was fond of saying that the public quickly forgets about you after you leave public office, and to a certain extent that is true. As time passes, fewer will remember Paul Laxalt as a former governor and United States senator from Nevada. That's too bad, because his is a classic American success story: the son of Basque immigrants who grew up in a small town in Nevada and went on to become a governor, a senator, a key advisor to one of our greatest presidents, and, for a time in 1988, a candidate for president of the United States.

One of his most significant contributions, I believe, is that because of his close relationship to Ronald Reagan, a number of Nevadans found opportunities in Washington that they might not otherwise have had. For example, Bob Broadbent, from Las Vegas, became director of the

U.S. Bureau of Reclamation. And, as I said before, Bob Horton, from Reno, became director of the U.S. Bureau of Mines. Frank Fahrenkopf, from Reno, became chairman of the Republican National Committee. Reese Taylor, from Carson City, was chair of the Interstate Commerce Commission, and Cameron Batjer, also from Carson City and a Nevada Supreme Court justice, became the vice chair of the National Appeals Board of the U.S. Parole Commission. That doesn't count the dozens of others who gained staff-level appointments throughout the federal government. Without Paul Laxalt's influence, none of those things could have happened for people from a small state like Nevada, regardless of their qualifications.

I learned a lot about campaigns, about politics and people by watching and learning from Paul Laxalt. And I wasn't alone. One of his greatest legacies will be the huge number of young people he brought to Washington to work in his office as interns or who volunteered on his campaigns. They were exposed to a big world outside of the Silver State, and many of them have returned to Nevada and started successful careers of their own.

Politically, Paul Laxalt was always true to his principles, but he was never doctrinaire. He was able to work with people from both sides of the aisle, from Republican Jake Garn to Democrat Ted Kennedy. He was respected by everyone as a man of his word and a man with whom you could work. He was a strong advocate for his conservative principles, some of them unpopular at times, but you could never accuse him of being harsh or excessively partisan. It is an example that more politicians would do well to follow.

The Laxalt influence will be felt in Nevada for many years to come. I know I felt it when I made my own decision to become a candidate. Decades of growth were reflected in the 1980 federal census, and Nevada was awarded a second seat in the House of Representatives. On the basis of all of my personal and political experience, I felt I was ready when Paul Laxalt and others encouraged me to run for the new Nevada seat that would be filled in the 1982 elections.

PART II

A Flamingo in
the Barnyard of Politics

CHAPTER SIX

A Tough Grandmother

When I ran television commercials in 1982 describing myself as a "tough grandmother," the message was that I was someone who was compassionate but strong enough to make tough decisions. It was a line I tried to deliver forcefully. After watching me on television, my young granddaughter Nora, daughter of my son Tommy and his wife, Cathy, turned to her mother and said, "How come Grandmommy has to be so tough?" Nora's sisters, Maggie and Katie, and her brother, Patrick, didn't understand either. Fortunately for me, the voters got my message.

Reflecting its status as the fastest-growing state in the nation, Nevada was given a second congressional seat after the 1980 Census. For the first time, Nevada would be electing two members to the House of Representatives in the 1982 election, and it created a considerable amount of political jockeying.

It was an open seat, without an incumbent, so many people considered it an opportunity. I was one of those people. First, however, the 1981 Nevada Legislature would have to determine how to apportion the two congressional districts. That decision would have a major impact on who would run and who could win.

There were two proposals, one dividing the state into north-south districts and the other dividing it into east-west districts. The first proposal had a southern district based in Clark County and a northern district for the rest of the state, including Washoe County and all of rural Nevada.

The east-west proposal would effectively give Southern Nevada two seats, since the majority of the population in both districts would be in Las Vegas. It would have made it almost impossible for a northern Nevadan to win a congressional seat.

The north-south division made sense for a number of reasons, most importantly because the issues in largely rural Northern Nevada were vastly different from those in metropolitan Clark County. However, some influential Southern Nevada legislators argued that because they had more than 60 percent of the state's population, they should have stronger representation. After considerable debate, the north-south separation carried the day, thanks to the influence of Governor Bob List. To ensure population balance between the districts, the northern district would include sixteen northern counties and a piece of northern Clark County. Geographically, with the exception of states that had only one representative in Congress, the northern district would be the largest congressional district in the House of Representatives. (After the 1990 Census, as Clark County continued to grow, the northern or Second District was expanded to include all of Nevada except metropolitan Las Vegas and Henderson, extending all the way to Boulder City; the 2000 Census gave Nevada a third member in the House of Representatives, with two seats in Clark County.)

The legislature's decision cleared the way for Northern Nevadans to run. Because I had represented Paul Laxalt in the northern part of the state for nearly seven years and because I was well known politically after thirty years of involvement, lots of people suggested that I become a candidate for the new seat. Paul encouraged me, too, suggesting in a casual way that I give some thought to running. He implied that I knew the district and the people and recommended that I talk with Jerry Dondero, his chief of staff, for political advice and support. At first I was a bit surprised by these comments. But after all, I had spent a great many years in politics and had worked for the people of the State of Nevada, and I knew a lot of people, so I started to think about it more seriously. It never really crossed my mind that being a woman was even a consideration. George and I spent private time alone discussing the pros and cons of what this would mean in our lives, and we included all of our kids in our discussions as our plans became more clear. The more I thought about it, the more my enthusiasm grew. I knew I was as qualified as any of the other candidates being mentioned. And I realized I could make a difference for the state and help on important issues.

I made up my mind that I would run—and run hard—but experience had taught me that political campaigns don't happen overnight. Paul Laxalt's saying that there are "no immaculate conceptions in politics" is true. I knew I had plenty of homework to do before I officially announced. So in June 1981, almost a year and a half before the election, I flew to Washington for a round of meetings that would be crucial to my future success.

I met with Anne Stanley and Larry Halloran from the National Republican Congressional Committee (NRCC) and with Paul Laxalt and Jerry Dondero, who arranged my first political action committee (PAC) meetings. I also met with Tony Payton, a political consultant with deep Nevada ties, and with Republican congresswomen Marjorie Holt and Margaret Heckler. They gave me some idea of what it was like to serve in Congress, but both were rather reserved, since it was my first meeting with them. As I would learn when I was in their position, they undoubtedly held meetings like this all the time, and they knew nothing about me or where I stood on the issues. As it turned out, Holt and I worked together on a variety of issues after I was elected. She had been in Congress since 1972 and had a reputation for good constituent service in a district that included many federal employees. After the 1980 Census, Margaret Heckler had been put in the same district as the virtually unbeatable Democrat Barney Frank. That was to be her last term in Congress.

I felt good about my reception in Washington, and on June 29, right after I returned to Reno, I announced the formation of an exploratory committee to investigate the possibility of running for Congress. I was the first candidate to do so, but I would not be the last.

My first task was to get organized. I set up a steering committee that would assist in developing and studying issues, lining up staff, creating lists of potential donors, establishing advisory committees in every county in the state, and determining an overall strategy for winning. As much as I knew about managing campaigns and about Nevada, I had no experience being a candidate. I knew I had a lot to learn, so I took advantage of some of the invitations I received to attend "campaign schools."

One of the best was put on by Joe Gaylord, a longtime advisor to Newt Gingrich at the NRCC. We learned about being a candidate from the ground up, everything from putting together an organization and dealing with the news media to how to dress and how to "work a room." During part of the school, we attended PAC receptions, which gave us an opportunity to meet the lobbyists and for them to meet us.

I was sixty-one years of age, the only grandmother and one of the oldest "students" in the class. My classmates were mostly young men, and lawyers, and many had held some elected office before running for Congress. I was really the new kid on the block, despite my experience at the grassroots level. For the first time, I was looking at an election through a candidate's eyes, and sometimes it seemed overwhelming. At the same time, I loved being in Washington with the other candidates and congressmen and congresswomen (although there weren't a lot of the latter). I enjoyed listening to their ideas for solutions to the problems facing the country.

The campaign school covered information on issues, campaign organization, fund-raising, tactics, strategy, targeting, polling, get-out-the-vote techniques, media relations, campaign advertising, and even candidate behavior. I learned a lot about campaigns; the most important thing I learned, however, was that I had to be myself—I couldn't be a phony.

I attended one of the campaign schools with a broken foot bone, suffered as a result of a slip during an early campaign stop. Part of the schedule included a reception at the White House, hosted by President Ronald Reagan and his wife, Nancy. Determined to go, I entered the White House on crutches. I'm glad I went, because one of the benefits was having my picture taken with the president for use in my campaign.

At the NRCC school, my speaking was constantly videotaped, and I hated it. I had never seen myself on camera, and it was dismaying to see that I wasn't perfect. My classmates offered critiques of my performance, and I did the same for them, but it was a painful process. As a result, I hired television consultant Roger Ailes (later president of Fox News) to help me with my public speaking. I met with him in New York several times between September 1981 and January 1982. His two-hour sessions cost about $500 each, and he was a brutally honest critic.

Roger would videotape me while I was "interviewed" and then offer an assessment. Once he noticed that I had a habit of bouncing my foot up and down. "You didn't like that question," he said. I asked, "How did you know?" He pointed out my bouncing foot. Anyone who could survive his critiques could handle any press interviews. The bottom line, he told me, was "You come across as a nice lady. That won't help you win. People will listen to what you have to say, but you have to say it with authority. You have to stand up and be tough."

I didn't necessarily agree with everything he said, but his training prepared me for the media scrutiny that is so difficult for most first-time candidates. My association with Roger was almost a love-hate relationship, but I believe it was critical on my road to victory.

One of the funniest campaign school invitations I received was from the Women's Political Caucus, which is basically an arm of the Democratic Party, with a membership mostly of liberal Democrat women. Either they sent me the invitation by mistake or they figured that I wouldn't come. But I couldn't resist, and the group was appalled when I showed up.

After a few school days, I ran into Democrat Mary Gojack in the ladies' room. She would become my opponent in the general election. To say she was surprised to see me would be an understatement.

Another part of the early stages of the campaign was polling to determine what the voters thought about the issues and the candidates. I took my first poll in July 1981, using Wayne Pearson of Las Vegas, Paul Laxalt's pollster. He concluded that Mary Gojack, expected to be my opponent in the general election, had come out of her 1980 Senate race against Laxalt in "damn good shape," to use Wayne's words. Although she was well known, Wayne said she had strong negatives. In a "head-to-head" matchup, she won among Democrats and I won among Republicans, but the majority of the voters were undecided—not surprising that early in the campaign. We also did a Republican primary matchup between me and Reno assemblyman Paul Prengaman, who was thinking about running. I came out ahead, 36 percent to his 28 percent. According to the Pearson poll, more than 60 percent of the people in the new congressional district were pro-choice on abortion, and less than 40 percent were pro-life, which was my position. For most people surveyed, however, the number one issue was jobs; taxes were second.

In June 1981 I made one of my most important decisions, hiring Tony Payton as my lead consultant for planning campaign strategy and tactics, a role he would play in every one of my campaigns. Tony was a westerner, the former publisher of the *Gardnerville Record-Courier,* who had gone to Washington with Congressman David Towell in the early 1970s and stayed there after Towell was defeated for reelection. I had known Tony from previous Laxalt campaigns and felt his knowledge of both Nevada and Washington would be beneficial. I also asked Reno attorney Dick Horton to be my campaign chairman and Thornton Audrain, a CPA and longtime friend of mine and George's, to be the campaign treasurer, with my daughter Susie acting as assistant treasurer.

We decided I should start reaching out to conservative leaders in the state to gain their support of my candidacy. For example, I met with Judy Brailsford, a pro-life leader in the Mormon community in Las Vegas, and with Helen Palmer of Hawthorne, a businesswoman and a conservative Republican activist. Both agreed to help, and I continued to meet with other community leaders throughout the campaign, lining up support for my candidacy.

We also made a strategic decision to run television advertising in the early spring of 1982, six months before the primary election. There were two reasons for it. First, and most important, we felt that we needed to tell people about Barbara Vucanovich, that I was an energetic conservative, a former businesswoman, a mother and grandmother, and a person in touch with Nevada. We ran one-minute spots, twice as long as most commercials, so we would have time to tell the story. The other reason for running early television was that we felt it would discourage fund-raising by other candidates and would demoralize them. The thinking was, if I could run television ads six months before the election, it would appear that I must have a lot of support and a lot of money. The first was true, the second only marginally true. But, just as in real life, in politics perception is often reality.

We hired political television consultant Jay Bryant of Washington to do the filming. He came to Nevada in March 1982, and we filmed television commercials outside Genoa in Douglas County, on a hill outside Reno along the Truckee River, and at the Winnemucca airport in Humboldt County. The ads Bryant created showed me jogging in the park, walking up a hill, flying and landing our Cessna, working at a desk, and at home surrounded by my family.

During one of the filming sessions, I was talking to the camera about the kind of person we needed in Congress. I said that we needed someone who had compassion for those less fortunate but was strong enough to make hard decisions. "Sort of like a tough grandmother" was the phrase I used. It caught on, and after those ads ran, I was known as the "Tough Grandmother." The phrase was an effective shorthand way of summing up my political identity for that campaign, but once I had a voting record I never used that theme again.

Some suggested that it was risky to emphasize my status as a grandmother. After all, I was in my early sixties and didn't want to come across as an old fuddy-duddy. By talking about it openly, and by portraying myself as an active person, jogging and flying an airplane, I wanted to turn a potential negative into a positive. The goal was to show that I had the maturity and the life experiences to which voters could relate. I believe it worked.

Of course, being "tough" certainly didn't mean that I had to start being rude to people or try to act like a man. It simply meant that I was assertive and firm in my beliefs and not afraid to express myself. After all, I had raised five kids, been a single mother twice, and been a small business owner, and I didn't do it by being a pushover.

Strategically and image-wise, this theme offered a great contrast to Mary Gojack, who could appear strident and aggressive at times. She portrayed herself as an active "feminist," which she was—a risky strategy to take in Nevada. We felt that positioning me as a "tough grandmother" would show the voters a clear difference from the image she projected. And, of course, a "tough grandmother" was an accurate representation of who I was. I emphasized my family because my family was an important part of me. But I also felt ready to make the hard decisions that being a member of Congress demanded.

Ultimately, my ads created a sensation and were talked about by everyone who saw them. Even the political reporters joined in the discussion by writing news stories about them.

In November 1981, I had taken a leave of absence from Senator Laxalt's staff and started campaigning in earnest, embarking on a campaign that ran virtually nonstop for the next twelve months. I opened headquarters, held campaign and finance committee meetings, and toured major employers, such as Nevada Bell, to meet employees. I attended and spoke at Republican functions and meetings, sent out my first direct mail piece, visited virtually every town of every size in Nevada, meeting with everyday Nevadans and opinion leaders in all parts of the state.

I also spent a lot of time raising money, both in Nevada and in Washington, D.C. No campaign will succeed without financial support, so it had to be an activity that I emphasized. Nate Topol held my first fundraising event at his Lakeridge Tennis Club in Reno, and many supporters hosted receptions in their homes to raise money for my campaign. I also held PAC receptions in Washington, San Francisco, and Houston. I met with businesspeople throughout Nevada to ask for financial commitments.

Nevada was—and is—a state that places a great value on face-to-face campaigning. In every community I visited, I would walk the business district, shaking hands and meeting business owners and customers. I also would walk door-to-door in many towns. I spoke to Rotary, Kiwanis, Exchange, and Soroptomist (of which I was a member) clubs; chambers of commerce and contractor organizations, Citizens for Responsible Government, women realtors, the Retired Officers Association, and in senior citizens' centers around the state. (One popular activity for political candidates is to work the food lines at senior centers, and I dished up more than my share of mashed potatoes, meat, and gravy.)

I attended Republican events, such as Lincoln Day dinners, Republican Women's Club luncheons, Republican Central Committee meetings, and local community events and parades. Outdoor community activities begin in May and run through late fall in Nevada, and these were "must-attend" attractions for candidates, whether it was Armed Forces Day in Hawthorne, Jim Butler Days in Tonopah, Carson Valley Days in Minden/Gardnerville, the Cantaloupe Festival in Fallon, Ione Days, Mason Valley Days in Yerington, Sons of Italy dinners, local church barbecues, Yugoslavs of Nevada receptions, the Harvest Festival in Pahrump, or Basque festivals in Sparks, Winnemucca, Las Vegas, and Elko. The schedule was hectic and it didn't stop.

Of course, not everything went as smoothly as we would have liked. On a wintry day in January 1982 I officially kicked off my campaign with what was supposed to be a traditional swing around the state. In my announcement speech, I stressed that I would be more effective than anyone else in the race because of my real-life experiences, my relationship with Senator Paul Laxalt, and my support for President Reagan. Little did I know I was about to add to those real-life experiences.

The first day we held news conferences in Carson City, Reno, and North Las Vegas, which went well. We then planned to take two days and fly in a rented twin-engine plane to several rural towns, where we would meet with supporters and the local media. On the morning of the first day, we flew out of Reno and were preparing to land at the small municipal airport in Fallon. The runway was covered with an inch or so of snow, and there was snow from previous storms piled up along the sides of the airstrip. In the plane were George and myself; Charlie Joerg, one of my campaign cochairs; Bill Martin, my public relations consultant; Dennis George, my rural counties campaign coordinator; and the pilot.

As we prepared to land, the pilot put down the landing gear but failed to notice that it didn't lock in place. It collapsed when we touched the ground, and the plane slid along on its belly for more than 1,500 feet, slowly executing a couple of 360-degree spins before coming to rest in a snowbank. It was a perfect "wheels up" landing, and fortunately no one was hurt, although the plane never flew again. The snow on the runway cushioned our landing, eliminating sparks and friction. Without that snow, the result might have been much different.

The incident ended up making the news, of course, and Mary Gojack dropped me a note about the incident. She jokingly wondered if I'd gone too far in getting free press coverage. She ended her letter by stating she was glad no one was hurt. Her letter was a good example of the relationship between candidates in Nevada. Candidates often know each other well, even their opponents or those of the opposite party. Mary and I disagreed on most issues, but we were always personally cordial to one another.

The old saying that lawyers should never represent themselves applies to campaign management as well, as I learned firsthand. Although I had as much experience as anyone in running campaigns, I realized that I needed a professional to take care of the daily nuts-and-bolts aspects, including organization, volunteers, and get-out-the-vote efforts. Unfortunately, I hired an inexperienced campaign manager, and from November 1981 to the following March I found myself going into headquarters every day, calling all the shots. I was acting like a campaign manager myself, not like a candidate, wasting time that would have been better spent meeting voters and raising money.

Another problem was that I did not have enough control over the campaign budget and quickly found myself spending money unnecessarily. Early money poured into the campaign and poured out just as quickly. If a campaign and candidate don't have tight controls on spending, the campaign can waste thousands of dollars.

George and I put up $50,000 of our own money to start the campaign, but by March 1982 we had spent close to $120,000 and had very little to show for it. Campaigns require a lot of money on the front end. I had paid for headquarters, brochures, signs, travel, staff salaries, and consultants' fees. The campaign spent money on things I didn't need, such as ten thousand Styrofoam coffee cups with VUCANOVICH FOR CONGRESS printed on them. I used those cups at every event I scheduled for fourteen years, but I still have a few boxes of them. I even used them—and still do—at family campouts.

Of course, one of the problems was that the manager I had hired, while well meaning, was simply not up to the job. A change had to be made. In the end, my daughter Patty agreed to temporarily manage the campaign until I could find an experienced person. She was planning to run for state treasurer that year, and she was experienced at running campaigns. She took the job on the condition that I would follow her orders.

Patty literally cleaned house at headquarters, even scheduling a moving van to take my desk out of the office. She took control of my schedule, arranging for me to meet with different groups and to travel around the state, and drafted a preliminary tactical campaign plan and budget. She made some staff changes and organized my volunteers. Bringing her in was one of the best decisions I made during the campaign.

Patty also started the process of targeting voter groups and geographic areas, something that proved extremely important as the campaign progressed. On the basis of my background and beliefs, we planned to target seniors, farmers, ranchers, mining people, and businesspeople, Mormons and Catholics, retired military personnel, Yugoslavs, volunteer women's groups, and gaming associations and professionals. She also divided the district into five areas, according to the number of voters, to determine the best use of my time. The purpose was to help me focus on getting my message out to the people most likely to vote for me.

Meanwhile, Tony Payton put me in touch with Tony Likins, who became my campaign manager in May 1982 (and my administrative assistant after I was elected). Tony had worked for the NRCC and on other congressional campaigns.

In addition to being a professional campaign manager, Tony knew Washington issues and people who were helpful. He brought focus and professionalism to the campaign, putting together a winning team and a successful fund-raising plan. He arranged for the volunteers to pump out a tremendous amount of direct mail, hired new staff, and helped map out a public relations and advertising strategy.

One night after I hired Tony, some of my family and I were eating dinner with him at the Santa Fe Hotel in Reno, and the subject of his age came up. When he said he was thirty-two years old, it gave me pause to think that I was putting my future in the hands of a young man barely half my age. But he did a great job.

When candidate filing ended for the new Second Congressional District, there was a long list of candidates in both parties, as you would expect with an open seat. Besides myself, the Republican candidates were Assemblyman Paul Prengaman, Assemblyman Dean Rhoads, Don Gustavson, Don Capps, and Joni Wines, former sheriff of Nye County. On the Democrat side, the candidates were former state senator Mary Gojack, state senator Rick Blakemore, Washoe County district attorney Cal Dunlap, John Gojack (Mary's ex-husband), Don Springmeyer, Assemblywoman Peggy Westall of Sparks, and Lloyd Williams. On both sides it was a mix of experienced and inexperienced candidates.

One quick way to assess the realistic chances of the candidates was to look at the money they raised. On that basis there were only a few serious players. When the first campaign finance reports were published in July 1982, I had raised $156,412 to Dean Rhoads's $30,252, Paul Prengaman's $5,000, and Mary Gojack's $49,777. By August I'd raised a total of $204,000. No one ever caught up with me.

As mentioned before, from the beginning of the campaign, the conventional wisdom favored a general election race matching me against Mary Gojack. Mary was a former member of the Nevada Assembly and the state senate and, of course, was coming off her run against Paul Laxalt for the senate in 1980. Although she was defeated decisively in that race, she was well known. I was not as well known, but I benefited from my association with Paul Laxalt and from his early and strong endorsement.

Usually, elected and party officials won't take sides in primaries, but Senator Laxalt's endorsement of my candidacy was clear from the beginning, despite the presence of five other Republican primary candidates. In fact, with the exception of a couple of my opponents, no one thought it was strange at all, because of our friendship and working relationship of more than twenty years. His wasn't the only endorsement I received, but it was easily the most important. It gave me credibility as a candidate, especially in Washington. Before the primary election, I was endorsed by the National Chamber of Commerce, Concerned Citizens and Victims of Drunk Drivers, BIPAC (a business and industry PAC), Citizens for Responsible Government, the National Association of Managers, the Builders Association of Northern Nevada, and the *Las Vegas Review Journal*. They all added credibility to my candidacy, but I knew that I still had to earn the endorsement of the voters themselves.

Of my primary election opponents, Paul Prengaman and Dean Rhoads were seasoned, experienced legislators and campaigners, but they had never put together a professional campaign outside of their assembly districts. Both candidates focused on local issues, rather than on the broader concerns of the nation, such as federal taxes, national defense, and federal budget deficits.

Prengaman was considered a maverick, liberal Republican, and his voting record in the legislature supported that assessment. He had voted against Governor Bob List's "tax shift" and with the liberals on social issues, such as abortion and the Equal Rights Amendment (ERA). He was considered very much out of the Republican mainstream. During the primary, Prengaman concentrated his efforts on walking door-to-door in Washoe and Churchill counties and handing out "Prengamints," a chocolate mint candy. Although his strength was in Washoe County, I beat him there more than two to one.

Rhoads, an Elko County rancher, was a well-liked rural representative and a conservative. His biggest problem was that he wasn't well known in Washoe County, where nearly half the votes would be cast. I'm not sure what Dean's strategy was, except to concentrate on the rural counties. He came in second in the primary, but carried only Elko, Eureka, Humboldt, Lander, and Lincoln counties. Like Prengaman's, Rhoads's campaign was mostly a grassroots effort.

In contrast, because of my previous political campaign experiences and my association with Paul Laxalt, I ran a professional campaign. I kept headquarters in Reno and North Las Vegas, ran top-quality ads, printed distinctive brochures and direct mail pieces. I had a staff that recruited volunteers, coordinated my schedule, and raised money. I traveled all over the state. Thanks to Paul Laxalt, I had the necessary Washington, D.C., contacts. In addition to the early television spots, we ran radio ads and bought newspaper advertising (in the rural counties only). Television spots were run with increasing frequency as the election got closer.

In any campaign there are substantive issues, and in 1982 they included public land use, the MX missile system, taxes, crime, jobs, and nuclear waste storage and disposal. There are also procedural or process issues, such as endorsements, debates, and campaign funding. As it turned out, those last three issues were what the primary campaign turned on. Although Prengaman was more liberal on social issues than the rest of the Republican candidates, we pretty much agreed on the substantive issues.

Both Prengaman and Rhoads complained bitterly about the Laxalt endorsement, claiming that their money dried up because of it. I don't know if that is completely true; no one would have given me money if they didn't like my candidacy, regardless of who endorsed me. The Federal Elections Commission reports showed I raised $120,000 more than Rhoads and $145,000 more than Prengaman. (I ultimately spent a total of $604,624 in both the primary and the general elections; my Democrat opponent, Mary Gojack, spent $248,865.)

The other big skirmish in the primary was over debates. Frankly, I was reluctant to debate with the experienced politicians. Although we made a number of joint appearances at candidates' night functions, we held our one and only television debate in late August, sponsored by the League of Women Voters. We were questioned by members of the news media and by each other. I was questioned by everyone regarding my endorsements and my source of contributions. My opponents might have wanted those to be perceived as negatives, but in the primary it only helped to emphasize that I had the broad-based support I needed to win. After the debate, the pundits said that Prengaman had won on style, and I was criticized for reading from my notes. Ultimately, the voters didn't seem to mind.

The last two weeks before the 1982 primary election were hectic, to say the least. Every day was filled with activities, including "walk-throughs" at major employers, media interviews, precinct walking, parades, picnics, and community festivals. I remember especially well a picnic in Ione on September 5. The main course for the "picnic" was a stew cooked in vats that were so large the chefs used canoe paddles to stir the contents. The entertainment was lady mud wrestling, a "sport" I had never seen. I still shudder when I remember it. When the first round began, Patty, George, and I were seated in the middle of the bleachers with no way out and I kept trying to slump down in my seat. Thankfully, after a couple of matches we were able to escape.

Family was also keeping me busy. In August, the day after Kenny's twins, Casey and Heather, were born my daughter Susie was married. George and I visited the twins at St. Mary's Hospital the day they were born, and then I cleaned house, went grocery shopping for the wedding rehearsal dinner, attended the rehearsal at the church, and hosted the wedding party for dinner that night. The next day I flew to Lovelock to ride in the Frontier Days parade. I shook hands in the park at the courthouse, then flew to Reno in time for Susie's four o'clock wedding there.

All of the hard work was worth it on primary election day when the votes were counted and I won easily. I received 16,453 votes, while Dean Rhoads finished second with 7,684 votes and Paul Prengaman got 7,306. Other Republican candidates received a combined total of 10,464 votes, so I didn't get a majority, but it was a clear and decisive victory and gave me the momentum I needed for the general election.

On primary election day George and I voted early in the day, then didn't know what to do with ourselves until the polls closed at 7:00 P.M.— so we went to the movies. I can't remember what we saw, but when the lights came up in the theater, Mary Gojack and her husband, Bob Gorrell, were sitting a couple of rows ahead of us. Apparently, Mary and I agreed on movies, but that may have been about all. As the "all-female" general election campaign unfolded, the differences on the issues between Mary and me couldn't have been any sharper.

Mary's campaign brochures said, "Together We Can Do Better." My campaign ads said, "She Can Do More for Nevada." The pundits asked, "Better than who? More than what? This is the first time anyone will hold this seat." At least the media treated us equally on that front.

It was clear from the beginning that Mary would conduct a more professional campaign than anyone did in the Republican primary. As a former state legislator, she was well known for spearheading the 1978 repeal of Nevada's sales tax on food. She had been on the ballot statewide in 1980, and her campaign network was in place, organized and professionally managed. She had support from organized labor and feminist groups and knew how to coordinate a grassroots campaign and use volunteers. She raised enough money to at least give her visibility. I wasn't surprised that she had an early poll that showed her beating me 25 percent to 8 percent with most people undecided, so she emphasized that she was the "clear front-runner" in the race.

In politics it is frequently the things you can't control that cause problems, and Mary had one distasteful problem: an extremely bitter ex-husband. In fact, John Gojack was so bitter that he ran against her in the Democrat primary, I think purely out of spite. He didn't have any money to campaign with, but the novelty of an ex-husband running against his former wife attracted considerable media attention. He spent a lot of time attacking her, referring to her frequently as "a former 21 dealer" and even "hired" a dog as his campaign manager. John claimed that her continued use of her former married name, Gojack, showed that she was hiding the fact that she was divorced and had married Bob Gorrell. Apparently some of what he said stuck because Mary said the questions she was most often asked on the campaign trail were "Why don't you use your husband's name?" and "Why are you Mary Gojack, not Mary Gorrell?"

In the general election the voters definitely had a choice, not just in political philosophies but also in styles and approaches to campaigns. Mary was a tall, attractive blonde who dressed in a much more casual manner than I did; she favored dresses or skirts with blouses. I was more from the "dress for the job you want" school. I preferred more traditional business suits, and I wore western clothes in the rural counties. I rinsed my graying hair a soft blue-gray color. Mary was forty-six years old and I was sixty-one when we started the campaign. More than my appearance, though, I think my experiences over the years helped me to look more "congressional."

Besides our outward appearances, of course, we were different philosophically. I campaigned as a supporter of the programs of President Ronald Reagan, which were popular with most Nevadans. Mary said that it would be tough for Paul Laxalt to transfer his popularity to me. She tried to balance my support for the president by arguing that Nevadans wanted independent thinkers to represent them.

My strategy was to make the campaign a choice between a liberal and a conservative. We stood on opposite sides of all the issues important to Nevadans, such as Reagan's economic policies, prayer in schools, gun control, government spending, balanced federal budget, the Equal Rights Amendment, states' rights, busing, and abortion. Mary also had a liberal voting record from her service in the legislature, which we had researched extensively. We sent out a direct mail piece on her voting record, showing that out of 256 votes to increase spending when she was in the Legislature, she had voted "yes" 244 times. As my mailer stated, "Mary voted 95.3 percent of the time for big spending." She objected to the characterization, of course, but it had the benefit of being true.

One of the great advantages I had was the personal support of President Reagan, which increased my visibility in the media. The president visited the University of Nevada in Reno for a rally, where he endorsed Chic Hecht, who was running against incumbent Democrat Howard Cannon for the Senate. Reagan also endorsed Governor Bob List and me before a crowd of more than ten thousand people. After the rally, the president attended a private reception at Rancho San Rafael Park. About a hundred people bought tickets at $500 each, and the proceeds were split between me and Bob List.

Later that same day, the president flew to Las Vegas for a rally where he repeated his endorsements (adding Peggy Cavnar, the Republican running against Harry Reid in the First Congressional District). He also attended a $1,000-a-plate barbecue at Wayne Newton's ranch; the proceeds were split between Chic and Peggy, with Chic receiving the larger share because he had a statewide race. On October 28 I was in Las Vegas when the president returned to give all of us a final boost before the election.

Mary and I debated during the campaign, but it really had very little impact. I was for Reagan's policies, and Mary was against them. She was also hurt by the fact that the first debate was scheduled by the Greater Reno-Sparks Chamber of Commerce and the Nevada League of Women Voters at John Ascuaga's Nugget on October 17. The Culinary Workers Union was picketing the Nugget at the time, and Mary refused to cross the picket line to attend. It gave me an opportunity to question her stance as an "independent thinker" when she was so closely aligned with the labor unions.

I also had a minor secret weapon in the person of Terri Vuceta, a Libertarian who was running for Congress and therefore participated in the debates. Before one of the debates, Terri called me and asked, "Barb, what are you wearing tonight?" She explained she wanted us both to look good enough to outshine Mary. Terry was not a fan of Mary's, to put it mildly.

My schedule during the general election was a repeat of the primary. I continued to travel the state, visiting every town once or twice again. I rode in parades, attended candidates' nights, community events, and fund-raising parties, walked door-to-door, toured major companies, worked with Roger Ailes in New York, went to Washington for meetings with PACs, met with the press, and spoke at service organizations. George and I attended most of the University of Nevada, Reno home football games and the National Championship Air Races, working the crowds at both events.

Another big advantage in all of my campaigns was the fact that George was a pilot. We owned a Cessna Skyline, so he was able to fly us around the state and the district. It meant I could attend events more than 400 miles apart in one day because we flew where commercial planes didn't fly, which is just about everywhere in Nevada. (Fortunately we weren't using our plane the day we made our wheels-up landing in Fallon.)

I had hired Tarrance and Associates of Houston to do my polling, and one of the final tracking surveys they did in late October showed that I had a 46 percent favorable rating and a 19 percent unfavorable, while Mary's favorable/unfavorable ratings were about even. It is a political fact that people won't vote for someone they don't like, even if they agree with that candidate on the issues. Seeing those polling numbers helped me believe I could win the election.

When the votes were counted on November 2, I received 70,188 (56 percent) to Mary's 52,265 (41 percent). The only county Mary won was Clark, which had a slight Democrat voter registration advantage, but that county accounted for only about 9 percent of the vote in the district. I won the other sixteen counties.

Before election night, I was too busy campaigning to think about what my reaction might be if I won. I was honored and thrilled, of course, but it seemed unreal. After all the hard work of the previous year, after virtually nonstop campaigning for all those months, knowing it was over left me numb. And almost as rewarding and just as exciting was to see that my daughter Patty had won her race for state treasurer. She became the first woman elected to the state treasurer's office in Nevada, and I became the first woman elected to a federal office in Nevada. It was quite a mother-daughter event.

I was told that some of Mary's supporters at her campaign headquarters shouted, "Blue hair, blue hair!" referring to my gray hair when they saw me that night on television thanking my volunteers. It became a description of me that stuck for another campaign or two, until I changed my hair color from gray to light brown. That was, by the way, a purely personal decision and not influenced by politics. Ralph Capozzi was my hairdresser for forty years, and I usually listened to his suggestions about my hairstyle.

A couple of years after the election, Mary and I were drawn together through shared experiences and worries when we both were diagnosed with breast cancer. But on election night she blamed my victory on "one of the dirtiest campaigns in Nevada." My response was, "She had to run on her record, and she didn't want to run on her record."

Immediately after the election, I spent a couple of days meeting with the media and responding to their questions. I gave a party for my campaign staff and volunteers three days after the election. I knew that I wouldn't have won without their help and support. Then, George and I, with Patty and her husband, Treat, flew to the Big Island of Hawaii for some rest and relaxation. George and I played golf, swam and snorkeled, and lounged in the sun. This became our post-election pattern for the next six campaigns.

I returned to Nevada on November 18, and the next day I was on the campaign trail again, traveling to Fallon for an event—also a pattern that I followed throughout my time in Congress. Since the terms for the House of Representatives are for only two years, a member of Congress never stops campaigning. We did manage to spend Thanksgiving with our children and grandchildren before I embarked on my first term as a member of Congress.

CHAPTER SEVEN

She *Is* the Congressman

Being a mother brings with it some extreme emotions, which I experienced in 1983. On January 3, while I was being sworn into office in Congress, my daughter Patty Cafferata was sworn in as Nevada state treasurer in Carson City. I could not have been prouder. In December of that year fear and worry dominated my emotions when my son Mike had his first heart attack. He lived in Las Vegas at the time, and I had a chance to visit him in the hospital. He sustained major damage to his heart and never fully recovered physically, although he was able to work for his brother, Kenny, in his roofing business for several years after that.

As I look back on it today, my first term in Congress seems like a whirlwind. In many ways, of course, that whirlwind set the tone for my entire career in the House of Representatives.

On November 29, 1982, excited about the challenges ahead of us, George and I flew to Washington for "freshman" orientation. I was one of the 81 new members of the Class of 1982 and was definitely in the minority. There were 23 Republican and 59 Democrats in the new class, including 2 Republican women and 2 Democrat women. The Ninety-eighth Congress would have 166 Republicans and 269 Democrats when it convened in January.

It is interesting to consider what has become of some of the members of that Class of 1982. Five of my classmates became governors of their states: Republicans Don Sundquist of Tennessee, Tom Ridge of Pennsylvania (later President Bush's director of homeland security), and John "Jock" McKernan of Maine, and Democrats Tom Carper of Delaware and Bill Richardson of New Mexico. Six of my classmates later served in the Senate, including Carper. The three Republican classmates were John McCain, Mike DeWine, and Connie Mack, and the two other Democrats were Harry Reid of Nevada, later minority leader of the Senate, and Barbara Boxer. Before being elected governor of New Mexico, Richardson served in the Clinton administration as ambassador to the United Nations and as secretary of energy. It was a diverse class of independent thinkers.

Most of the initial orientation period was spent learning how congressional offices operated. Republicans and Democrats met separately for two full days, with PAC receptions in the evenings so the lobbyists could meet the freshman members. A newly elected member arrives in Washington as part of his or her political party's team, loyal to the leadership, platform, and agenda. At the Republican orientation sessions, we met our leaders, who established our Republican agenda for the coming year. I assume that the Democrats did the same at their orientation meetings.

Unlike the real world, where one's political party has little influence on one's daily affairs, political party membership in Washington controls every aspect of your life. Most people, unless they are familiar with or have worked in Washington, may not appreciate the significance of the role that a member's party has in Congress. While Democrats and Republicans share the common goal of making America a better place, their philosophies and approaches as to how to achieve this goal differ.

Representatives are like members of a ball team. Team members don't sit in the other team's dugout or on their sideline bench. For example, University of Nevada, Las Vegas ballplayers don't usually make nice comments about, sit with, or socialize with University of Nevada, Reno ballplayers or vice versa. Likewise, Republican and Democrat members wouldn't dream of sitting on the other party's side of the aisle on the floor of the House. Republicans always sit to the right of the center aisle facing the Speaker—either the Speaker of the House or the Speaker Pro Tem—while Democrats sit on the left. Members may cross over the center aisle, of course, to chat with a colleague about congressional business, but they would seldom sit down there. That is not to say that members are not

My classmates after we were elected in 1982, at the White House with President Ronald Reagan. *Back row, left to right:* John Kasich, Rod Chandler, Jock McKernon, and Tom Ridge. *Middle row, left to right:* Don Sundquist, Ed Zschau, Mike DeWine, Sherwood Boehlert, Ron Packard, George Gekas, Dan Schaefer, me, Steve Bartlett, and Connie Mack. *Front row, left to right:* Mike Bilirakis, Tom Lewis, President Ronald Reagan, Web Franklin, and Howard Nielson. Several others in the Class of 1982 were missing from the photograph, including Nancy Johnson. Collection of Barbara F. Vucanovich

congenial toward members of the opposite party. They are, but they are rarely "buddies" with them.

Every activity in the House is governed by political party. Even seat assignments in committee are determined by political party. The chair of the committee sits at the center of the table, with the ranking minority member next to the chair. The Republicans sit on the right of the chair by seniority, with the more senior members closest to the chair, while the Democrats sit on the left, also by seniority.

The majority party decides even the number of members from each party assigned to the committees, location and number of parking slots, size of office, and number of staff members. It determines control of the floor, including who is recognized to speak at any given time, although speakers are usually recognized in an order that alternates between the parties. The Democrats had been in the majority for more than two decades when I arrived at the House.

Republicans were not allowed to forget who was in control. On most of the "housekeeping" issues we did not have a vote, nor were we even consulted. No matter what the activity was, members were constantly reminded that they belonged to their party's team.

Although there are a few mavericks in both parties, such as Republican John McCain and Democrat James Traficant Jr., they are the exception, not the rule. Mavericks rarely accomplish much by trying to oppose their own party's agenda. The members who support their leadership advance in the ranks and receive the committee assignments they seek.

There are, of course, bipartisan activities, too. Every time the House meets, both parties are present to vote. And during the year there are a few other bipartisan events. For example, on December 3 a bipartisan meeting was held, with the leadership from both parties addressing the new representatives. In the following days, the Republican Conference, to which all House Republican members belong, held all-day sessions to talk policy and politics.

I learned about the federal budget process and about my office budget. My salary for the 1983–84 session was $60,662.50 annually, and each member was permitted a "clerk hire allowance"—staff salaries—of $336,384, for up to eighteen employees. I could distribute the salary any way I wanted, but no employee's annual salary could exceed $50,112.50. Ultimately I hired three employees in my Reno office, two in North Las Vegas, two in Elko, and six in Washington. Members were also authorized to hire a "Lyndon Baines Johnson Congressional Intern," with only one intern permitted at a time. During my terms in Congress, these internships presented wonderful opportunities to bring young Nevadans to Washington, where they could work and learn about government and help with my congressional duties. More than seventy-five young men and women served as interns in my office, and I appreciated their help. Along with my staff, the interns contributed to my success in the House.

Also during this time committee assignments were made. I felt being on the House Interior and Insular Affairs Committee was vital to the interests of my district and was pleased to be appointed to it. My initial subcommittee assignments were Energy and Environment; Mining, Forest Management and Bonneville Power Administration; and Oversight and Investigations. I also served on the Indian Affairs Task Force. Almost all had direct benefits for Nevada.

At this hearing of the Mining and Natural Resources subcommittee of the Interior Committee, we were listening to a witness testify. Ron Marlenee (Montana) is in the right foreground. Behind him on his right is his staffer Cy Jamison, who later became director of the Bureau of Land Management. Collection of Barbara F. Vucanovich

Getting the Interior Committee assignment wasn't easy. My competition was a newly elected freshman Republican from Arizona, a former POW by the name of John McCain. We both felt we needed the assignment for our states, and we lobbied the party leadership and anyone else we thought would help us. In the end, the Democrats, who controlled the ratios on the committees, added one more seat to the committee on their side, which in turn meant one additional Republican seat. That allowed both McCain and me to be appointed to the committee. Our chairs were jammed so close together, we sat almost arm to arm. I remember him as an intense individual, and sometimes I could actually feel the tension radiating up and down his arm when he didn't like what was happening at a committee meeting.

Because House members typically have two committee assignments, I was also named to the Committee on House Administration, with sub-committees on Accounts and Contracts and Printing. It was not a high-profile committee and had little impact on Nevada, but as a freshman, getting my first choice (Interior) was enough of a reward. I also received an assignment to the Select Committee on Children, Youth, and Families, popularly referred to as the "Kiddie Committee," because it was an area in which I was particularly interested.

Throughout the years I was in Congress, I tried to be conscientious about committee meetings. Some members were not. Once a man walked up to me in the Washington airport, introduced himself, and told me he served on the Interior Committee with me. I looked him over carefully and expressed surprise because I had never seen him at a meeting. He said he felt comfortable with his absence because he had given his proxy vote to the chairman. I asked him if he knew the chairman was casting his vote against the best interests of his state. He had no idea because he wasn't there. Proxy voting was the norm when the Democrats were in control of the House, and it gave the chairmen enormous power that they wouldn't ordinarily have had. In 1995, when Republicans won control of the House, we eliminated proxy voting.

When I arrived in the House there were many special-interest caucuses, all funded by Congress, many of them large, often militant and seldom bipartisan. For the most part, members were recruited to join these caucuses because they wanted the members to pay dues from their official office budget. The caucuses ran their organizations with these funds. I paid dues to the *Congressional Green Sheets,* a daily publication that covered natural resources and environmental issues, and the Republican Study Committee, which provided research and information on conservative issues.

Later I served on the executive committee of the Republican Study Committee and eventually became its chair. Originally this study committee was formed by conservative Republicans who felt that the issues they cared about were not being considered by the Republican leadership. We often had speakers from the Reagan and Bush administrations discussing current issues. Republican Study Committee members also reported on what was happening in their House committees, and we discussed strategies on various issues. For several years, I was the only woman who attended the weekly meetings of this group.

There were other caucuses that collected dues and put the money in outside checking accounts with no accountability as to how the funds were later spent. This was taxpayer money, of course. When the Republicans became the majority party, we abolished many of these caucuses, including the Democrat Study Group, the Women's Caucus, the Republican Study Committee, and others.

I was also appointed one of five members of the Republican Personnel Committee by Minority Leader Bob Michel. We met only if there was business to be decided. This committee interviewed potential applicants for openings on the floor, such as the cloakroom attendants, the doorkeepers, and elevator operators. We also had jurisdiction over the Republican pages and their housing and schooling arrangements.

More important was Michel's decision to name me as the freshman class representative to the Republican Committee on Committees. Our responsibility was to interview members who wished to serve on a committee, to change committee assignments, and to settle disputes over committee assignments. It was a powerful committee because it had the final word on assignments. The other members of the committee were the senior members of the major committees, the leadership, and a sophomore class representative. We met only when a member was seeking a committee change, which rarely happened.

At various times I took advantage of opportunities to serve on ad hoc committees, because they either helped Nevada or involved a personal interest. I served on the Congressional Arts Caucus, the Republican Task Force on High Technology Initiatives, the Task Force on Education, the Insurance Caucus, and the Human Rights Caucus.

Of these caucuses, my favorite was the Congressional Arts Caucus. Every state was encouraged to set up an arts caucus to invite high schools to contribute art for display in the hallways from the Capitol to the Cannon House Office Building. I formed such a caucus in Reno and in Las Vegas so Nevada students could participate in the program.

One of the bipartisan caucuses I was recruited for was the Pro-Life Caucus, which met when votes on pro-life or abortion issues were coming up. Usually it involved anti-abortion amendments or appropriation bills, such as opposing the funding for overseas military personnel for family planning purposes funded by the taxpayers. Other members of this caucus included Republicans Chris Smith, Henry Hyde, Ileana Ros-Lehtinin, Democrat Harold Volkmer, and many others of both political parties.

I also joined a number of nonofficial committees during my first

Minority leader Bob Michel (Illinois) with me at my first political action committee (PAC) event at the Capitol Hill Club in Washington. This photograph was taken only weeks after my mastectomy for breast cancer in 1983. In my freshman year Michel appointed me to two important Republican committees, the Personnel Committee, and the Committee on Committees. Collection of Barbara F. Vucanovich

term in Congress, such as the National Advisory Council of the Citizens Committee for the Right to Keep and Bear Arms, the National Republican Congressional Committee (NRCC) (which recruits, trains, and contributes to Republican candidates for Congress), the Congressional Advisory Board of the Committee for the Survival of a Free Congress (a conservative organization), the Honorary Board of Advisors of the Close

Up Foundation (a nonpartisan, nonprofit forum for the involvement of youth in government), and the United States Space Foundation. In most cases, these committees did not take much of my time, but I felt my membership was important.

After committee assignments, probably the most anticipated aspect of the freshman orientation process was the assigning of office space. It is a formal procedure based first on class seniority, then drawing of numbers to determine the order for selecting your offices. When people leave office, naturally their offices become vacant, so after every election a list of vacant offices is posted for members' consideration. As members gain seniority, they generally try to get into offices that are larger or in a better location. As a result, by the time freshmen are allowed to select their office space, the best offices are gone. I didn't expect much, so I wasn't disappointed.

My first term, I ended up in Room 507 in the Cannon House Office Building, above the air-conditioning units. All member offices consist of three rooms, and I was lucky that my storage area was right across the hall from the main office. Some of my staff worked in that cramped room with a chain-link fence instead of a wall along the hallway. There was no privacy, and anyone walking by could look in the office. It wasn't one of the worst offices ("split" offices, with some rooms on another floor from your main office, were worse), but it was inconvenient. From my office on the fifth floor, it was necessary to take two different elevators to get to the main floor and then to the floor of the House. Since members have only fifteen minutes to respond to the bells signaling a vote, I was usually out the door at full speed when the bells rang. Still, I was satisfied with the space for the time being, knowing that if I was reelected I would move into better and more convenient offices.

I couldn't move into my offices until Congress convened in January, but there was still work to do. Tony Likins, whom I had hired as my administrative assistant (chief of staff), and I sat in the Longworth Building cafeteria, reviewing résumés and interviewing potential employees. The first person we hired was Jackie Troy as my office manager. She had worked for a congressman from South Dakota, so she had Capitol Hill experience and knew all the procedures for running a congressional office. Some members who hired only staffers from their home states had a difficult time figuring out the system on the Hill. Some literally spent weeks figuring out simple things like how to get to the floor. I wanted a good mix of people who knew Washington and who knew Nevada.

Once I knew where my office was to be located and that Jackie would be answering the phone in January, I left Tony to continue interviewing for office staff. I set off to rent furniture for the condominium George and I were buying in Alexandria, Virginia. On December 14 we signed the papers on the condo and flew home for two weeks. We enjoyed the holidays with our family, then returned to Washington in time to celebrate New Year's Eve with my sister, Patsy, and her husband, Jerry, at the home of my brother, Peter, and his wife, Joan, who lived near Mount Vernon, about twenty minutes from our condo.

The Ninety-eighth Congress was sworn in on January 3, 1983. The swearing-in ceremony was a family affair. Members of Congress are allowed to bring their young children onto the floor, and many of them do. Each member was also allowed two guest passes for the House Gallery, and I used mine for George and for Patsy. The rest of the family joined my staff to watch the ceremony on C-Span in my office, where later we gathered for a small buffet.

Three days later, George and I attended our first-ever White House dinner, with all of the newly elected members of Congress, their spouses, Cabinet members, and the president's staff. It was a bipartisan affair, with perhaps 170 to 200 people present. Naturally, we were excited to be invited to the White House.

The guests arrived in their own personal vehicles and parked on the White House grounds in an area off Fifteenth Street, close to the east entrance. We were issued a parking pass for the area. Security was always tight and even more so in later years. During the Clinton administration, Pennsylvania Avenue in front of the White House was closed to public traffic. At this first event for us, and at all later events I attended at the White House, guests' names were checked off the list of invitees by the guards at the gate. When you responded to your invitation to the White House, your staff gave certain information about you, such as your social security number and, perhaps, your birth date. My staff took care of the details, so I'm not quite sure of the exact information that was required, but it had to be supplied or you wouldn't have been permitted inside the grounds. When you passed through the gate at the security area, your purse or briefcase was opened for inspection (even though you shouldn't be a security risk, as a member of Congress).

There was so much to take in—after we arrived I did not know where to look first. The event, the famous guests, and the White House itself were overwhelming. We entered the White House through the covered entryway of the East Wing at ground level, walking past the large oil portraits of the first ladies. We also passed a few of the public rooms, such as the Library, the Vermeil Room, the Diplomats' Reception Room, and the China Room. where each president's china, some personal and some official, was displayed.

I'm not sure whose china was used at the dinner that night, I didn't dare turn a plate over to look at the bottom to see the hallmark and the name of the administration on the china, but I know it was not Nancy Reagan's. The china she commissioned had her favorite color, red, in the design, and the plates used that night did not have any red on them.

The social events I attended at the White House were held one flight above the ground floor. Usually the Marine Corps Band or the Air Force Band was playing music in the north entrance hall as you arrived. Finger foods were set out on a long table or tables in the center of the State Dining Room at the west end of the house. We served ourselves and ate standing up, while waiters circulated with trays of wine and soft drinks.

At most events, except formal sit-down dinners, the guests were allowed to wander into other rooms, such as the Red Room, the Blue Room, and the Green Room, to see the panorama of the Washington skyline and monuments. The rooms were furnished with antiques, and the paintings, photographs, and other artwork on the walls changed from president to president or changed to reflect current events in the administration, but the formal portraits of the presidents and first ladies remained the same.

I'm not sure if it happened this night, but oftentimes a big band played in the East Room, the largest public room in the White House, at the opposite end of the house from the State Dining Room. The band, located at one end of the room, played dance music, while the president and the first lady circulated among the guests at the other end.

White House events were always formal, never casual, except for the

To Barbara Vucanovich
With best wishes, Ronald Reagan

In December 1983, George Vucanovich and I are attending our first White House Christmas party with President Ronald Reagan. President Reagan is on my left, and George is behind me, shaking hands with First Lady Nancy Reagan. The others are unidentified military personnel and guests. Collection of Barbara F. Vucanovich

barbecues on the lawn. I was aware of how few people in the world were invited to the White House, so I always believed I was fortunate to be there. I didn't know what to expect as far as presidential conduct was concerned. The Reagans were more reserved but as warm as George and Barbara Bush and the Clintons, but I didn't know that at this first White House event. That night the only time I actually spoke to President Reagan and Nancy was in the receiving line.

After dinner, the guests lined up to shake hands with the president and the first lady. A Marine honor guard directed the receiving line, with a young guard telling all the guests that the congressman was to be the first of each couple in line to greet the president. George and I lined up accordingly. The guard repeated to us that the congressman was to be first. Neither George nor I changed places. The guard indicated that George should stand in front of me because the congressman was to be first. He repeated his command, "Congressman first." George finally said, "She is the congressman." Very chagrined, the guard simply said, "Oh, sorry."

I guess I should say something about the word "congressman." I always looked at it as the title of the office. My letterhead and business cards said, "Congress of United States, House of Representatives, Member of Congress," so it wasn't much of an issue with me. It struck me as funny, when people were trying to figure out how to address me. I always was sort of practical about it; after all, Vucanovich is a long name, so "Congressman Vucanovich" is a little shorter than "Congresswoman Vucanovich." Later on it seemed silly to change, so I just stuck with "congressman," but I did refer to the other women members as "congresswoman."

CHAPTER EIGHT

A Day in the Life of a Congressman

Obviously, once I was elected to the House, most of my time was spent in Washington. George and I saw some family members each weekend we were home, but we weren't getting to see our family as much as we would have liked. So at the end of my first year in Congress, we started the Family Christmas Brunch for our children, their spouses, our grandchildren, and eventually our great-grandchildren. It was a family tradition that would last for thirteen years, until George died. (We resumed the tradition three years after his death.) It was always held on the Saturday before Christmas, at John Ascuaga's Nugget, in the Captain's Room, a banquet room off Trader Dick's restaurant. Each year different family members decided upon and staged a "game" or other entertainment. My daughter Patty always read "'Twas the Night Before Christmas" for the younger members of the family. The party ended after we went around the room hearing each person describe the major events in his or her life that year. It was one way for me to keep in touch with my family and their daily lives.

My day in Washington typically started early. My commute time from our condo to "the Hill" was about forty-five minutes to an hour. Traffic was heavy, but I tried to travel in the off-peak times. Members have assigned parking spaces, with the leaders and the majority party members receiving the best slots. Mondays were considered a "travel" day for members, but I usually returned to Washington on Sundays, so I was in my office on Monday. That was the day we held a staff meeting

My family photograph taken in 1988 during our annual family Christmas brunch at John Ascuaga's Nugget. *Front row, left to right:* Mike Dillon Jr., Jennifer Dillon, Nora Dillon, Maggie Dillon, Trevor Dillon. *Middle row, left to right:* Farrell Cafferata, Patrick Dillon, Cathy Dillon, Casey Dillon, Sandra Dillon, Katie Dillon, me, Heather Dillon, Patty Cafferata, Scott Anderson, David Anderson, Susie Anderson. *Back row, left to right:* Mike Dillon Sr., Kenny Dillon, Tommy Dillon, George Vucanovich, Butch Anderson, Steve Farrell, and Treat Cafferata. Missing from the photograph are family members Elisa Cafferata Erquiaga, Dale Erquiaga, Brendan Erquaiga, and Reynolds Cafferata. Collection of Barbara F. Vucanovich

that included everyone—the receptionist, the scheduler, and even the interns—to review the schedule and plans for the week.

We discussed legislation due to be on the floor and what votes could be expected, as well as my positions on the upcoming bills. If I planned to speak on the floor, I would outline my views and the staffer who was most knowledgeable about the public policy in the bill would prepare remarks for my final approval later in the day. I often made corrections or additions right up to the time I delivered my remarks.

During my freshman year I didn't speak on the floor too often unless an issue affecting Nevada or an issue from one of my committees was being debated. Gradually I was asked by the leadership to take part in the debates on core Republican issues. The time allotted to each speaker was usually two to three minutes for any given debate.

Most days started with an early breakfast meeting and ended with a dinner or a reception. These events were put on by PACs, associations, or other special-interest groups, for example, the National Restaurant Association or Women in Mining, and they were usually held on "the Hill" so that members could easily leave if a vote was called. Votes are held open for fifteen minutes, so there isn't much leeway when you're away from the House. I often didn't get home until eight or nine o'clock at night, and some nights I got home after midnight.

Committee meetings were regularly scheduled on Tuesday, Wednesday, and Thursday. Very often, floor votes were called during committee meetings. We would recess for a short period, go to the floor to vote, and then hurry back to the committee to continue business. On Fridays, if we had scheduled votes, they were taken before 3:00 P.M., so members could go home or return to their districts. That meant I could catch a plane from Dulles International Airport for home at 5:30 P.M. and still attend a Nevada event that night if needed.

Visitors from the district (Nevada) came to the office quite often. I always tried to see them and, if possible, take them to the Capitol to see the House in action. I would give them a quick tour of the Capitol and show them our Nevada statue of Senator Pat McCarran, located in the hallway next to Statuary Hall, if it was their first time in Washington.

Party conferences were held quite often during the week as well, perhaps to hear from the administration on an issue or to debate the pros and cons of expected legislation. Oftentimes the party leadership would outline the Republican position and urge support. Our conference meetings were attended by all of the elected Republican members. The Democratic members met in their caucus for the same reasons.

Congress is generally in session from January until October, with several "District Work" weeks during the year, most notably in January, the week after Easter, and in August. Members also took some days off around the three-day holiday weekends, such as Presidents' Day, Memorial Day, and the Fourth of July. We tried to adjourn early in October, but often I was still in Washington in December. In December my Nevada staff came to

Washington for a week to meet my staff there and to work on issues that were important to me.

As previously mentioned, my staff was always a mix of Nevadans and Hill-experienced men and women, with my Washington staff being younger than my district staff. My Washington staff members were more likely to be college graduates, with some expertise in an issue of importance to me or to Nevada, but they were not necessarily from the state. They came recommended from other offices, committees, or members. My interns came from Nevada, and usually I knew them or their families before we hired them.

On the other hand, for my district staff in Nevada, I hired only two men in fourteen years. Of the women I hired, almost all had volunteered in one of my campaigns, so they knew me, my concerns, and many of my Nevada friends. Most congressmen hire campaign volunteers for their staff because they know them and are familiar with their abilities. Of course, people looking for positions with an elected official know that if they volunteer and do a good job on a campaign, they will have an opportunity to be hired if their candidate wins. And volunteers continued to help out in my district offices after my elections, generously contributing their time and talents.

While I had a lot of campaign volunteers over the years, many of them were not looking for a job, like Lee Smith, a mining lobbyist; my grandsons, Reynolds Cafferata and Mike Dillon Jr., who put up my campaign signs in different races all over the state; and my children, Patty, Mike, Kenny, Tommy, and Susie, who volunteered in various capacities. Of course, I couldn't have legally offered them a job anyway.

Staff members did a myriad of tasks. My Washington staff handled legislative and committee matters. Some of my employees were specialists in areas like mining and so were assigned to me for the Interior Committee. One staffer usually attended committee meetings with me. If you were speaking or handling a bill on the floor, you were permitted to take one staffer to help you; beyond that, the floor was restricted to members only. Staffers had to sign in with the doorkeeper to receive a pass before entering the chamber.

Many staffers dealt with the mail received and sent from the office. A typical mail day could bring anywhere from one hundred to five hundred letters. If there was a "hot button" issue pending, we might receive a thousand letters on the subject. I'm sure that computers and e-mail are the norm in the offices today, but while I was in the House the mail came in by letter and fax machine. Naturally, we tried to answer every letter I received.

Responding to your constituents is a must. I can't remember where I heard this story, but it circulated in Washington: An old man died, and when his heirs opened his safe-deposit box at the bank expecting to find some valuables, the only thing in the box was a letter from his congressman that he had received years before his death. Clearly, the man valued the letter so highly that he had paid rent on his safety-deposit box for years so that it could be kept safe.

Constituent service is one of the most important activities that any good congressional office performs, and it is often the most tangible reason for House members' success in bids for reelection. People that you help feel that you care about them because you took your time and made an effort to help them. Both my district and my Washington staff were called upon daily to help with problems people had with the federal agencies, such as Social Security, immigration, and military and veterans affairs, as well as with the Bureau of Land Management. My staffers were frequently on a first-name basis with the staff in those agencies, so they were able to work the problems out on behalf of the Nevadans in my district. My district employees also attended federal agency meetings to listen and collect information, and they wrote reports on the meetings so I could be informed on what was happening in Nevada.

To this day, I meet people who stop me to thank me for some problem we were able to solve for them during my years in Congress. For example, when I was in the Eldorado Hotel for a social event, one of the employees took one look at me and said, "Barbara?" I nodded. He said, "I am grateful to you. You helped me with my immigration problem when you worked for Senator Laxalt." Even though more than twenty years had passed, he had not forgotten my assistance.

In addition to office staff, members have committee staffers to assist them with legislation. Every committee has Republican and Democrat staff employees, with the majority party, of course, having the most staffers. There is no question that congressional staff, especially committee staffs, wield a great deal of power. Oftentimes fewer than half a dozen staff members actually know all the details in any given bill. Committee staffs also often meet without the members present to develop the legislation under consideration. A member's legislative office staff will attend these meetings to represent the member and to learn the details of proposed bills.

Congress could not function without staffers to advise members on legislation. No one individual could read every bill in its entirety. For example, during the appropriations process, there are so many details and billions of dollars being considered that the staff are often the only ones who have looked at every word and every dollar. I and the other members of the House have no choice but to rely on staff to pay attention to these details and to trust that they are working for our best interests.

I began my first year in the House by learning about the public policies I would be addressing in Congress. George and I took Amtrak to Williamsburg for a three-day bipartisan orientation sponsored in part by the American Enterprise Institute. The seminar, which was voluntary, was attended by about ten Republican and twenty Democrat members of Congress, all newly elected, including Harry Reid, from the First Congressional District of Nevada. I was the only woman in either party to attend. I considered the seminar to be part of the learning process for being a good representative for Nevada.

A great deal of the program was spent on the budget and how it affects legislation, with presentations from the Congressional Budget Office, the White House Office of Management and Budget, the American Enterprise Institute, and Democrat Leon Panetta and Republican Ralph Regula, both members of the House Budget Committee. We spent a lot of time discussing "entitlement programs," such as welfare, food stamps, unemployment, and health care. The federal government was and is committed to those programs, with the benefits determined by certain eligibility criteria, such as income and age. Any suggestion of changing the criteria always meets with stiff opposition. I learned that spending on entitlement programs increased automatically as more and more people used these programs. Congress couldn't do much to reduce the bureaucracy and to make these programs more efficient.

Paul Volcker, then chairman of the Federal Reserve Board, was another informative speaker. He was a bit intimidating, but he answered our questions. The new congressmen who were former bankers or had some banking experience asked most of the tough questions. Volcker was candid, but he didn't concede any ground to us. When he was asked why the Federal Reserve Board met in secret and why it didn't disclose its decisions and activities, he basically said, "That's the way it is." And that's still the way it is.

The other policy area discussed was national defense, including arms control, levels of defense spending, and preparedness. The most forceful speaker was Edward Luttwak from the Center for Strategic and International Studies, a scholarly, conservative group. Luttwak covered the programs I was interested in, such as the MX missile deployment and the nuclear freeze proposals.

Unfortunately, while we were attending this seminar, we received word that George's mother, Anna Vucanovich, had died. George flew home as soon as we learned of her death, and I returned to Reno for the funeral a few days later.

George's mother was born into a Serbian Orthodox family in what was then Austria, later Yugoslavia, now Serbia and Montenegro. She was a naturalized citizen who loved America. When I was elected, she said with great pride, "Barbara has gone to work for the government." She was the mother of three sons and two daughters and had outlived two husbands when she passed away at the age of ninety-four.

Congress scheduled a "District Work" period in late January 1983, a time for all of us to return home. I attended the opening of the Nevada Legislature and a reception at the Governor's Mansion that evening, hosted by the new governor, Richard Bryan. I flew back to Washington in time to attend the State of the Union address given by President Ronald Reagan. It was the first of seven such speeches I attended while I was in Congress.

The delivery of the State of the Union speech is always a traditional and solemn occasion. It is held in the House Chamber, which is much larger than the Senate Chamber. The House has seats for about 450 people, even though there are only 435 representatives. To seat the 100 senators and several dozen other dignitaries, including Supreme Court justices, the president's Cabinet members, and others, extra chairs are set up on the floor. House members filled the chamber first, as mentioned, Republicans on the right facing the Speaker and Democrats on the left. The senators file in next, followed by the Cabinet. (It is traditional that one member of the president's Cabinet remains away, so that in case of disaster or attack our government can still function.) The justices of the U.S. Supreme Court arrive in the chamber after the Cabinet, followed by the diplomatic corps.

After the president's wife is escorted into the second-floor gallery, to a front-row seat to the left of the podium, the president is escorted down the center aisle of the chamber. As anyone who has watched this event on television knows, members on both sides of the aisle jockey for position to shake the president's hand as he makes his way toward the podium. I was amused that Congresswoman Helen Bentley figured out how to always get a good seat: She put her purse down on an aisle seat early in the day. When the president walked in, she was able to greet him and be seen on national television.

During any State of the Union address, both political parties stand out of courtesy and respect when the president arrives, but most often after that applause is pretty much divided along party lines or reserved for statements upon which there is broad agreement.

For me, that first State of the Union speech was exciting and memorable. President Reagan gave an upbeat, sometimes humorous speech. But he also laid out his agenda for the Ninety-eighth Congress. He received many standing ovations and much applause from the Republican side of the aisle, although the Democrats were not as kind, nor were the media. The press gallery was located directly above the Speaker on the second floor. The members of the media were given copies of the speech just before the president arrived, and sometimes they rattled the papers if they disagreed with the speech, as they did on this night. They were not very courteous.

Another tradition is for House and Senate members to rush out after the speech and swarm to the Capitol Rotunda to make their comments to the media representing their television stations and newspapers back home. It was quite a sight, and I was right in line myself. Nevada had several "stringers" who reported for the Reno and Las Vegas papers and broadcast outlets. It was a great opportunity for press coverage because Nevada is three hours earlier than Washington. The speech often ran until 10:30 P.M. or so, Washington time, giving plenty of time to make newspaper and television deadlines back home.

While I of course was aware that Washington is awash in partisan politics, it was still somewhat of a surprise to see that in action, especially how petty and disrespectful it could become. For example, the first week in February, Interior Secretary James Watt appeared before the Interior and Insular Affairs Committee. Watt was not popular with environmentalists, but he should have been given the respect and courtesy that came with being a member of the president's Cabinet. Democrat Jim Weaver of Oregon, however, was absolutely awful and rude to him. I was shocked, never having seen such blatant animosity on public display from an elected official. Watt was respectful to the congressman but not intimidated.

Weaver was a small man in stature, balding but with some gray hair. Others describe him as hot-tempered and inflexible, and I would not disagree with those characterizations. Elected in 1974, he was certainly not a typical low-key, agreeable congressman. An avid environmentalist, he clashed again and again with Interior Secretary Watt, even ridiculing Watt's belief in an imminent Second Coming.

In 1986 he ran against Republican senator Bob Packwood but dropped out of the race. Subsequently, the House Ethics Committee charged Weaver with violating the law that barred personal use of campaign money.

February is the month when most Lincoln Day dinners are held by local Republican central committees and other Republican organizations in Nevada. As a newly elected Republican, I was much in demand on that year's circuit. I also saw it as an opportunity to thank my supporters. I attended dinners in Churchill, Clark, Humboldt, Elko, Storey, Douglas, and Washoe counties and in Carson City. I was the keynote speaker in Pahrump and Elko. My attendance at these events meant that I sometimes took the "red-eye" back to Washington so I wouldn't miss any votes. Congressmen representing districts in the East certainly had an advantage in that regard.

On February 18 I addressed the Nevada Legislature on Nevada issues and needs. I knew many of the Republican legislators and felt welcome. And it was particularly pleasing to have my daughter Patty Cafferata, the newly elected Nevada state treasurer, present when I spoke. It had been a long tradition for Nevada congressmen and senators to come home to address the legislature when it is in session. During my remarks, I made a statement about Governor Dick Bryan, suggesting he was not being flexible on nuclear waste storage in Nevada. He was not pleased, but it did not bother me.

At that time the storage of nuclear waste was perceived by many people, especially businesspeople and labor leaders in Southern Nevada, to be a good project for Nevada because of the infusion of federal money and the creation of new jobs. The Nevada Test Site was a major employer in Southern Nevada, with many high-tech jobs. When Dick was in the legislature, he voted for a resolution in support of the storage of nuclear waste in Nevada, and when I was elected to the House, I supported the project too, but we both changed our minds when we learned more about the dangers of nuclear waste.

My comments about Dick reflected my views and the conventional wisdom at the time. During the late 1970s, however, as more became known about the risks involved, public opinion about nuclear waste storage began to change. Within a year or so of my comments, the people in Nevada were overwhelmingly opposed to the storage of nuclear waste in the state for health and safety reasons. As their representative in the House, I made it a priority to study the issue, and I came to agree that the downside of nuclear waste storage in Nevada far outweighed any perceived economic benefits.

Those early months in Washington were filled with many "firsts" for me as a member of Congress. I attended my first Republican leadership dinner in Statuary Hall to hear from our leaders, including minority leader Bob Michel, minority whip Trent Lott, House Republican Conference chair Jack Kemp, and Dick Cheney, chair of the Republican Policy Committee. Their message was largely to welcome us to the House, as well as to offer assistance in our new roles.

Statuary Hall in the U.S. Capitol Building once served as the U.S. House of Representatives chambers. Today it is adorned with statues of eminent Americans, a collection started by an act of Congress in 1864. Every state has been invited to contribute statues of two individuals, although not all states have done so. For years, the statue of Senator Pat McCarran was the only one provided by Nevada; recently, however, there was the unveiling of the statue of famous Native American leader Sara Winnemucca in the Capitol.

I attended the regular weekly Republican Conference meetings. Our first leaders were strong conservatives, Dick Cheney and Jack Kemp. The conference was made up of every elected Republican member, and most attended the meetings. In these meetings legislation was discussed and party decisions were made, and it was an opportunity for members to lobby one another for their positions on bills. It was a place to air differences between our members, but also a place to promote the party programs. Occasionally, outside speakers, usually someone from the administration who shared information on legislation, gave presentations to the group. The Democrats' corresponding group is called the Democrat Caucus, and although I never attended one of their meetings, I'm sure that they promoted their agenda to their members, too.

In March I attended my first Central Intelligence Agency briefing, one of many such bipartisan briefings that I attended over the years. It was quite a production. Just off the floor of the Rotunda in the Capitol is an unmarked door that opens into a small elevator. That day we took this elevator to the fifth floor, where we stepped through metal doors and signed in before a security guard. This particular briefing was about Nicaragua and the Sandinista National Liberation Front. The speakers were those in the administration who were knowledgeable about the country. The briefings invariably reminded me that the reality of a situation was often much different from what was being reported in the news media. The press, with little real information, constantly attacked President Reagan's Nicaragua policies. Knowing the facts, I resented this unfair assault on the president's policies, but I couldn't respond because of the secret nature of the information.

On March 10 I attended a breakfast meeting as a guest of Secretary John R. Block at the Department of Agriculture with other Republican members of the Interior Committee to discuss western agriculture issues.

That afternoon I participated in my first White House briefing with other newly elected Republican congressmen and our leader, Bob Michel, meeting with President Reagan in the Roosevelt Room. I was awed, of course. President Reagan sat in a leather armchair at the middle of the table, with Vice President George Bush across from him. Their staffs sat behind them. The congressmen sat at assigned seats around the long conference table by seniority.

Reagan was always cordial and pleasant, a generalist on public policy and certainly not a detail-oriented person. He opened the meeting by thanking us for coming. He presented his views on upcoming legislation and explained why the legislation was important to the country. Then he let us know that we could assist him by voting and supporting his bills. We did not debate the merits of any particular bill, nor did we question the president. We were, after all, the "new kids in town." When he finished speaking, the meeting was adjourned.

On that day, the only other president I had spent any time with was Richard Nixon, who always knew everyone's name and was specific about how to accomplish his goals. Reagan and Nixon were both effective in pursuing their own public policy agendas, but they certainly had different strengths and different personalities.

Later on, I attended President George Bush's and President Bill Clinton's White House briefings, usually held in the State Dining Room. They both used a microphone to address the members, who stood during the briefing. Bush knew many of the members because he had served with them in the House, so he was much more relaxed and informal than Reagan was. It seemed to me that Bush knew everyone, while Reagan, for the most part, knew only our leaders. Reagan was more reserved and conventional in interacting with members than Bush was. Clinton was informal as well.

My first day on Leadership Desk duty was April 25. This duty rotated among all the members, who served in this capacity for a few days every session. The functions of this position are like those of a traffic cop. You must be present during the entire floor session, directing the order of debate and making sure that the Republican members are present when they are supposed to speak. The usual procedure is for the presiding officer to acknowledge each speaker, alternating between the Republicans and the Democrats.

On June 7 I flew to Albany, New York, to give the commencement address at my alma mater, Albany Academy for Girls. The subject of my speech was how much things had changed since my graduation and how the school had prepared me for my future. It was my first visit to my school since my graduation in 1938, and, of course, much had changed, including the campus.

When I attended, the school was in a formidable-looking three-story building in the downtown Albany business district. Now the school was outside of the center of town and surrounded by lovely grounds. As a student I wore the required green uniform of a blouse, matching skirt, and sensible shoes. I saw no uniforms when I returned. It was hard not to think about the improbability of seeing myself as a member of Congress in 1983. When I had graduated forty-five years before, I never could have imagined such a thing, nor, probably, could anyone who knew me back then.

The highlight of my June schedule was attending the early-morning launch of the Space Shuttle *Challenger* at the Kennedy Space Center in Florida on June 17, when Sally Ride became the first woman to fly into space. The National Aeronautical Space Agency (NASA) invited about a dozen new members of Congress and members of the Space subcommittee to attend the liftoff. The agency arranged for our transportation from Andrews Air Force Base in Maryland to Patrick Air Force Base in Florida. They put us up in a modest motel near Cape Canaveral, we met the five-person crew, including Sally Ride, and we were briefed on costs and procedures of the flight.

I continued to fly back and forth from Reno to Washington all summer long. When I was in Nevada, I was giving speeches, attending events, or meeting with the news media. I also attended Republican events and conferences, giving speeches across the country in places like Denver and Scottsdale. In August I took the Association of Pilots exam to get my pilot's license. I passed the written exam but didn't qualify on the performance part. I needed more actual flying experience, but never seemed to have enough time.

The first session of the Ninety-eighth Congress adjourned on November 18, 1983. I flew home, and for the most part George and I spent time with the children and grandchildren, although official business frequently intruded. I participated in a two-day Interior Committee hearing in Ely and Elko on proposed Ruby Marshes legislation, attended the dedication of the University of Nevada's Medical School, flew to Salt Lake City for a "Kiddie Committee" hearing, spoke at an education conference in Indianapolis, and flew to Washington to take part in a meeting of the Conservative Opportunity Society, which had just recently been founded by Newt Gingrich.

Like most first-term congressmen, I learned quickly how different governing is from campaigning. Instead of just talking about the issues, you have to vote on them. And often the issues involved things that you just wouldn't talk or think about during your campaigns, when you are selling yourself and your ideas. Your votes are part of the public record and the source of good or bad publicity, depending on the issue. As a result, you need to be prepared on every single vote and on every issue that is discussed in your committees.

That first term, it often seemed to me that I was trying to drink out of a fire hose. Colleagues from other states urged me to vote for bills I didn't know much about. Sometimes it was hard to say no or to be noncommittal, but fortunately most legislation was discussed and digested in committees. There were newspaper clippings, letters and memos from numerous sources, and of course, staff people who kept me informed. Party leadership held meetings to share its views, as did the White House. The information we received came from every side and was overwhelming at times. Like most members of Congress, I came to rely on my staff to help me sort things out. Having a staff member read all of the voluminous material on an issue, then brief me on the pros and cons was extremely useful. Eventually it would come down to what fit with my convictions and what was good for Nevada.

Committee assignments drive a member's activities in the House, and I was no different. I was, of course, most active in mining, gaming, and other Nevada issues. First and foremost, I represented Nevada's interests. Being a conservative Republican, I wasn't interested in creating new laws or government agencies. The Republican philosophy isn't about more government, but rather about limiting the power of government. That position reflected my own philosophy as an individual and the opinions of the people of Nevada who were my constituents as well. For the most part, I followed the Republican Leadership Conference's and the president's agenda. I was a freshman, after all.

As my first term in Congress came to an end, the *Congressional Quarterly* reported that I voted the Republican Party line in 88 percent of 206 House votes. That was about right, as far as I was concerned. On the 65 Conservative Coalition bills, I rated a 97 percent voting record. On the 53 White House–supported bills, I had voted for 39. When asked by the press for my comments, I said, "It would be surprising if I were voting any other way." I did not take the lead on many particular pieces of legislation, but spent a lot of time working with and getting to know the other members of the House, building relationships that would be extremely important in the years ahead, and learning about the issues we were voting on every week.

Generally, my record during that first term reflected the positions I had taken during my campaign on issues like the economy, lower taxes, strong national defense, and American values of faith, family, and hard work. I had a 94 percent attendance record, and I was the primary sponsor of 15 bills and cosponsor of another 151. I had answered 50,000 letters, flown more than 32,000 miles, and visited sixty towns and cities in Nevada. I had returned $25,000 to the federal treasury from my office budget, despite opening and maintaining offices in Reno, North Las Vegas, Elko, and Washington, D.C.

In my first term I supported Ronald Reagan's programs for a free-market economy and his conservative philosophical ideas, including prayer in schools. I voted for the 1984 Tax Simplification Plan, lower government spending, incentives for businesses and entrepreneurs, local government control, states' rights, and stronger families. Even though a majority of Nevadans supported abortion rights, I opposed any legislation that might have funded abortion with taxpayers' money. I supported the pro-life position, of course, because of my Catholic upbringing. The Catholic

Church teaches that abortion is murder, and I agree. I realized early on that you had to be true to your convictions, even if it meant you might not win the next election.

When the Federal Aviation Administration planned to close or automate flight services stations across the country, I successfully fought to keep the stations open in Nevada communities, such as Battle Mountain, Boulder City, Elko, Ely, Fallon, Hawthorne, Lovelock, North Las Vegas, Silver Springs, and Tonopah. I also was able to ensure that the law gave Congress the authority to regulate or prevent any further closures.

By any standard, it was a good record, especially for a first-term member of Congress. My performance was reflected in a wide range of early reelection endorsements from groups such as the U.S. Chamber of Commerce. Watchdog groups that supported lower taxes and less government gave me a perfect voting record on issues important to them. One of the most significant achievements came when my Republican and Democrat colleagues voted me one of the top three most effective and promising freshman.

CHAPTER NINE

Reflection and the
Temptation of the Senate

*While I was in the House, my family also added new members, by marriage.
My daughter Susie married for a second time, to Butch Anderson. I was
actively involved in the plans because they were married on my back patio in
May 1985. The ceremony was performed by Judge Bob Schouweiler in front
of both families and close friends. Two weeks later, my granddaughter Elisa
Cafferata married Dale Erquiaga at Our Lady of Snows Church in Reno.
Dale was from Fallon, but he and Elisa met in Washington, D.C., when she
was interning for Senator Paul Laxalt and Dale was interning in my office.*

Being a member of Congress was, of course, a full-time job. But it is a
fact of political life that you also have to find time to campaign if you
want to keep that job. Although I considered myself by now a seasoned
campaigner, I learned even more as I ran for reelection in 1984 and 1986.
Between those campaigns I had to make one of the toughest political
decisions I ever faced.

My first reelection campaign, in 1984, was a challenging personal experience, although politically it wasn't a close election at all. I was reasonably
comfortable that the voters would recognize the job I had done for them
and return me for a second term, and that became more likely when no
prominent Democrat indicated a desire to run against me. I'm sure that
if there had been any sign of weakness, Democrats would have lined up
to run. I felt my record showed no obvious vulnerabilities—no political
blood in the water, as the saying goes—and that, combined with the fact

that the Second District was conservative and leaned Republican, seemed to guarantee that I would not have serious opposition. That turned out to be true because I got an opponent who was hard to take seriously.

The Democrat candidate was Reno publicist, labor union advocate, newspaper columnist, and political gadfly Andy Barbano. He launched a series of personal attacks that, nearly twenty years later, are still distasteful when I remember them. His campaign, I believe, exemplified everything that many think is wrong with partisan politics. Barbano labeled me a "mobster" and attacked me, and George, continuously. (In later years, in his newspaper column, his name-calling abilities at least took a more original tone. He usually referred to me as "The Vuke," although when I came out in opposition to state senator Joe Neal's initiative petition to raise gaming taxes in 2000, he dubbed me the "Wicked Witch of the West.")

The 1984 campaign began late because neither Barbano nor I faced primary challengers. In 1982 I had started campaigning a year and a half before the general election. In 1984 (although in reality a congressman never stops campaigning), I didn't officially start my campaign until July 2, when I held press conferences in Reno, North Las Vegas, and Elko.

My campaign strategy was a simple one—and effective. I would run on my record. Barbano tried to bash it from the beginning, attempting to make himself king of the sound bite, struggling to be quotable even if he wasn't electable. When he filed for office in May, he charged that I had "hoodwinked" Nevadans, failing every segment of Nevada's population, except the "radical right." Trying to justify what virtually everyone knew would be a long-shot campaign, he claimed that my record meant that even Smokey the Bear would be a viable candidate against me. I won't disagree that Smokey the Bear would have been a better candidate than Barbano—and most Democrats agreed. Not one prominent Democrat endorsed him, campaigned for him, or helped him raise money. Even the news media did not take him seriously. The ability to raise money is a good measure of a candidate's viability, and Barbano raised only $13,390 to my $398,177.

Barbano took classic liberal positions, which did not resonate in Nevada. He favored Big Government and Big Labor, often sounding like a spokesman for the Northern Nevada labor unions, which, in fact, he was. His little digs continued throughout the campaign. According to him, he was the fighter, I was the follower. Nevada's congressman should be a statesman, not an overpaid pen pal, he alleged. He called me anti consumer and pro utilities and big business.

Because he was on the wrong side of almost every issue important to most Nevadans, Barbano adopted a strategy that underfunded and undersupported candidates have traditionally used. He started going through my contribution reports looking for reasons to attack me. For instance, he accused me of being captive to special-interest groups because of my (relatively small) contributions from the nuclear power and energy utilities. He called me a "typical garden-variety overpaid member of Congress, who maintained a low profile while serving out-of-state interests."

The time Barbano called me a mobster, he alleged I had mob connections because I had accepted campaign contributions of $500 each from Al Sachs and Herb Tobman, former operators of the Stardust Hotel in Las Vegas. He claimed Sachs and Tobman were under indictment for skimming, a charge that was not true. He also criticized a contribution I accepted from William T. O'Donnell, the CEO of Bally's, who had been denied a gaming license in New Jersey. He followed this attack with a call for full disclosure of George's salary from Bally Distributing.

With only a few contributions, Barbano's campaign relied on as much free media as he could obtain. His was a campaign of press conferences, and most of the time the media had better things to do. He would send news releases to the smaller newspapers in the state, hoping to get them published. He also appeared on radio talk shows that didn't cost him any money.

One of his few successes came in October, when KVBC/Channel 3 in Las Vegas ran an editorial urging people to vote for Barbano, "even though he didn't have a snowball's chance in hell" of unseating me. The editorial came after Barbano had called a press conference to publicize a poll I had done, which included a couple of questions about a possible Senate race if Paul Laxalt retired in 1986. The television station attacked me for "ambition that was totally unrealistic," and then went on to criticize my support of slot machines in the army's overseas recreation facilities. The station stated that I owned stock in Bally Distributing, the company that supplied the slot machines to the military. George and I owned a few shares of the stock as a result of George's joining the company's stock option plan when he worked there, but of course I wasn't involved in the selection of the slot machines by the army. Bally won the contract through an open bid process.

Truthfully, I found this attack about slot machines bizarre. It is hard to assail Nevada's main industry, gaming. I see nothing wrong with adults playing slot machines, and for servicemen and women it is good, clean fun. It is certainly better entertainment for the soldiers than using drugs or participating in other illegal activities. And suggesting that a candidate in Nevada should not take contributions from people connected to the gaming industry is like suggesting a candidate in Michigan should not accept money from people associated with the auto industry.

I don't remember seeing Barbano much at all on the campaign trail, although I would occasionally get reports from others who ran into him. On one occasion, my grandchildren, Elisa and Reynolds Cafferata, then twenty-two and eighteen, respectively, ran into him at a fireworks show on the Fourth of July. Without telling him who they were, they told him they were interested in learning about politics. Andy's comments about me were less than flattering, to say the least, as he said things like "She's out of touch. She is a dinosaur. I'm one hundred eighty degrees different from Barbara Vucanovich." Elisa and Reynolds politely thanked him and walked away. Two nights later, at a function at the Governor's Mansion in Carson City, Barbano spotted Reynolds wearing a name tag and helping me hand out brochures. When Barbano read the name tag he went ballistic, pointing his finger at Reynolds and shouting, "I know you! I know you!" This episode illustrates the fact that Nevada is a small state and it always pays to be careful what you say about people.

While Barbano was running a marginal campaign, I assembled a statewide campaign organization. George and I flew all over the state, participating in community events, including the usual parades, picnics, and barbecues. I met with the news media in every town and appeared on local television and radio shows. It was a pleasant surprise when the *Reno Gazette Journal* endorsed me, stating that I wasn't a Paul Laxalt clone after all and that I'd been effective in dealing with constituents' problems and questions.

My campaign goals—in addition to winning, of course—were to increase my image and issue base in the congressional district, increase the size of my donor base, and raise my name identification in Southern Nevada. I achieved my goals. On election day, I received 71 percent of the vote to Barbano's 26 percent; the margin of victory was 63,645 votes. I believe some of the victory margin was attributable to the fact that I had done a good job in the House. But Barbano's negative attacks were also a factor. They were so ludicrous—for instance, his accusation that I had underworld ties—that they seriously backfired on him. He attempted to make me into someone I wasn't by making wild accusations, but the voters knew who I was and his attacks weakened any credibility he may have had.

In the 1984 election, and in every election thereafter, I had the powerful advantage of being an incumbent. An officeholder's name is better known, just by the nature of the news coverage and the visibility of being in office. Incumbents repeatedly connect with the people in numerous ways, helping constituents with problems and speaking out on issues about which people care. Often the people who agree with you become your advocates with others.

Still, none of that matters if you don't represent the philosophy of the people who elected you. You have a voting record that people can examine to see if you have been voting the way they expect, and the electorate can take you out of office just as quickly as they put you in. One of the clear advantages I had in 1984, and in future years, was that I kept in touch with the voters and my votes reflected the positions of most Nevadans. As a result, people knew me and didn't believe the false claims of my opponent—in 1984 or in any other campaign.

Unfortunately, while I quickly put the 1984 election behind me, my opponent was able to continue attacking me in his newspaper columns during and after I was in office. And, in one respect, my campaign with Andy Barbano continued for nearly two years after the election was over. After I was quoted in the *Reno Gazette Journal* as saying that the poll of mine that Barbano had made an issue of earlier in the campaign had been stolen, he sued me, filing his complaint on the Friday before the general election, using his legal pleadings to continue his personal attacks on me and my reputation. Eventually, he would file more than twenty motions or pleadings before the case was dismissed "with prejudice," meaning it couldn't be refiled, on April 11, 1986. This poll is the one I previously mentioned. A young intern in my congressional office had copied confidential data concerning a potential run for the U.S. Senate and sent the information to the press.

After winning reelection, I had no plans but to continue to do a good job for the people of my district in the House of Representatives. I fully expected to run for a third term in 1986. But when it became clear that Senator Laxalt would not seek a third term that year, I felt I had an obligation—to Nevada, my supporters, the Republican Party, and myself—to give serious consideration to running for the United States Senate.

Early in 1985 there was considerable speculation over Paul's plans. My gut feeling initially was that the pressure he was feeling from President Reagan was too strong and he would run for a third term, but on August 18 I met with Paul at the Dreyfus estate (formerly the Whittell estate) at Lake Tahoe, and he let me know that he wasn't going to run for reelection. He and I met several times over the next few months to discuss his replacement and the possibility that I might be a candidate. While he didn't discourage me, he was noncommittal, as one might expect. Early and enthusiastic support for my candidacy for a brand-new House seat was one thing; support for a Senate race, with its national implications, was entirely another. I understood that.

As the only Republican in the House from Nevada, I knew that in many ways an effort to succeed Paul seemed like the logical next step in my political career. My Southern Nevada counterpart in the House, Democrat Harry Reid, and I were both elected in 1982. When Harry made it clear that he planned to run for the Senate, other Democrat hopefuls simply evaporated and he became the front-runner—and then the nominee—without much effort. That would not be the case for me if I decided to run.

While I received expressions of support from many people, my decision was complicated by the fact that there was another prominent Republican candidate who also wanted the job, former congressman Jim Santini. After he had lost to incumbent senator Howard Cannon in a hard-fought

Democratic primary in 1982, Jim had changed political parties and become a Republican. He was being urged to run by many people—in Washington and in Nevada—who felt he had represented Nevada well when he served in Congress and would have the best chance of keeping the Senate seat in Republican hands.

I quietly explored whether I had the support I needed to win. Even though my own congressional district covered nearly the whole state, including parts of Clark County, I also would have to run in the heavily Democratic First Congressional District, Harry Reid's home base. I hired a pollster to assess my chances, as did Santini. Both of us saw encouraging signs in our polls, so for a while we had a mini battle of the polls, with both of us claiming the better position.

During the late summer and fall of 1985, I discussed the campaign and the likelihood of my success with conservative leaders in Washington and with my political and financial supporters in Nevada. I continued my schedule of attending events around the state, giving speeches to groups, and raising campaign money. But I was busy with my congressional duties, so I didn't devote full time to analyzing the senatorial race. It never reached the point of setting up an official exploratory committee, but I did the appropriate due diligence just in case. (My daughter Patty, who was then the state treasurer, was doing her own exploratory work, looking into running for my congressional seat if I ran for the Senate. Surprisingly, a few Republicans contacted me seeking my endorsement if they ran for my congressional seat. I found it strange that anyone would think that I would support someone over a family member.)

By November 1985, a year before the election, some conservative leaders outside Congress began to put pressure on my colleagues in the House to urge me not to run for the Senate. It became clear that Santini's party change had taken place with encouragement from Senator Laxalt. They had worked together while Jim was in the House, and the senator was very knowledgeable about Santini's record. I realized that I probably would not have a strong endorsement from my mentor. I could see the handwriting on the wall, so on November 18 I announced that I would run for reelection to the House.

I was happy with my decision not to run for the Senate. I had a "safe" seat in the House as long as I kept doing a good job for Nevada. I was

My daughter Patty Cafferata and I are standing on the steps of the Capitol in Washington, D.C. She encouraged me to write my memoirs. Over a five-year period after I retired from the House, Patty interviewed me about my life and wrote my story down. Collection of Barbara F. Vucanovich

accumulating seniority on my committees and got along well with both Democrats and Republicans in the House. After all, as I told people facetiously, "the pay was the same and so were the hours."

I've never been one to think much about "what might have been." I had a rewarding and successful career in the House of Representatives. Of course, looking back, I felt that I would have had a good chance to defeat

Harry Reid for the Senate seat in 1986 or I never would have considered it in the first place. I had strong Republican credentials, I had proven myself in Congress, and President Reagan was immensely popular in Nevada. There has been a lot of speculation about how the race would have turned out between Harry and me. But political speculation is just that—speculation.

For all his strengths, Jim Santini was hindered in his race because many Democrats, although they had liked him as a congressman, still blamed him for Howard Cannon's defeat in 1982. Throughout his campaign, he was on the defensive over his switch from Democrat to Republican, and Harry Reid ended up winning narrowly, by about 14,000 votes out of 263,000 cast. All I know for certain is that I was satisfied with my decision and comfortable as a member of the House of Representatives.

It was while I was wrestling with that "run-or-don't-run" decision that I had one of the greatest thrills of my life in Congress or elsewhere. On August 16, 1985, at the age of sixty-four, I got to fly in an F-16. It was one of the few times that George Vucanovich was truly jealous of my job. Members of Congress get these opportunities occasionally, usually if there is a military base in their district or if they have appropriate committee assignments. Since my district included both Nellis Air Force Base and Fallon Naval Air Station, I was delighted to accept the invitation to fly in the F-16.

The one caveat for taking the ride was passing a complete physical examination, including a workout in an altitude chamber wearing a special pressurized suit. After spending some mandatory time in a simulator and in a briefing on what to expect during the flight, I was cleared to fly. I wore a helmet and a pressurized flight suit—with my name on it—to help withstand the G-forces during the flight. It was heavy and bulky, and I felt like I could barely waddle out to the plane. When I stared up at the cockpit, there was my name stenciled on the fuselage. While the F-16 is a one-person aircraft, this was a two-seater used for training, with a pilot in front and a passenger behind.

Nothing can quite prepare you for the flight itself. We taxied out onto the runway and before I could catch my breath, we were at 10,000 feet altitude. We flew a course close to the ground and then pulled about three

I am at Nellis Air Force Base, getting ready to take off in an F-16 Falcon on August 16, 1985. I had to pass a rigorous physical examination at Andrews Air Force Base before I was allowed to take this flight. Official U.S. Air Force photograph

G's as we rapidly ascended. My G-suit pressed against my body, and I forced air out of my lungs as I had been told to do during training. I had to work to see over the oxygen mask, but there was a "heads-up" display screen in front of me showing the course we were flying. At one point my pilot, Air Force lieutenant colonel Roger Riggs, invited me to take the controls. I timidly touched the stick and had the plane on its side in a split second. I suspect he was prepared for that, for he quickly righted the aircraft. I turned him down the next time he offered to let me fly.

I will never forget the feeling. We flew over the Nellis Bombing and Gunnery Range in restricted airspace, flying a typical training mission—hitting simulated targets and then ascending rapidly from the target area. All too soon we were back on the ground, but it was the thrill of a lifetime!

Meanwhile, my decision not to run for the Senate caught some people by surprise. Certainly it surprised the man who would become my opponent in the 1986 congressional race, Reno mayor Pete Sferrazza. Pete had already announced that he planned to run for Congress, fully expecting me to run for the Senate. It never made complete sense to me that he followed through on running for the House even after I announced that I was running for reelection. He was a stronger candidate than Andy Barbano because Reno was the largest population center in the district, and he came into the race with excellent name identification. He was, from the start, a significantly more credible candidate, and I expected a serious challenge.

Sferrazza was an unusual candidate for many reasons. As someone who was electable as a populist "anti-growth" mayor, he had trouble translating that popularity into a race outside of Reno. Another of his challenges, which worked to my benefit, was that he came across as less than warm and friendly while he was campaigning one-on-one, which was one of my strengths and is still extremely important in Nevada campaigns. Also, he was not popular with the business community. In fact, more than one person said that the only good thing about sending Sferrazza to Congress would be that it would get him out of Reno. Finally, my family was one of the strengths of my political persona. Pete had a reputation as something of a playboy. In those days, compared to me, he was almost the anti-family candidate.

My campaign team for 1986 was virtually identical to the group that had performed so well in my previous two elections. Based on Tony Likins's and Tony Payton's recommendations, I hired Mike Pieper as my campaign manager. We also hired a paid staff that included a finance director, an organization director, and an office manager/scheduler— my oldest granddaughter, Elisa Cafferata. Jay Bryant produced all my television and radio spots, Tony Payton was the general campaign consultant, Lance Terrance did the polling, and Bill Martin served as the campaign spokesman, designed my print ads, and handled all the press releases. I printed thousands of yard signs, brochures, newspaper inserts, and buttons. (I didn't need, however, any more Styrofoam coffee cups with my name of them.)

I added one staff person because of his success in fund-raising. Originally, Pete Ernaut volunteered to be my rural fund-raising chair. I didn't know I needed one because I'd never raised much money in the rural counties. Pete put together an exciting event at the Searles ranch in Elko County. The entire length of the driveway to the ranch was posted with my yard signs and American flags. The money raised at this party made it my best rural fund-raiser to that time, and naturally I put Pete on the campaign payroll after the event.

Strategically, we planned for me to spend 50 percent of my time in Washoe County, 30 percent in rapidly growing Clark County, and 20 percent in the rural counties. I targeted Republicans, senior citizens, and even Democrats in the rural counties. I had volunteer coordinators in every county, volunteers operated a phone bank to identify favorable voters, and we called back the undecided voters with advocacy calls.

I filed for office at the secretary of state's office in the capitol in Carson City on June 30, 1986. Once again I would run on my record. I talked about the bill I had introduced to protect Nevada from nuclear waste and the first-ever Nevada wilderness bill. My intent was to protect our lands for future generations to use and enjoy, while respecting traditional multiple use of the public lands. When I filed, the issues concerning Nevadans were a balanced federal budget, lower taxes, and a strong national defense. My record showed I was on the "Nevada" side of all of those issues.

We decided early that my campaign would revolve around five key themes: I cared about Nevada and its people; I worked hard to represent the people; my conservative views were in tune with the views of a majority of Nevadans; I offered a stable, positive voice for Nevada; and I had valuable legislative experience that Nevada could not afford to lose. I summed up my position by stating, "I think and act like a Nevadan." In all cases, we expected it would offer contrasts with the positions that Pete would be taking.

I opened my Reno headquarters in late June and the Las Vegas office in September. My tentative budget at the beginning of the campaign was $222,000. It was optimistically low. By the end of the campaign, I had raised and spent that $222,000 and another $145,000.

From the beginning, Pete Sferrazza tried to position himself as a "Champion of the People." Like my other opponents, he tried to make my age an issue. For example, early in the campaign he rode a bicycle all the way across U.S. Highway 50 in Nevada to show he was young and energetic. I responded by saying I would ride a Harley-Davidson instead. This was another example of how small-town candidates used tactics more appropriate for local races. Pete was out in the middle of sparsely populated rural Nevada on a bicycle, which meant he wouldn't be talking to many voters. And few of them could relate to his marathon bike trek.

As I noted, Sferrazza was a different sort of candidate. He was an attorney, not a typical cowboy or a traditional Nevada type. He wasn't interested in mining or agricultural issues. I always considered him more of a politician, which, in that regard at least, made him not much different from many of my other opponents. True Nevada issues, such as mining and public land use, important priorities for most the Second District, were not really that important to him. I don't think any of my opponents—Gojack, Barbano, or Sferrazza—really understood the rural areas. If they talked about public lands at all, for example, it was from an environmentalist's perspective that favored wilderness areas and restricted access. That was not popular in rural Nevada. My opponents all ran on the standard Democratic issues, including Big Labor concerns, the environment, and abortion. In politics, it's all about putting together enough groups of voters to garner a majority on election day. On my campaigns, we never underestimated the possibility that a Democrat could put together enough urban and labor votes to win.

In contrast, most of my experience in Nevada politics was in the rural areas, especially when I worked for Paul Laxalt. I understood the "cow counties," and I thought a big part of my job was to protect the Nevada lifestyle. None of my opponents seemed concerned about that. The voters, however, were interested; even those in urban areas cared about rural Nevada.

In the 1986 campaign I found Sferrazza to be generally distant and aloof, a liberal Democrat whose views on the issues were directly opposite from mine. He was pro-choice, but I don't remember that being a big issue in our campaign. His radio and television advertising I remember as particularly personal. For instance, in attacking me on the nuclear waste issue, he ran a television ad that showed me with brightly glowing eyes bouncing out of my head. He also ran a takeoff on the television program *Lifestyles of the Rich and Famous,* with a Robin Leach–style announcer claiming that I traveled to glamorous places at taxpayers' expense. I'll give him points for creativity, but the voters deducted points for accuracy. The charges were not true, and the election results reflected the public's disbelief.

At that time the Second District, while conservative, was almost evenly divided between registered Republicans and registered Democrats, with a huge number of independents. I ended up with 58 percent of the vote, defeating Pete by 24,046 votes. Members of the media called it a landslide. The pundits thought I would lose, mainly because of the age issue. Yet I carried every county in the state, with a margin of victory ranging from 51 percent in Storey County to 74 percent in Eureka County. It would not be my last encounter with Pete Sferrazza. We would meet again in the general election of 1992.

CHAPTER TEN

Elections—
Forgettable and Not So Memorable

I remember many family birthdays or events by relating them to election years or campaigns. My daughter Susie was particularly helpful with election-year babies. Her older son, Scott Dillon Anderson, was born in February 1986, and David Christopher Anderson arrived in March 1988. In both years I had already started planning for that year's reelection efforts when they were born. Scott and David are my youngest grandchildren.

If you don't enjoy campaigning, you should not be a member of Congress. Because your name is on the ballot every election cycle, you are always on parade—literally if not figuratively. I have known members of the Senate (not necessarily in Nevada) who, since they run every six years, can spend four years picking and choosing which home state events they want to attend, and then during the two years before they have to run for reelection, they are everywhere. Members of the House don't have that luxury of time off from the campaign trail.

There are three things to be considered when it comes to running for reelection. First, you must make the commitment to be everywhere you can be, to shake as many hands as possible, to be willing to attend all of the small-town community fairs and festivals, visit local businesses, and keep a schedule that is brutal. Fortunately, I have always enjoyed meeting people with George at my side, and I didn't mind the wear and tear of steady campaigning. It was what drove us to take a lot of red-eye flights between Washington and Nevada and to try to get home virtually every weekend when Congress was in session.

Coping with the three-hour time difference between Washington and Nevada was difficult. If it was 6:00 A.M. and time to get up in Washington, it was only 3:00 A.M. in Reno, or if it was 9:00 P.M. when I was at a Reno event, it was midnight in Washington. To adjust, I immediately set my watch for the time where I was and acted accordingly.

Travel picked up during election years because I didn't want to miss any Nevada events. Probably the busiest weekend of the year was the Labor Day holiday. On average, we covered more than 1,000 miles over those three days because there were events and parades in Elko, Winnemucca, Ione, Pioche, Fallon, and Carson City. George flew me to each town, except Carson City. We didn't always make Pioche, but I got there as often as I could. It was always a relief when the weekend ended and I flew back to Washington to go to "work."

Second, a political fact of life is fund-raising, and you have to make a commitment to that as well. With a campaign coming along every two years, fund-raising was almost a year-round activity. I would spend about 50 percent of my time campaigning and 50 percent raising money, although those proportions would change during the course of the campaign. Early on, I spent more time raising money, and as election day neared, I spent much more time campaigning. Still, for almost all of my campaigns, probably the most important person in my campaign was the one who coordinated my fund-raising activities.

For large donations, there were two parts to the money puzzle. The first was soliciting money from the PACs that supported you or that you supported, and the second was good old-fashioned one-on-one check collecting. No one, with rare exceptions, would give you money unless you asked for it, which meant a lot of telephone calls and personal visits. If you expected to collect $5,000 from a PAC or $1,000 from an individual, the contributor had every right to expect to be able to personally hand you the check.

The types of PACs that scheduled events for me included mining, gaming, home builders, contractors, Realtors, pro-life, pro-business, insurance, tourism-related, restaurant industry, and other industries with Nevada interests. Obviously, it would be unusual for a PAC that didn't care about Nevada issues to contribute to my campaign.

Congressional leaders, industries, and special-interest groups create PACs because of the limits on individual campaign donations. When I served in the House, individuals could give no more than \$1,000 per election (since raised to \$2,000), while a PAC could give up to \$5,000 per election.

My PAC events were mostly held in Washington, but I attended some in Denver, Texas, Arizona, and, of course, Nevada. These events were often held in the evening, usually with food served, although breakfast events were also scheduled. In general, I would speak about that group's legislative interests, what I was doing to support its positions, and the likelihood of success. I answered questions and mingled with the guests. Typically, I raised \$5,000 to \$10,000 at a PAC event. As I gained in seniority and had better committee assignments, I raised more money at these events than I did at the beginning of my House service.

The importance of PACs increased during my time in the House. Today, all the leaders in both parties and many members establish their own PACs, so they can donate to other party members, both incumbents and challengers. That was not the norm when I was in the House, although I often supported others with my own personal donations.

For an individual member of Congress, the efforts to form a PAC made it worthwhile because a donation from a PAC helped affirm the loyalty of the receiving candidate to the donor and his or her agenda in the House.

It would be an understatement to say that fund-raising was my least favorite aspect of campaigning. I dreaded it, but I did what I had to do to fund my campaigns, never raising more than I needed for any race. I found one of the dynamics of fund-raising was that people were more inclined to give you money if they thought you had a tough race ahead of you and less inclined if they thought you didn't. As a result, during those campaigns where it was perceived that I might have a difficult time getting reelected, people were apt to donate more and larger sums. Since that was rarely the case, I always felt as if I simply eked by, barely receiving the funds I needed for most campaigns.

For me, the most successful fund-raising activity was direct mail. By the end of my time in Congress, I had more than five thousand names on my "House List" that I mailed materials to several times during the campaign year. They were people who had a history of giving to me. I mailed to these donors between elections as well, but not very often. I also mailed "prospecting" fund-raising letters to members of targeted groups whose political philosophies were similar to mine, such as Republican committees, the National Rifle Association, pro-life organizations, and business groups, not only to raise funds but to expand my House List for future mailings.

Generally, each mail piece mentioned my achievements or the Republicans' successes in the House. It was also important to create a sense of need and a sense of urgency, so I included an explanation of how their donation would be spent on a specific campaign activity, such as television spots, yard signs, or radio ads, and I mentioned a deadline of when the money was required. The conventional wisdom still is that the most likely person to give you money is someone who has already given you money. After the first contribution, the donor usually gives more money to protect the "investment."

My second most successful fund-raising tool was scheduling parties in private homes. The campaign finance reporting laws permitted people to pay for events in their houses without the expenses being subject to the contribution limits. The host or hostess would invite their friends and family members to a picnic, barbecue, dinner, luncheon, wine tasting, cocktail party, breakfast, or coffee to meet me. Depending on the event, the guests who wanted to attend were asked for a $25 to $1,000 donation to my campaign. During any campaign cycle, my supporters gave twenty to thirty parties in communities all over the state.

Both direct mail and the private parties generated for the most part numerous small donations. The parties at the $1,000 contribution level obviously raised larger sums of money, but I held only a few of those over the years.

While raising political money was never fun, it wasn't necessarily as unsavory as some people would like you to think it is. I can honestly say that I never—in seven terms—had someone say they would give me money only if I voted a certain way. I would not have accepted the contribution if that had been the case, of course. Certainly, people aren't going to support you financially unless they generally agree with your political positions. But there was never even a suggestion that I was receiving a campaign check in exchange for my vote. Such a thing was never asked, and of course it was never promised.

The third consideration in running for reelection was the level of the opposition. I ran for office seven times. Four times—in 1982, 1986, 1988, and 1992—I had what I considered to be my toughest opponents, capable of raising enough money and getting enough support to be serious threats. Even in the other years—1984, 1990, and 1994—I never made the mistake of underestimating my opponents. I had seen too many candidates, at all levels, get defeated because they assumed they were invincible, only to find out they were not. I ran a professional, fully funded campaign every time my name was on the ballot, regardless of who was running against me.

After I toyed with the idea of running for the Senate in 1986 and then defeated Pete Sferrazza, I was committed to staying in the House of Representatives as long as my health was good and as long as the people wanted me. Once I was in Congress, I had what was considered a "safe" seat by the party professionals and political pundits, meaning that I should be reelected. But I also knew that the voters of Nevada were smart enough to figure out that if I wasn't representing them well and wasn't voting the way they expected, they could send me into an early retirement. I had learned over the years what it takes to stay in office: a solid record, being responsive to constituents' problems, and a professional campaign. Every two years, I campaigned to remind them that I had been doing exactly what they sent me to Washington to do and that I deserved to be reelected. I always felt my record was a good one, but two of my last four elections were hard fought against determined opponents.

1988—The "Oops" Campaign

The general election ballot in 1988 listed three candidates for Congress—Democrat Jim Spoo, Libertarian Kent Cromwell, and myself. Even with my so-called landslide against Pete Sferrazza in 1986, there was speculation in the news media that Spoo, who at the time was the mayor of Sparks, would be the most formidable opponent I had faced thus far. It was déjà vu all over again. The media had said the same thing about Sferrazza two years earlier.

A pattern that I noticed over the years was that reporters often seemed to expect my opponents to do better in elections than they actually did. I suspect the reason for that was that most reporters didn't understand the importance or the impact of my style of grassroots campaigning.

One seldom saw reporters on the campaign trail, and they tended to focus on high-profile events, like debates, and not the nuts and bolts that make a campaign work. I also think they were open to any talk from Democrats that "this will be the year we get Vucanovich." After all, it can make election coverage more exciting if the race is considered a close one. Perhaps some of their own political leanings colored their perceptions as well. But truthfully, I didn't mind being underestimated.

I formally announced for reelection in March and officially filed on June 20 at the state capitol. In announcing, I emphasized my voting record, including positions designed to reduce the federal deficit and improve the economy, repeal the 55-miles-per-hour speed-limit law, keep nuclear waste out of Nevada, improve health care for senior citizens, strengthen our national defense, and preserve traditional family values.

With my early announcement, I was off and running for the rest of the year. We quickly had an organization in place with campaign coordinators in every county. Originally, I hired Linden Heck to manage the campaign, but after a short period of working for me she was offered another opportunity for a better position outside Nevada, so she recommended Bill Ulrey to replace her as my campaign manager. He had worked on several other campaigns, including one for another woman candidate, and came highly recommended by Tony Likins, Tony Payton, and Mike Pieper.

Fund-raising was its usual hard work. I made a lot of telephone calls, sent numerous pieces of direct mail, and held several special events, including some with such guests as Congressman Larry Craig of Idaho and Secretary of the Interior Don Hodel. When the secretary was in Reno, we combined congressional and campaign business when I took him on a tour of the Oxbow geothermal energy plant in Dixie Valley. Every opportunity to expose Washington officials to lesser-known areas of Nevada was always an advantage for the state.

One of the stories the media liked to focus on was which candidate was raising the most money, so it was news that during the first half of 1988 I raised about $500 less than Spoo. However, I had raised more than $100,000 in 1987, and although Spoo's campaign collected close to $150,000 before June 30, I had more money in the bank. In addition, I remember he was burning through money quickly for items like staff and headquarters equipment. I felt that money not used for direct voter contacts was money not being used to its best potential. Spoo's money was coming from the usual Democrat supporters, including unions and pro-abortion groups. The latter I found odd, because Spoo was pro-life. I suppose the pro-choice crowd figured he would be a lesser evil than the Republican Vucanovich.

While I had made "tough grandmother" a positive phrase in my campaigns, Jim Spoo once referred to me as a "tough old grandmother," perhaps in an effort to reinforce the obvious fact that he was younger than I was. He called himself a new kind of politician and tried to contrast that with what he said were my "old-style politics." "Old" seemed to be a popular word to describe me. Of course, as did all of my challengers' campaigns, his misrepresented my voting record, claiming I had voted against senior citizens, education, veterans, and the environment. One of the more outrageous statements he made was that I defended defense contractors' right to defraud the government. For the most part, I framed the election around the question "Who can best represent Nevada in the 1990s?" Of course, we took the offensive when he made factual errors, which he did frequently. And I challenged his hypocrisy for calling his campaign employees "private contractors" so he wouldn't have to withhold and pay income and Social Security taxes on their salaries.

Because neither of us had primaries, it was clear early on that we would face each other in the general election. One of the real challenges of my campaign was that we didn't know where Spoo stood on many federal issues. As a municipal mayor, he had never had to take a position on issues like national defense, federal control of public lands, federal budget, or Social Security. We made a calculated decision to challenge him to an early debate in Elko. We felt that Elko would provide a friendly audience for me and would, at the very least, give me a chance to find out where Jim Spoo stood on the issues.

The decision paid big dividends for us. We met on July 19 in the Elko Convention Center, and Spoo committed one of the biggest mistakes he would make during the campaign. In answering a question, he said that he believed people ought to "qualify" for Social Security benefits (what was called in those days "means testing"). I pointed out that Social Security wasn't meant to be a welfare program and that people who paid into the system should receive their checks regardless of any income qualifications.

Because there was virtually no media coverage of the debate, we held a news conference in Reno a few days afterward to attack his position, accusing him of saying that Nevadans might be denied the Social Security benefits to which they were legally entitled. I said it was callous and insensitive to suggest that when people reached retirement age their Social Security benefits might not be available to them. Spoo had to try to explain himself, and it put him on the defensive early in the campaign. I'm not sure he ever really recovered.

He also made a number of other mistakes and changed his positions on some issues. That inconsistency led to a television commercial that my campaign staff members still considered one of the best ever produced in Nevada politics. The "Oops" spot was a play on Jim Spoo's name, spelling it backward, of course. We were fairly certain we wouldn't be criticized for making fun of his name because he had frequently referred to himself as "Mayor Oops" in self-deprecating fashion. Jay Bryant created the spot, which opened with a picture of Spoo and an announcer talking about a position Spoo had taken on an issue. Then the picture (and his name) would reverse, and the announcer would talk about his new position. For instance, Jim Spoo claimed he was for a cleaner environment, but "oops," he had lobbied Congress against enforcement of the Clean Air Act. He said he was a fiscal conservative, but "oops," he had proposed new federal spending and taxes amounting to tens of billions of dollars. The ads were memorable, and many voters told me they were effective.

Although we debated two more times during the campaign, in Las Vegas on October 18 and in Reno on November 2, I have no clear memory of Spoo doing much campaigning, and I seldom ran into him on the campaign trail. As a candidate I tried to attend every event that I could, even though I had to spend a great deal of time with duties in Congress. I felt he was perhaps a reluctant candidate whose heart never was in the campaign. Although those who know him well say he has a good sense of humor in person, he never seemed very comfortable as a candidate. He was not an aggressive guy, and if he had strong convictions I never heard him express them.

In the end, his campaign never really got off the ground. I ran hard and won by nearly 31,000 votes. The 105,981 votes I received gave me the highest total I had ever collected and exceeded my margin of victory over

Pete Sferrazza in 1986. I won all seventeen counties, including the portion of Clark County that was in the Second Congressional District. At that time Clark County represented 15 percent of the total voters in the district, second only to Washoe County. In the rural counties, I received 65 percent of the votes and even ran ahead of presidential candidate George Bush in several counties.

After this election, I was the only Republican left in the Nevada delegation. The others in federal office were Harry Reid, Dick Bryan, and Jim Bilbray. When a member of the press asked me how I would work with those three Democrats, I said something like "I've raised three boys of my own, I can handle those three Democrats."

1990—The Rocking Chair

We started planning for the 1990 election even before we knew who my opponent would be, with the first strategy meeting in Dick Horton's office on January 17, nearly eleven months before election day. In an effort to discourage anyone from even thinking about running, I filed for reelection very early, on February 12.

As I mentioned earlier, I hired Polly Minor from Washington as my finance director, assisted by Marsha Berkbigler of Reno. Family was also involved, as usual. My granddaughter Farrell Cafferata worked in campaign headquarters, and my grandson Mike Dillon Jr. put up my campaign signs in rural Nevada.

Curiously, 1990 was the first time since I had been elected in 1982 that I had primary election opponents. Anyone with the filing fee is entitled to run, and it was probably unusual that I was a candidate for three elections without a primary. Most of the time, unknown primary candidates run for one of three reasons. First, they are hoping for lightning to strike or for a miracle to occur. Second, they have a single-issue agenda that they want to promote. Third, they really believe they can win if they can just get their vital message out. In 1990 two Republicans, Dick Baker and Brooklyn Harris, filed against me. I had never heard of either one of them, but the fact that they were running didn't change my strategy at all. As it turned out, neither ran much of a campaign. I ended up getting almost 85 percent of the votes in the primary.

My general election opponent was Democrat Jane Wisdom, a two-term assemblywoman from Las Vegas. She was virtually unknown outside of Southern Nevada and clearly hoped to capitalize on the growth of the voter base in the Clark County portion of the Northern Nevada Congressional District. When the district was created in 1982, only about 9 percent of the votes came from Clark County. By 1990 that number had nearly doubled, to 17 percent, and about 52 percent of the voters were in Washoe County, with the rest in the rural counties.

Wisdom turned out to be another opponent who tried to use my age against me. She ran a television ad showing a woman in a rocking chair (supposedly me) knitting, while a voice-over said, "Babs should stay home and tend to her knitting." Even when political advertising is supposed to be humorous it has to be believable, and the image of me sitting in a rocking chair was so far from what people thought of me that the joke was on her, not me.

At the press conference when she announced her candidacy, her comments about me were insulting and outrageous. The press called me immediately to get my response. I declined to join Wisdom in her name-calling but said I looked forward to discussing the issues.

One thing I remember about her campaign was that she had the help of consumer advocate Ralph Nader. Right before the election, on October 30, he sent out a news release attacking me for voting to increase my congressional pay by $35,000 a year. It was misleading because the raise applied only to the new congressmen, not to the sitting members. I didn't like the last-minute nature of the attack, but of course I always felt that criticism for such votes was fair game.

Nader also attacked me for the size of my PAC contributions. I raised $176,367 from individuals and $129,950 from PACs, with some additional money from Republican Party organizations. I thought it was a good sign when challengers attacked incumbents for accepting PAC money. It shows that they think the incumbent's PAC support isn't a weakness. The amount of money a candidate raises is almost always an indication of how much support the person has, regardless of where it comes from. From what I've heard, voters understood how expensive campaigns had gotten, something we all wished wasn't true. In a state like Nevada it was important to understand that many voters felt that their concerns were represented by PACs, for example, the PACs that represent mining, ranching, and gaming interests. Bottom line—Wisdom's attacks didn't work. On election day, I received 103,508 votes to 59,581 for Wisdom and 12,120 for Libertarian Dan Becan.

It was after this election, as the House was organizing for the 1991 session, that my Republican colleague Jerry Lewis (not the comedian) suggested that I make a bid for a seat on the prestigious House Appropriations Committee. Appropriations is the "money" committee, and a seat on it would allow me to have a bigger voice in federal spending, particularly for Nevada. Jerry served on the Committee on Committees and was always supportive of Republican women moving up in the House. With Jerry's support and encouragement I solicited the support of my Republican colleagues and was appointed to the Appropriations Committee. The Republicans needed a replacement for Virginia Smith, who had retired. The only Republican woman on the committee, she was from the small rural state of Nebraska.

Normally members of Appropriations had to give up all other committee assignments, but I was allowed to stay on the Interior Committee because of its importance to the public land issues in Nevada. (Eventually, in 1995, I gave up the Interior Committee when I became chair of the Appropriations Military Construction subcommittee.) Part of my Appropriations Committee assignment, however, included sitting on the Interior Appropriations subcommittee, which amounted to a double benefit to Nevada. I was in a position to influence the expenditure of funds on programs to promote Nevada's interests.

My seat on the Appropriations Committee was a big victory for me. I had tried to get the assignment in 1988, but I was passed over. After I missed out that year, I asked for a seat on the Armed Services Committee, hoping to get off the House Administration Committee. I didn't get that seat either, but I did become the ranking member of a couple of subcommittees on House Administration, so I finally received additional staff because of my ranking member positions. I also moved up on the Interior Committee, so I was able to hire Bill Condit for help with resources issues.

My last really hard-fought campaign was in 1992, a rematch with Pete Sferrazza. We knew he was gearing up to run again, and the campaign started early. I had already held my first campaign meeting and my first PAC fund-raiser in Washington by the time I filed on February 11 at the secretary of state's office.

This was different from my previous campaigns in that the 1991 Nevada Legislature had reapportioned the state's two congressional districts after the 1990 Census. Fortunately, reapportionment was accomplished without too much debate. Southern Nevada congressman Jim Bilbray and I sat down and divided up the state, and the legislature agreed. Jim wanted to pick up North Las Vegas and other parts of my district that were heavily Democratic, and he wanted to get rid of the Republican areas of his district, such as Boulder City. That sounded like a good idea to me.

I ended up with a district that went literally border to border in Nevada, while Jim had a district that was virtually a pocket inside my district. It meant that a large percentage of my district was located in Clark County, reflecting the phenomenal growth in that part of the state, but I was not concerned because it included a lot of Republican voters, so that year, for the first time, I got to ride in the Boulder City Fourth of July parade.

(Ironically, while the purpose of our reapportionment plan was to give us both relatively safer districts, Jim Bilbray's part of the deal didn't work out so well for him. He was defeated for reelection in 1994 by John Ensign, now a senator from Nevada.)

I intentionally waited until July 18 to open my campaign offices. Campaign headquarters were important in my campaigns as the place for my volunteers to gather to make telephone calls, put together mailings, hold events, and give visibility for the campaign. But headquarters are expensive to operate; they require rent, telephones and other utilities, equipment, and staff. Usually I tried to delay the opening of headquarters as long as I could.

I defeated my three Republican primary opponents, but the night of the primary election would best be remembered by an incident that immediately put the Sferrazza campaign on the defensive. In a late-evening telephone call with a reporter, he caused a sensation by calling me an "old bag." I immediately organized a committee of "Old Bags for Barb," and many of my women friends and volunteers rushed to sign up. Of course, Sferrazza denied making the remark, even claiming that a friend was impersonating him on the phone when the comment was made. The reporter had spoken to Sferrazza several times on the phone, so the reporter stuck by his story. We had a lot of fun with it. This incident showed how close to the candidates Nevada voters can be. Many people told me they could imagine Sferrazza making exactly that kind of comment, so it was believable. Even people who weren't usually my supporters told me that his comments were out of line.

For all of that, it turned out to be my closest election. Pete ran an extremely aggressive campaign and so did I. This campaign was more difficult than I had originally thought it would be, and I was concerned enough to ask Mike Pieper, my administrative assistant, to take a leave of absence from the federal payroll to manage the campaign. We ran a tough-minded campaign, giving the voters reasons to compare our records.

The *Reno Gazette Journal* endorsed Sferrazza, sort of. It said nice things about me, especially my work in obtaining funds for the federal courthouse, the Reno airport, and breast cancer research. They mentioned my attempts to help the "Notch Babies," people born between 1917 and 1926 who received fewer Social Security benefits than other seniors. But they disapproved of my support for "trickle-down" economics and stated that I was nothing more than a rubber stamp for the Republican administration. In endorsing Sferrazza, the editors said they were not endorsing his performance as mayor of Reno, but they liked his desire to trim defense spending, his support of social needs, and his favoring a light increase in taxes.

This also was my most expensive campaign. In 1986 Sferrazza spent $69,777 to my $367,044; in 1992 he spent $202,888 to my $688,379. There were three other candidates on the ballot in 1992—a Libertarian, a Populist, and an Independent American. While third-party candidates had little chance of winning, they diluted the vote and certainly tended to draw conservative voters away from me. They usually didn't actively campaign by advertising, attending events, participating in parades, or giving speeches. For example, Dan Becan, a Libertarian, ran for Congress in 1984, 1990, and 1992, but I met him only once. In 1992 Dan Hansen was the Independent American Party candidate, but I hardly ever saw him either.

I debated Sferrazza on public television two days before the election, and the debate was broadcast simultaneously in Reno and Las Vegas. The thing that stuck with me most about that debate was that Sferrazza said something negative about my son Mike, and it made me furious that an opponent would attack one of my children. I couldn't get out of the studio fast enough. My longtime public relations consultant Bill Martin remarked afterward that he had never before seen me get angry. But I was certainly mad that night. It was probably the only time I ever lost my temper at an opponent.

On election day, I received 129,575 votes, Sferrazza 117,119, and the minor-party candidates a total of 23,687 votes. It was a comfortable margin of victory, although I received only 48 percent of the vote, which some in the press claimed was an indication of vulnerability. I attributed it to the fact that there were five people on the ballot.

Nor was it a good year for Republicans in general. It's hard to believe now, but George Bush lost nationally to Bill Clinton and also lost Nevada. Third-party candidate Ross Perot made the difference. In Nevada Perot got 132,580 votes, Bush 175,828, and Clinton 189,148. I think some of that voter dissatisfaction with the political establishment spilled over into my race and made it closer than it probably would have been without Perot on the ballot.

1994—The Last Campaign

Although I didn't realize it at the time, 1994 would be my last campaign for Congress. I began planning for reelection early, just as I always had, holding my first campaign planning meeting in mid-January. My record on issues important to Nevadans was strong, and I felt it offered voters a clear understanding of my accomplishments for the state.

I supported the presidential line-item veto, a $500 annual tax credit for each child, school choice, cost-of-living increases for Social Security recipients, a "three strikes, you're out" bill on sentencing repeat offenders, and a crime bill on violence against women. These bills, for the most part, were part of the Republican agenda supporting the family and seniors.

The crime bills were to improve the protection of society and women from violent offenders, and, of course, the line-item veto gave the president power over the bloated federal budget proposed by the liberals in Congress.

I had worked hard to save regularly scheduled air service for Ely and assisted in the implementation of the Truckee River Negotiated Water Settlement. I opposed an effort to institute a federal gaming tax and continued to support the 1872 Mining Law with responsible reform and the multiple-use philosophy for public lands, which included opposition to increases in the grazing fees.

Through my position on the House Appropriations Committee, I helped to obtain funding for a research center at the Nevada Test Site, a critical minerals program at the Mackay School of Mines, a park in North Las Vegas, the Reno Veterans Hospital, a post office in Mesquite, a Clark County bus maintenance and storage facility, the Hawthorne Army Depot, a Clark County flood control project, the Nellis Air Force Base, housing and improvements at the Fallon Naval Air Station, the Reno National Guard Armory, and the Las Vegas Armed Forces Recruitment Center. Overall, it was a record of which I was extremely proud.

Joe Emmet Fay, a small businessman from Carson City, was my primary election opponent, and I defeated him by almost a 4–1 margin. Democrats struggled to come up with a credible opponent to run against me. Their primary election favorite was Pat Clary, a Las Vegas attorney, but he finished last behind Janet Greeson and James Roberts, a retired University of Nevada political science professor. On election day, there was no clear choice among the Democrats, with barely 1,000 votes separating the three candidates. Greeson won by 366 votes.

One of the highlights of this campaign was that Charlton Heston appeared at a fund-raising dinner at Harrah's in Reno for me on September 25. He came because of my support for the National Rifle Association and the Second Amendment right to bear arms. He spoke on the subject of gun control and also on the importance of electing conservative Republicans.

Greeson, my Democrat opponent, tried to depict me as indecisive, even running a television spot showing a white chicken dashing back and forth across a road because it couldn't make up its mind where it wanted to be. This was probably a stock ad that the Democrat National Congressional Committee, the fund-raising arm of the Democrats in the House, was using around the county, and it showed that these types of ads work only if they're based on fact. If there was anything that voters knew about me, it was that I took strong and consistent stands on the issues important to Nevadans. I received the biggest vote total ever, with 64 percent of the vote, even running ahead of Senator Dick Bryan in every county except Clark.

It was a great Republican year across the state and country. The Republicans became the majority party in the House for the first time since the 1950s. John Ensign beat Democrat incumbent Jim Bilbray in the First Congressional District in Las Vegas. And, from a family standpoint, my daughter Patty Cafferata, the former state treasurer and Republican nominee for governor in 1986, was elected district attorney of Lander County. It was quite a victory, and my role in the House changed significantly.

CHAPTER ELEVEN

A Front-Row Seat at the Revolution

Some of my grandchildren share my love of politics and my political gene and had an opportunity to see Washington, D.C., firsthand. Not only did Elisa intern in Paul Laxalt's office, but later she worked for the Republican National Committee. Her brother, Reynolds Cafferata, interned in Chic Hecht's office in 1988, and Mike Dillon Jr. interned for the Republican Study Committee in May 1990. Reynolds later told me that given what he observed while he was in Washington, he was shocked when the Republicans took over the House, but I certainly was not.

While I was gearing up for the two-month general election campaign in Nevada in 1994, I also found myself heavily involved in national events. This was the year that we gained the majority in the House for the first time since the Eisenhower era in the 1950s. The shift in power was sparked by the leadership of Newt Gingrich, and Dick Armey and the Contract with America. They envisioned the contract as a tool for Republicans incumbents and challengers to focus their campaigns on issues important to all Americans. They came up with the idea at a House Republican Conference meeting in 1993 and formed a task force to draft the components of the plan. Congressman Henry Hyde and I cochaired a committee that drafted two of the ten bills that became part of the contract.

The first bill was House of Representatives (HR) 6, the American Dream Restoration Act, which eliminated the marriage income tax penalty, created a $500 per child tax credit, and established individual retirement plans called American Dream Savings Accounts. The second bill was HR 11, the Family Reinforcement Act, which created an income tax credit of up to $5,000 for adoption expenses, amended the federal sentencing guidelines with respect to sexual exploitation and abuse of children, and required states to enforce child support orders from other states. Both bills were passed by the House as part of the Contract with America but were not acted upon by the Senate.

Helping candidates get away from the old adage "All politics is local," the contract let candidates focus on positive national themes. As a unifying strategy, the contract was extremely successful in the 1994 campaign and in the next session of the House. The plan resonated with the public because it committed Republicans to vote on specific issues and bills. It goaded the House Republicans toward radical reform and forced the House members to take action on issues they would have preferred to debate endlessly rather than act upon. I'm not sure whether Gingrich anticipated that the contract would so effectively unify the electorate to vote Republican, but it certainly did.

The Contract with America was a blueprint for what we hoped to accomplish. Its beauty was in its simplicity: It offered voters a clear plan and a promise that it would be implemented right away when Congress opened in 1995. The contract also promised more than a detailed policy agenda. The preamble said it would "restore the bonds of trust between the people and their elected representatives . . . transform the way the House works . . . restore accountability to Congress . . . end a cycle of scandal and disgrace . . . [and] make us all proud again of the way free people govern themselves." The language may have been extravagant, but the contract was something that candidates and voters could understand. Almost every successful Republican candidate incorporated it into his or her campaign.

On September 27, 1994, I took time out from my own campaign and joined other incumbent Republican congressmen and virtually all of the Republican challengers for the House to announce the Contract with America in a major media event on the west steps of the U.S. Capitol. My role that day was as a "spear carrier," one of the dozens of members who stood on the steps behind Newt Gingrich and nodded in agreement while he unveiled the contract that committed Republicans to vote on specific issues and bills.

I was privileged to have had a front-row seat at that revolution and to have been an active participant in that watershed moment in American political history. When we elected seventy-three Republican freshmen and became the majority party in the House, it had been a long time coming. The contract we had all signed avoided argument over our agenda and pushed the Republicans toward radical reforms when they might have otherwise balked. Nine of the ten contract planks passed the House substantially intact. The one casualty was term limits, although it was supported by 83 percent of the House Republicans.

In many ways, the contract was the last step in a march to overthrow the four-decade domination of the Democrats as the majority party in the House. When I arrived in Congress in 1983, there was a conservative group of about fifteen Republicans called the ACORNS. I can't remember the complete name for this group, but it was the forerunner of the Conservative Opportunity Society (COS) that Newt was in the process of organizing. As the name implied, we were small but hoped to become mighty oaks in the congressional forest. The ACORNS consisted of the older, longtime Republican members, including William Dannemeyer, Dan Burton, Tom Bliley, Ed Derwinski, Bob Dornan, and Phil Crane. The ACORNS discussed conservative ideas and planned strategy for getting our legislation passed. Members helped each other on issues, discussed committee work, and encouraged each other to speak on different issues.

Shortly after I was first elected, I was invited to join the ACORNS. I was usually the only woman member present, although Bobbie Fiedler attended the meetings occasionally. I attended as regularly as I could, but after a while I stopped going. When Congressman Tom Bliley asked me why I wasn't attending anymore, I explained I was tired of listening to the sexist, anti-woman jokes that one particular member made at the opening of every meeting. Tom urged me to come back to the meetings and promised to talk to the member. He apparently did so, because off-color jokes were never told again at meetings I attended.

In 1983 I was also asked to join COS, which at that time had maybe ten to fifteen Republican members. It was not unusual to belong to both groups, but COS was made up of mostly younger, more activist Republicans and ultimately had more impact on the changes that would come. Although both groups were interested in pretty much the same issues, COS became much more aggressive in seeking change and promoting the conservative agenda. Some of the other initial COS members were Dan Coats, Dan Lungren, Dave Dreier, Duncan Hunter, Judd Gregg, Connie Mack, Vin Weber, Bob Smith, and Bob Walker. Tom DeLay joined us when he was elected in 1986.

Our goal was simple: to get a Republican majority in the House. A change was necessary for both institutional and political reasons. It became clear to me as soon as I arrived in Washington that the system was broken, captive to an iron-handed Democrat majority. Used to having their way, Democrats had become arrogant in their exercise of power, completely silencing Republican participation and suppressing the minority in the deliberative process. We felt that the people's confidence in the House of Representatives as an institution had deteriorated and could be restored only by a complete overhaul of the way the House was being run. Politically, we felt that the Republican values and programs we supported were closer to those held by a majority of Americans than were those promoted by the Democrats. Our challenge, initially, was to sharpen the distinctions between the agendas of the Democrats and the Republicans. In 1983 victory seemed far in the future. It would take twelve years of hard work to achieve, but it finally paid off.

In the early and mid-1980s the goals of COS were the same as those held by most traditional conservatives. We wanted to cut the size of government, reduce taxes and the deficit, and promote family values. We began meeting regularly to accomplish that, deciding which pieces of legislation we would support or oppose and who would take a leadership role in the debate.

The Democrat majority in the House would not, of course, give the Republicans a voice or allow our input on legislation. We devised a strategy to get our message out, taking advantage of what was then the latest in modern technology—C-Span. Since all of the proceedings on the House floor were carried live without commentary, we began to utilize the time to give one-minute speeches during what was known as "Special Orders" on the floor. One of the established rules of the House was that the C-Span cameras were to be focused on the speaker at all times during the

Special Orders speeches. There was seldom anyone in the chamber except the speaker and those talking. But there were hundreds of thousands of people watching at home. Speaker of the House Tip O'Neill got upset at Bob Walker during Special Orders one day and ordered the cameras to sweep the chamber to show the folks back home that no one else was in the chamber listening to the impassioned one-minute speech being given. It didn't matter.

We knew that although we could work as hard as we wanted for change inside the House, we were the minority party and it wouldn't happen without support from outside. Our objective was to reach out beyond the House to the general public all over the country who tuned in to C-Span.

It certainly wasn't network television, but at any given time there were maybe five hundred thousand people watching. Vin Weber tells the story of Newt Gingrich arguing to one reluctant Republican, "If you could be guaranteed that you could have an audience of half a million people in a stadium listen to you, you'd never turn down a speaking engagement." We couldn't see the people, but we knew they were in their homes or their offices watching. We found proof of that when we traveled because people told us they had heard our message. Even Republicans who perhaps weren't strong supporters of cos started paying attention because when they were in their home districts the people would come up to them and say how great it was. So, well before we gained a majority, we were getting the Republican message out to people.

Of course, most of the established Republican leadership was not too happy with the way cos was rocking the boat. Minority leader Bob Michel, whose retirement in 1994 paved the way for Newt to become Speaker, had spent his whole political life trying to get along with the Democrats, to get what he wanted by being accommodating, not confrontational. While Bob tried to be a calming influence, cos felt that the only way to win was to have a showdown.

It is interesting to look back on the seeds we were planting in cos and in acorns. I don't think any of us had any idea of the profound changes we would be part of; certainly I didn't see it coming when I was first elected. It wasn't until the Republicans elected the majority in the House that we were able to enact some of the conservative agenda, much of which was determined in the meetings of COS and ACORNS and was articulated so well by Newt Gingrich.

It reminded me of my introduction to politics. When the "Young Turks" in Washoe County took over the Republican Party, they believed, as we did, that the political system should be used to solve real problems, not just serve as a tool to maintain the status quo or protect individual power bases. Like those Young Turks, we believed that traditional conservative approaches of limited government and lower taxes would be the most effective public policies.

The shift of power from Democrat to Republican in the 1994 election was dramatically apparent in the 104th Congress, in 1995–96. It was a true revolution in every sense of the word and represented a bitter change for the Democrats, who were terribly unhappy and did not accept being in the minority well. Sometimes they were more than feisty; they were rude and belligerent toward Republicans. You can imagine what a shock it was to them after so many decades of control.

Admittedly, it was a heady time for the Republicans. We started getting organized in November 1994 for the coming session, even though the current Congress had not adjourned. One of my first tasks was to meet with Bob Livingston, who would become the new chair of the Appropriations Committee. He wanted to have the committee members get to know him better and he them. In the past when the power shifted between the political parties in the House, the ranking member of a committee in seniority became the chair of the committee. For Appropriations, that should have been my friend Joe McDade of Pennsylvania, but unfortunately he was at that time under an ethical cloud (later cleared) in his home state, so Newt passed over Joe and two others to indicate his choice of Livingston.

In December all the Republicans met again, including the new freshmen, even though they had not been sworn in. We held several all-day meetings to plan our strategy and to understand how to manage committees and subcommittees, a new experience for all of us. Various members conducted the training sessions, but Bob Walker and Newt Gingrich led most of the meetings. Walker was sort of the Republicans' man on the floor, our procedural expert. We even held mock floor sessions to train us on how to preside, something we had never done.

At our Republican Conference, we officially elected Newt as Speaker of the House. Dick Armey became majority leader and Tom DeLay became majority whip. I was privileged to nominate Don Young as the new chair of the Interior Committee. John Boehner was elected chair of the Republican Conference, Susan Molinari was elected vice chair, and I was elected secretary. This was a time of firsts for me. Susan and I were the first women ever elected to leadership in the House, and I was the first Nevada Republican to hold a leadership position.

I actually had started campaigning for secretary a couple of years before I knew that we would be in the majority. Discussions about leadership positions typically begin right after the last leadership election in December of election years. In this case in December 1992, minority leader Bob Michel announced his retirement, which meant everyone would be jockeying to move up the Republican leadership ladder. The key to winning these elections is starting your campaign early and getting as many commitments (votes) as possible before anyone else gets into the race. With Bob's retirement, there was going to be a vacancy for the secretary's position, and I wanted it so I could be in House leadership.

My staff was surprised when I told them—they'd had no idea I had my eye on a leadership position. Mike Pieper, my administrative assistant, said, "You want to do that?" Although they were all surprised, they quickly got excited and energized about the opportunity. Mike developed a campaign plan and Dennis Parobek, my legislative director and later my administrative assistant, and my staff and I worked the plan throughout the 103rd Congress.

I listed all the Republican members in a notebook, along with their telephone numbers, their committee assignments, their states, their seniority position, and any other important information I knew about them. When I talked informally to a member, I pointed out that I was a woman (not too hard to figure out, but I reminded them), mentioned my conservative credentials and my seniority. After each conversation, I wrote down what the member had said beside his or her name in my notebook. I kept track of votes as I collected them. Most members willingly supported me without any quid pro quo, but I sometimes made commitments to other members who were running for the other leadership positions. Early on I committed to vote for Cliff Sterns for vice chairman because he was a nice guy and we had worked together on several bills. The vice chair's race became difficult later on when my friend Susan Molinari got into the running. I wanted to support her and told her so, but I had committed to Cliff, and I voted for him.

I began a more concerted effort on my candidacy, but in a low-key manner, starting in June 1994. I wrote all the members several times, describing my philosophy and Republican credentials and asking for their support. It was like any other grassroots political campaign. I made personal contact with as many members as possible and met one-on-one with the members I thought were influential and those who were the "old stalwarts." Mike Pieper and I believed that the members with seniority would support my candidacy. I also looked for support from those who agreed with my conservative political philosophy and ideology. I reminded members who were pro-life that I agreed with them on that issue and that I needed their vote. I targeted my efforts to those I believed would be supportive and did not contact those I was sure would not vote for me. There was no point in stirring anyone up to work against me.

I didn't have any opposition until sophomore Tim Hutchinson got into the race in the fall of 1994. After the freshmen members were elected in November, I contacted them asking for their votes. I jotted down in my notebook whom they had beaten in their election. I had campaigned for several of the new westerners during the year, so I was hopeful they would vote for me. I was conservative, and so were they. Some of them had been active party people, so I mentioned my party activities before I was elected to Congress, including my service as president of the Nevada Federation of Republican Women and my campaign experiences for such officials as Senator Paul Laxalt. I also spoke to all of the different Republican groups, each class organization, the Republican Policy Committee, of which I was a past chair, and the National Republican Congressional Committee, on which I had served as one of the regional campaign chairs. One of the last letters I sent to the Republicans was an endorsement letter signed by several other members. I hoped that if they signed a letter endorsing me they would vote for me and their endorsement would persuade other members to vote for me too.

When he nominated me at the Republican Conference, Henry Hyde called me a "flamingo in the barnyard of politics." It was, of course, a compliment, and he gave his usual persuasive speech for my nomination. My election was not a foregone conclusion, however. On the morning of the vote the *Washington Times* predicted that Hutchinson would win.

Hutchinson relied on the large classes of freshmen and sophomores for his votes. These members were not only conservative on social and fiscal issues, they were more confrontational than even Newt Gingrich. Even though I was a conservative with a voting record to match my rhetoric, I was perceived by the newer members as part of the House institution that needed to be changed. Fortunately, I won.

As a result, Susan and I had a seat at the table in the Speaker's conference room when all the Republican decisions were discussed and made. As a member of the elected leadership, I sat in on the two-hour weekly strategy meetings of the Republican leadership on Tuesday mornings.

These discussions were led by Newt's old friend and confidant Congressman Bob Walker, with Newt participating as one of the members of the leadership, rather than as the chair of the meeting. This allowed Newt to advance his ideas without having to be neutral. Bob had been defeated for the whip position by Tom DeLay; there was some uneasiness, I'm sure, on the part of DeLay when Bob remained in the leadership circle. Seated at the table were our leaders Dick Armey, Tom DeLay, John Boehner, Bill Paxon, Susan Molinari, and chairs of the major committees: Gerald Solomon, Rules; Bill Archer, Ways and Means; Bob Livingston, Appropriations; John Kasich, Budget. In addition, Denny Hastert, the current Speaker of the House, in his role at the time of chief deputy whip; Mike Crapo, freshman class representative; David Hobson; and Jim Nussle attended most of our meetings.

The purpose of the meetings was to discuss the legislative and message strategy for the coming week. If legislation was anticipated to be introduced from a committee whose chairman was not part of the group, he or she was invited to make a presentation and take questions. It was in these meetings that the disagreements within the caucus would first be aired, and we attempted to solve the disputes before the regular Wednesday-morning conference meetings with all the Republican members.

With the new majority, other Republican women received leadership positions, including Jan Meyers as chair of the Small Business Committee and Nancy Johnson as chair of the Ethics Committee.

The Democrats could not believe that the power in the House had shifted away from them. After all, they had been in the majority for more than forty years and were "Kings of the Hill." They chaired all the committees and subcommittees. They had the best offices, and there were secret rooms and even buildings controlled by the Democrats that the Republicans did not know existed. With the shift in power, there was a lot more confrontation.

Having served in the majority, Democrats were masters of the procedural process, and they made the passage of legislation a tedious event. They did everything they could to undermine our legislative agenda through delaying tactics. On the floor, they would introduce amendment after amendment to stall the passage of every Republican legislative proposal. Voting on each amendment took time and slowed the process down considerably. Often if they did not get their way, they would call for adjournment.

There were also ugly fights over committee assignments, offices, and staff. Because the Republican majority was only 26 votes, Democrats for a time wanted their ranking members on the committee to be known as "cochairs." Republicans rejected that proposal outright. In committee rooms, we played musical chairs by moving to the center of the table, with more Republican and fewer Democrat members on each committee.

As previously mentioned, at the beginning of every new session of Congress, all members drew for new offices, except for the leadership, who usually retained the same offices. This year Newt Gingrich moved into former Republican minority leader Bob Michel's office, with its commanding view of the Mall. That suite of offices became the Speaker's office. Newt took over additional space that adjoined his suite because of his enlarged staff as Speaker. He also got a hideaway office close to the floor that made it convenient for him to have quick meetings during floor sessions.

The suite of former Democratic Speaker Tom Foley, next to Statuary Hall, became the office of the new minority leader, Dick Gephardt. I understand that in the past, when the majority changed in the House, the Speaker and the minority leader actually switched offices, but apparently they got tired of moving back and forth, so each party kept its leaders' offices.

Majority leader Dick Armey evicted the House Administration Committee from its prime third-floor location one floor above the Speaker's office to claim that space for his suite of offices. Majority whip Tom DeLay took over a large suite of offices on the first floor in the Capitol, facing the Supreme Court, where the Clerk of the House had been located. The clerk moved across the hall to offices previously occupied by the doorkeeper. The Office of the Doorkeeper, merely a ceremonial post, had long been a fixture in the House patronage system; the Republicans abolished it. Most of its staff positions were folded into the Clerk's and Sergeant at Arms' offices.

The new Clerk of the House was Robin Carle, who was not only the first woman appointed to this top administrative position in the House, but who also had deep Nevada ties. Robin had served as the executive director of the Nevada Republican Party in the early 1980s, when Frank Fahrenkopf was chairman of the state party.

One of our major battles with the Democrats was over staff. For years Republicans had complained about the size of members' staffs. Sometimes it seemed the Democrats had so many staffers you had to stumble over them to get into committee meeting rooms. The Democrats gave committee or subcommittee chairmen extra staff. A good example was John Dingell, chair of the Energy and Commerce Committee. He had about a hundred employees to staff his office, committee, and subcommittee. Some of his staffers were lent to other committees, such as Ways and Means, to work on special projects. From any federal agency advising his committees, he received additional staff, which meant that the executive branch of the federal government, not the House, paid their salaries. This extravagance was one of the first to be eliminated by the Republicans. We had agreed to reduce our own staffs, or at least not to increase them, when we became the majority party. My office staff was reduced by one person. Of course, some Republicans were disappointed that they could not have extra employees now that we were in control, but it was the right thing to do.

Contrasted with being in the minority, being in the majority in the House was much more rewarding, but still challenging. I became the chair of the twelve-member Appropriations Subcommittee on Military Construction, which gave me a stronger voice for Nevada military installations, such as Nellis Air Force Base and the Fallon Naval Air Station. Without seven terms of seniority, that would not have been possible. I was now responsible for getting legislation passed and for providing leadership for our conference. Because of my position as subcommittee chair, at first I received two staff positions funded by the Appropriations Committee. Later, the Republicans reduced these staff positions to one and eventually eliminated the position.

On the Military Construction (MIL CON) subcommittee, I had been the ranking minority member when I became the chair. I replaced Democrat Bill Hefner, who now became the ranking minority member. He was a pleasant guy and we got along, so the transition wasn't subject to as much discord as some of the other transitions were. He was a fair chairman, but he could be partisan on the floor. On the downside, he was never on time for the committee meetings as the chair, and that didn't improve when he was in the minority.

In my subcommittee we kept our Republican staff, while the Democrat staff remained, but they were not in charge. On the other hand, Bob Livingston, the new chair of Appropriations, kept the top Democratic staff of the committee on the payroll to assist in drafting the upcoming appropriations bills. While he brought in Republican Jim Dyer as his top aide on the committee, the fact that he retained several Democrat staffers caused some concern among the more conservative Republican members. They thought the Democratic staffers would inject liberal spending priorities into the appropriations bills. Dyer remains the chief clerk of the committee, even though Livingston has retired. While Dyer is a Republican, he remains a favorite whipping boy of the conservatives led by columnist Bob Novak for his alleged free spending and pork barrel projects that are inserted in appropriations bills.

Many of the committees, such as Agriculture and Veterans, worked well together after the initial shock of the shift in power, largely because the issues were not overtly partisan. The biggest clashes occurred in the Ways and Means, Appropriations, Budget, and Judiciary committees because the two parties had totally opposing views on how to approach or solve the issues or set the public policies that these committees addressed. Even worse was the House Administration Committee, which practically had brawls over the location and size of offices, parking spaces, and staff size. This seemed almost criminal to me and was a clear example of what was wrong with Congress. After all, I thought it was my job to represent my state, not to be concerned about having a fancy office.

In the spirit of reform and in order to eliminate the private fiefdoms that the Democrat committee chairmen had created in the past, Newt Gingrich required that all committee chairmen present their new proposals to the Republican Conference before introducing a bill. Since the Democrats had not operated that way, several chairmen balked at the idea, but everyone fell in line eventually.

I also served on the Republican Policy Committee, chaired by Chris Cox. The committee included not only me but also Susan Molinari, Helen Chenoweth, and Sue Myrick, so women had significant input into the party policies, strategy, and solutions to issues. The big states like New York, Illinois, Florida, Texas, and California had the most members, but we tried to balance the committee geographically.

Newt Gingrich also asked me to chair a special committee called the Corrections Day Committee. The idea was to create a mechanism to correct laws and regulations that defy logic. Newt got the idea from the mayor of San Diego. The city needed to extend its wastewater discharge pipeline farther into the Pacific Ocean to reduce the amount of pollution at the shoreline, but the Environmental Protection Agency wouldn't permit it. Fixing this problem was the first bill the committee passed.

The committee members were appointed by their own parties, with one or two more Republicans than Democrats. The purpose of the committee was to look at past legislation to see if it was still relevant or perhaps should be corrected by further legislation or repealed. I received an extra staff person to review the *Federal Register* to look for laws or regulations that were onerous and should be repealed.

Newt asked me to figure out a method for Congress to pass these obvious corrections in an expedited manner. Traditionally, the House Rules Committee controls when, how, and if a bill will be introduced. Gerry Solomon, chair of that committee, was on my committee to ensure that he did not lose control of the process for bringing legislation to the floor. My committee was a threat to Gerry's power.

Because the Corrections Day Committee had no legislative standing and could not mark up or file committee reports, we had to rely on the standing committee of jurisdiction to file reports before we could recommend that a bill come to the floor. This caused some friction between us and the other committee chairmen, who were not excited about moving bills that might take away some of their floor time. Only with Newt's help were we successful in persuading all the chairmen that we needed to move our priorities so that we would have bills available every other week for the Corrections Day Calendar.

I held the first committee meeting on May 15, and we met about once a week for the rest of the year. I presented bills first to the Republican Conference for support. If there was agreement, then I set them for a hearing in my committee. I tried to have a Republican and a Democrat testify in support of each bill. Conservatives Democrat Collin Peterson and Republican Joe Knollenberg stand out in my memory as particularly helpful in supporting the committee's mission. I invited members to submit foolish regulations and laws that they wanted to change.

The committee was able to eliminate quite a few outdated laws, although we occasionally ran into resistance from the members who had originally gotten the laws passed. The most notorious was Democrat Henry Waxman, who had authored many of the laws we were trying to repeal. A member of the committee, he assigned one of his staff members to review all our proposals to make sure his legislation was not repealed. Anytime a bill of his came up, he showed up with an entourage to testify against our proposal.

In retrospect, we didn't move our bills much faster than was done by following the normal procedure. The regular committee chairmen insisted on marking up all of our bills. My corrections day process is still included in the House Rules, but it is used infrequently.

The Appropriations Committee and my chairmanship of the MIL CON subcommittee was another story. The thirteen chairs of the Appropriations subcommittees were among some of the most powerful members of the House because they had nearly total control over the contents of the budget for the various federal agencies for which they are responsible. The "Cardinals," as we were called, determined the total level of funding for each of the bills among ourselves, and then we determined how much money would be available for each function within our individual allocations.

In recent years, the Cardinals' power had been reduced considerably by two laws. The Congressional Budget Act of 1974 created the House Budget Committee and established the current budget process, and the Balanced Budget Act of 1985, also known as the Gramm-Rudman-Hollings Act, limited overall spending and required that reductions be made before spending could be increased. Nonetheless, the Cardinals remain a powerful force in the House with their ability to reward and punish other members by approving or not approving earmarked projects for their districts.

In the spring of each year, a letter-writing campaign was waged by nearly every member of the House as they sent thousands of letters to the Cardinals, asking for funds to be appropriated for projects. An elaborate tracking system was established in each subcommittee office to catalog and record every funding request that was received. The actual drafting of an appropriations bill was relatively easy, since Congress had been writing these same bills every year for well over two hundred years. With rare exceptions, and now with the aid of computers, last year's bill would simply be cut and pasted into this year's bill with the numbers changed to reflect the increases and reductions in funding for the various programs. The difficult part involved total spending levels and the earmarks (some refer to them as pork barrels). The process also got bogged down by the increasingly frequent attempts to legislate change in the appropriations bills, which is against the rules of the House.

As chair of the MIL CON subcommittee, I was, of course, one of the thirteen Cardinals. MIL CON was one of the smaller appropriations bills and dealt exclusively with defense construction projects and base closures.

For the most part, the allocation of earmarks was decided through an agreement between the subcommittee chair and the ranking member of the other party. Since I had an easy relationship with Bill Hefner, the ranking Democrat member, we agreed on how much would be available for the members of our committee in special projects, and that amount was signed off on by the chair of the full committee. From that point, we determined which projects among the many requests we received would get additional funding above the agreed amounts.

One particularly memorable request involved construction of a national army museum in Arlington, Virginia. The museum was requested by the army in its annual budget. There was considerable controversy over the expenditure of $14 million to purchase the land near the Pentagon where the museum was to be built. Speaker Gingrich asked that the museum funding be included in our bill. Since he was the son of an army officer, he had a particular interest in seeing the project move forward. It is difficult, if not impossible, to oppose your own Speaker, so we included the funding in our bill and reported it to the floor.

Traditionally, the MIL CON bill is one of the first appropriations bills to come to the floor each year because it is usually noncontroversial and relatively small. That year, my bill was actually the first on the floor under the Republican majority, and I expected it to pass easily; however, that didn't happen. Usually a lot of deference is given to the Appropriations subcommittee chairmen when they bring their bills to the floor, especially by their own party. After all, the Cardinals are not going to look kindly on members who challenge their bills.

It was my maiden voyage guiding my own appropriations bill on the floor. My bill introduction was a historic moment in the House, but I didn't know it until Democratic congresswoman Marcy Kaptur spoke. I was surprised, although Marcy and I were classmates and had a cordial relationship, because Democrats usually don't applaud Republicans and vice versa. Her words were memorialized in the *Congressional Record* on June 16, 1995. She said:

> Mr. Chairman, I would like to congratulate the gentlewoman and
> inform the membership that not only is this bill historic, but, in fact,
> the moment we are about to experience here with the gentlewoman from
> Nevada [Mrs. Vucanovich], the chair of the Subcommittee on Military
> Construction handling this bill, is a truly historic moment for women
> and for men in our country, because, in fact, as she moves this bill today,
> this will only be the second time in the 200 year history of our country
> that a woman has chaired any of the subcommittees of the Committee
> on Appropriations, which is an exclusive committee.
>
> The last such woman to handle such a bill was Julia Butler Hansen
> of Washington State who, at age sixty-seven, retired from this institution
> and chaired the Subcommittee on Interior and Related Agencies at the
> end of her career.

I just want to congratulate the gentlewoman. The road here is still a difficult one for women and to rise and chair one of the most exclusive subcommittees is truly an honor. We are proud of you. Good luck with the bill and congratulations to the people of Nevada for sending you here.

Even having heard that, no one deferred to me, including the members of my own party. Republican Wally Herger proposed an amendment to delete the army museum from the bill. He claimed that the expenditure of funds was wasteful and unnecessary. I have to admit I didn't disagree, but as chair of the committee I was bound to defend the bill, warts and all. A hard-core group of liberal Democrats was determined to hand a defeat to the new Republican majority. They could be counted on to join any effort to embarrass the leadership and with Republican support from budget hawks, such as Jim Nussle and freshmen Mark Neumann, the amendment passed by a wide margin. The army museum was scrapped.

In addition to the amendment to delete the funding for the museum, Neumann proposed eliminating funding for upgrading officers' housing at several bases around the country, including the dilapidated officers' quarters at Nellis Air Force Base. He argued that the cost exceeded $200,000 per unit and was excessive. As a successful building contractor in his home state of Wisconsin, he thought this funding should be eliminated. Fortunately, he had not done his homework, his facts were just flat wrong, and his amendment was easily defeated.

This incident, however, showed that it was a new day in the House. Under Democrat control, a freshman, especially a member of the Appropriations Committee, would never have attempted to amend an appropriations bill. While my bill happened to be the first appropriations bill introduced, it was not long before the same tactics were used against other Republican bills. Needless to say, I was relieved when the MIL CON bill passed.

One of the biggest struggles for the more senior members of Congress like me was riding herd on the large number of Republican freshmen swept into office by their commitment to the Contract with America and their own campaign promises to shake things up. Because of their numbers, they were able to drive many of the decisions we made, including the refusal to negotiate over the budget that led to the 1995 shutdown of government.

There were many late-night caucus meetings during that time, in which Newt tried to sell the newer members on the idea of making a deal, only to be told by them that they wouldn't support him.

The attempts of the freshmen to amend bills on the floor, as I previously mentioned, were an example of the precarious situation the Republicans were in during those early days and the fragile nature of Newt Gingrich's leadership. While he had a reputation in the press and outside of Congress as an inflexible ideologue, he was in reality easily pushed to compromise and unable to tell people no. Neumann and many of his freshmen colleagues learned that they could push Gingrich to get what they wanted, even when it was not in the best interests of the Republican Party, the House, or the nation. This same trait became evident when Gingrich later negotiated with President Clinton. Newt was more inclined to take a deal than he was to stand and fight.

Having said that, I should also note that though Newt's style turned a lot of people off and he made some missteps in handling power, I gave a lot of the credit for the Republican successes to his leadership. It is difficult to describe Newt in only a few sentences. His beliefs had been honed thoughtfully and actively over a long career as a scholar, a professor, and a politician. He advocated a coherent and consistent set of ideas and held to certain Republican policies whether people agreed with him or not. When we were in the minority, one of his constant stands was that Republicans should fight Democrats' bills and not compromise with them in exchange for a few crumbs. He strongly believed that the Republicans should challenge Democrat ideas, no matter what. Naturally, the Democrat leadership felt under attack from him and were not happy when he achieved his goal of becoming Speaker.

Certainly the conservative philosophical seeds were planted during the administrations of Presidents Ronald Reagan and George H. W. Bush, but it took the careful cultivation of Newt to bring in a new crop of conservative members to the House of Representatives. He recruited Republican candidates by committing them to sign on to the conservative platform. By fashioning an agenda—the Contract with America—he enabled Republican incumbents and challengers to articulate positions that the voters could support, in house district after house district, all across America.

It soon became obvious that the freshmen were more loyal to their class and each other than they were to the Republicans or the House. The freshman class was a tight-knit group of nonpoliticians, young businesspeople, and independent self-made men and women. Many were a little arrogant, but they were articulate and outspoken on issues they believed were important. Many of them were born-again Christians and devout believers. Just before a "critical" vote, they would adjourn to a room on the fourth floor and pray about the vote. There had been nothing like that when I arrived in Congress; even the prayer breakfasts I attended did not deal with specific issues. The freshmen brought a different focus and approach to legislation, usually good but sometimes not particularly effective.

The demands of our freshmen for reform led, with Newt's support, to six-year term limits on committee chairs and leadership positions. Most of the senior members were opposed to this but did not have the votes to block it. As mentioned earlier, the Class of 1994 also pushed the Republicans to abolish several caucuses funded by Congress. They didn't believe that funding certain caucuses was an appropriate use of tax dollars. Consequently, we abolished the Black Caucus, the Women's Caucus, the Republican Study Committee, and some other conservative caucuses. Additionally, certain subcommittees were either combined with others or totally eliminated; the numbers of joint committees were also reduced; members were limited to serving on only five subcommittees; a seven-year plan to reduce the budget deficit was established; and proxy voting in committee was abolished. The freshmen created their own mini revolution within the Republican ranks in the House.

One of the things the freshmen had campaigned on was term limits, so many came to Washington intending to serve only three terms and leave. They wanted to change Congress, so they were willing to upset the House and bring it to a halt if that was necessary to accomplish their agenda. They had not learned to seek consensus and had no desire to do so; they came simply to change the system and often voted their conscience at every opportunity and against the leadership. As a group, they were difficult to deal with and impossible to convince to change their positions because they couldn't be swayed to do things for the good of the country. Because of their pledge on term limits, many retired during the 2000 election cycle, but I believe a number were reluctant to do so after seeing how the system worked and realizing the importance of seniority.

It was remarkable that we not only passed the Contract with America, except for term limits, but we did it within one hundred days of the opening of the session. The 104th Congress began on January 4, 1995, and we actually had votes later that day, which was unusual. Republicans had promises to keep and were eager to get under way. On the opening day, during a fourteen-hour session, the House adopted eight major rules changes and passed the Congressional Accountability Act to transform the way the House operated. We also adopted some two dozen changes in House rules. It was interesting to me, as someone who had been a witness to the unfairness of Democrat rules for twelve years, that almost all of the recorded votes drew substantial Democrat support for these changes. Even they could see the handwriting on the wall and knew the system needed to be changed.

We worked nearly nonstop from early January through April, often late into the night. As conference secretary I was expected to attend all meetings of the conference and record the minutes. Usually Mike Pieper or Kathy Besser, my legislative assistant, attended the meetings with me to take notes. After they were typed up, I reviewed and corrected them, if needed.

This year, John Boehner chaired the regular conference meetings on Wednesday mornings. Newt acted as the chief strategist and visionary for the Republicans. All the Republicans were present, and we freely discussed our views on the bills that were coming to the floor. Since we were now in control, legislative discussions became more lengthy, so we held additional meetings.

February marked two important "firsts" in my congressional career. On the first day of February I chaired my first MIL CON subcommittee hearing. It was an exhilarating feeling to be the chair and not to have to wait to be recognized by my former chair. Then, on February 7, I presided over the House for the first time. While not necessarily exhilarating, it was an honor, and it underscored the fact that we were finally the majority party in Congress. It was remarkable to think how far we had come.

When I arrived in 1983, the Ninety-eighth Congress had 269 Democrats and 166 Republicans. The 104th Congress in 1995 had 230 Republicans, 204 Democrats, and 1 Independent. It was the first Republican majority since the Eighty-third Congress, in 1953. This victory of party principle and philosophy resulted from the hard work and vision of many people. House Republicans were convinced that we best reflected the views of a majority of Americans and that we could change the way the Congress conducted business. I believe we were right on both counts.

The revolution occurred not only because of the Contract with America, but also because of certain policies pursued by President Clinton that were unpopular with the people. One of the issues was NAFTA (the North American Free Trade Agreement), supported by the Clinton White House. During the 1992 campaign, presidential candidate Ross Perot claimed that passage of this bill would cost Americans jobs. He famously said that if NAFTA was passed we would hear "that giant sucking sound" when jobs left this country for Mexico. Clinton was successful in obtaining passage of this legislation, but the average citizen, especially in Nevada, was opposed to NAFTA, and I voted against it. The other issue was even bigger and more unpopular; it was Bill and Hillary Clinton's health care plan, which was extremely controversial and ultimately did not pass.

Additionally, welfare programs were viewed skeptically by many. The feeling was that numerous recipients were abusing the system at the expense of hardworking people. Only the people who really needed help should receive welfare. People also wanted to reduce the size of government programs and even abolish entire agencies. It all added up to the fact that the people were ready to vote for a change in the way the federal government was conducting business and in the public policies offered by the Democrats.

Certainly, the Contract with America agenda continues to resonate today, attracting candidates and voters to the Republican Party and to conservative issues throughout the American heartland. Similarly, the Gingrich legacy of reform in the way the House did business continues to have a lasting influence on the institution.

I am proud to have been part of it.

PART III

Not Your
Average Congressman

CHAPTER TWELVE

A Tough Irishman

Hospitals are not places where anyone wants to spend a lot of time. In 1982 I did my share of visiting my twin granddaughters, Casey Evonne and Heather Brown Dillon, Kenny's girls, at St. Mary's Hospital. They were born prematurely in August 1982, my first election-year grandchildren. Casey was almost average size, but Heather was tiny, earning the nickname "Heather the Feather" from the nurses. At one and a half pounds, Heather was in the hospital for several months. I was a patient myself in 1983, shortly after I was elected to the House. In some ways I was more fortunate than they were because I spent only a few days in the hospital. On the other hand, my diagnosis was different. I had breast cancer. Heather would outgrow her medical problems, while I faced an uncertain future.

During my campaign in 1982 I was too busy for my usual annual physical checkup. After being sworn in early in 1983, I canceled two doctor's appointments for a checkup because my schedule was constantly full from early in the morning until late at night. A checkup wasn't a priority for me. I felt fine. I was active and in good physical shape for a woman sixty-one years of age. So I put off seeing the doctor.

Thankfully, Jackie Troy, my newly hired office manager, insisted that I make time for my appointment. So on Monday, March 14, I went to see a navy ob-gyn doctor who came to the House clinic twice a year and offered physical examinations for congresswomen and women senators. It was convenient, so I took advantage of it.

During the examination, the doctor asked me if I knew that I had a lump in my breast. I had not noticed it. The doctor did not seem particularly worried but suggested that I arrange an appointment at Bethesda Naval Hospital within the next ten days for a needle biopsy and a more complete examination. I made the appointment, of course, but in the meantime I saw no reason not to keep my regular schedule. At the end of the week, I flew back to Nevada, then returned to Washington on Sunday. On Tuesday I introduced Frank Fahrenkopf, a Nevadan and chairman of the Republican National Committee, to a group at the Capitol Hill Club. The next evening George and I attended a National Rifle Association reception.

I checked into Bethesda on Thursday, March 24, for tests and a biopsy. When the results came back and I was diagnosed with breast cancer, I was shocked. No one in my family had a history of breast cancer, and cancer of any kind in my family was rare. I was also scared. In my more fearful moments, I was sure I would never see the end of my second term in Congress. Worse, I would not see my grandchildren grow up. George and I, both of us pretty well shaken up, drove to Williamsburg for a couple of days to ourselves. We shed lots of tears over many of our fears, but in the end I was very lucky. When we returned, we met with the doctors to discuss a course of treatment. In 1983 my options were limited. No one discussed lumpectomies or other treatments. I had two alternatives, a modified radical mastectomy or radiation. George and I talked it over and I felt the mastectomy was the best choice for me. Surgery meant a shorter recovery time, and I could go back to my job of serving in Congress that much more quickly.

Surgery was set for Wednesday, March 30, during the congressional Easter recess. We called each of the children, starting with Patty and her husband, Treat, a surgeon. When I asked for his advice, he was cautiously optimistic. Because there are no secrets in the lives of public officials, we also made a public announcement of the diagnosis and the plans for surgery to the Nevada press. People were overwhelmingly supportive.

On March 28 I checked into Bethesda. I was in the operating room for three and a half hours, during which they removed the malignant lump, my right breast, and some muscle tissue. The operation was performed by Captain Robert Cochran, chair of the Naval Hospital's Department of

Surgery, with Dr. William Hamilton, chief of resident surgery, assisting him. There were no complications and no sign that the cancer had spread to my lymph nodes. The malignancy was limited to the one breast lump.

Looking back, I realize that with early detection my prospects for recovery were excellent, and I am thankful that I went for that routine physical examination. My breast cancer was deceptive because I felt well at the time and never felt ill. My experience made me a strong advocate for annual physical exams for early detection because that was what saved me. Without an early examination the cancer could easily have gone unchecked and become incurable. After surgery I had no reason to fear more problems. My breast cancer was a curable disease.

My daughter Susie had flown to Washington as soon as the initial diagnosis was made and stayed with me for two weeks after I left the hospital. George took me home from the hospital on Monday, and on Tuesday I was back at work, six days after my surgery.

That first day I went to the floor of the House to tell my colleagues that I had breast cancer. In my speech I said, "I'm not sick. I'm recovering from surgery." I thanked the doctors for their care, and I praised the Reach for Recovery organization, an American Cancer Society–sponsored group of recovered mastectomy patients who support women with breast cancer and who had visited me in the hospital.

In reviewing my calendar for that day now, I can't believe I put in a full day at the office and that night we attended the Cherry Blossom Festival on the Hill. I continued all my activities. My colleagues in Congress didn't treat me any differently after my surgery, nor did I use it as a crutch.

It is remarkable to think how dramatically times and attitudes had changed from when I grew up to when I discovered my cancer. Years ago people would speak in hushed whispers about someone having the "Big C." People thought it was the end of life if someone had cancer. Today, thanks to early detection and treatment, a diagnosis of cancer isn't always a death sentence. At the time of my surgery in 1983 I was the only member of Congress who had had breast cancer. I had always been a supporter of annual physical examinations and cancer prevention and treatment programs, although, remarkably, at the age of sixty-one I had never had a mammogram. Now, with my personal experience driving me, I became an advocate for early prevention and cure. I became more aware of all cancer-related issues, and my legislative agenda was also affected. For the rest of my years in Congress, my staff reviewed all bills knowing that I was interested in legislation on cancer, so I was always prepared on the subject. I got to know the American Cancer Society's lobbyists, and they kept in touch with my staff. If there was a bill that appropriated money for cancer education, research, and treatment, the lobbyists let us know, and I usually supported it.

I never missed an opportunity to speak on the floor if the topic was cancer. My speeches were reasoned, not emotional; factual but certainly not scientific. I wasn't strident. I don't think that my colleagues ever thought, "There she goes again." I wasn't labeled "Mrs. Anti-Cancer"—I had other issues I was interested in promoting too. But because I could talk from experience, on a personal level, I believe my words carried weight.

I actively worked to obtain federal funding for cancer research and to pass bills on early detection. Since then several other women members have been diagnosed with breast cancer. In 1983, most of the women members of Congress were supportive of issues that dealt with breast cancer, but it was rare for a male member to be interested. One exception was Republican John Myers, whose wife had been diagnosed with breast cancer. To his mind his wife's medical care for breast cancer left a lot to be desired, and he cosponsored legislation, gave speeches, spoke out in support of federal funding, and hosted American Cancer Society forums with me.

Early on, I encouraged other women to become advocates for breast cancer research and funding. With fellow Republican representative Lynn Martin, I met with Dr. Antonia Novello, the surgeon general under President George Bush and the first woman to hold the position. Less than five feet tall, dressed in her uniform, Novello looked like a doll sitting in her big desk chair. We asked her for support of breast cancer research and treatment. We reminded her how difficult it was for male congressmen to get involved in the issue. We pointed out that women leaders had to be active in raising awareness. While her top concern during her tenure as surgeon general was children (she was a pediatrician by training) and young adults, she did agree to make breast cancer a priority.

Legislatively, one of the most important things I did was to introduce a bill to extend Medicare coverage to annual mammograms for women. Truthfully, I had not been aware that Medicare didn't provide such coverage until many of the cancer support groups urged that the law be changed. Breast cancer is a bipartisan issue, but passing legislation is a long, involved process, and I knew it would take support from members on specific committees and subcommittees. With that in mind, I enlisted Democrat Mary Rose Oakar to cosponsor my bill. Mary Rose's sister had died of breast cancer, so she knew of the need for early screening and detection, and she served on the Select Committee on Aging and on its Health and Long Term Care subcommittee.

Another member who was helpful to the cause was Republican Olympia Snowe. She also was a member of the Select Committee on Aging and on its Human Services subcommittee, which dealt with issues such as education and health. Both women pushed the legislation through their committees. Then we battled it out again on the floor, working together for passage. Even with considerable bipartisan support, it took us two sessions of Congress to win passage, a testament to how slowly the process works.

Because of that long struggle, I was even more dismayed when President Bill Clinton's health care reform program in 1993 replaced the annual mammogram coverage requirement we had fought so hard to secure with coverage only every two years for women over the age of sixty-five. I reintroduced legislation for annual exams in 1994, but was unsuccessful in getting the bill passed before I left Congress in 1996. Fortunately, Representative John Ensign of Nevada's First Congressional District was able to get annual mammogram coverage reinstated in 1997.

Health funding was always a fight, even in 1994 when I was on the Appropriations Committee. I did not serve on the Labor, Health, Human Services, and Education subcommittee, which determined who was going to receive federal health care funds and how much. Some of the Republicans, such as John Porter and Bill Young, whose daughter had cancer, cosponsored legislation that was helpful. But Democrat David Obey, the ranking member on the other side, obstructed my quest for more money for breast cancer programs.

Vice President Dan Quayle's wife, Marilyn, whose mother had died of breast cancer, joined me to testify at hearings before several committees. Both Dan and Marilyn Quayle helped in the fight against cancer. They held a reception at the vice president's residence for the participants in the

I am testifying in the 1980s on a breast cancer or mammography bill, and Vice President Dan Quayle's wife, Marilyn Quayle, is on the left. Both Dan and Marilyn were activists for breast cancer legislation. Marilyn's mother had died from breast cancer. Collection of Barbara F. Vucanovich.

first Race for the Cure, which was held in Washington on June 16, 1990. Both of them ran in the race, along with some eight thousand people who helped raise $500,000 for breast cancer programs.

Nancy Brinker from Dallas, Texas, had started Race for the Cure, which has since spread across the country, to raise awareness of breast cancer. Her sister, Susan Goodman Komen, had died of breast cancer at age thirty-six. Nancy, who discovered her own breast cancer four years later, had promised her sister that she would dedicate her life to being an advocate for breast cancer education, research, screening, and treatment. After her sister's death, Nancy established the Susan G. Komen Breast Cancer Foundation in 1982.

Because research has shown that the mortality rate of breast cancer will decrease by 30 percent if every woman in need of a mammogram receives one, the foundation began an educational campaign that led to the enactment of the Mammography Quality Standards Act of 1992. The foundation has a national network of volunteers supporting the Race for the Cure and fighting for legislation requiring insurance companies to cover mammograms and pap smears as medically recommended for women over the age of thirty-five, as well as for other programs on breast cancer.

I first met Nancy in 1988 when she visited me to get my support for the race. I agreed to contact other women members of Congress to ask them to participate in the event. Almost all agreed to help; some even participated in the race. My staff contacted the staffs of all the federal departments and asked them to participate. I personally called anyone who agreed to join the race and asked them to run with me. After the first race, I ran again in 1991 and 1992 and in a few local races in Nevada. I understand that the Race for the Cure is now one of the largest 5K runs in the world.

Race for the Cure acquired one of its first major sponsors when the Ladies Professional Golf Association added the Susan G. Komen Foundation to its list of charities. LPGA golf balls carry the looped pink ribbon symbol that represents breast cancer. Currently, there are many national sponsors, including some of the men's golf groups and Chevron. Reno also has several sponsors of Race for the Cure, including Nevada Bell, Sandy Pearce Raffealli of Bill Pearce Motors, and Steve Johnson, general manager of Chevron at Winner's Corners. Ward Hinckley, the owner of Winner's Corners, is also supportive because his first wife, Dorothy, died of breast cancer.

When I was first asked to give speeches on cancer and on the importance of early detection and treatment, I could barely get through my speech without crying and bringing tears to the eyes of those in the audience. But I always told my audiences I could handle what came my way because I was a "tough Irishman."

One of the first times I spoke about my surgery in Las Vegas, I described my meeting with a volunteer from the American Cancer Society's Reach for Recovery program. She was an attractive woman who visited me in the Bethesda hospital a couple of days after my surgery. Wearing a form-fitting knit dress, she announced that she had had breast cancer and the same surgery that I had. I told her I didn't believe her. She said, "Put your hands on my breasts and tell me which one has been removed." I did as she asked and was surprised that I couldn't feel the difference.

So here was Barbara Vucanovich, a conservative Republican, standing up in front of a room full of men and women, describing putting my hands on a woman's breasts. I have to tell you, I can hardly believe that I would even mention my breasts before an audience like that. After I described this event in a speech, Claire Haycock, a relative of Harry Reid, I think, stood up in the back of the room and shouted, "I'll be happy to do that for you anytime, Barbara." The audience and I erupted into laughter. It is a story I've told many times over when I talk about the Reach for Recovery volunteers. Laughter is part of the healing.

Gradually, as time went by, and I spoke about my disease and my surgery, I became more comfortable with my situation. I had accepted early the fact that the diagnosis wasn't a death sentence for me, and it was wonderful to be able to share my experience with others. Generally, I have curtailed my public speaking since I retired from Congress in 1996, but I still accept the invitations to speak about cancer.

Still, having a mastectomy is not like having other types of surgery, such as the removal of an appendix or a gallbladder. Because so many women feel that the loss of a breast is an attack on their femininity and sexuality, a mastectomy is almost always traumatic.

Both men and women have a difficult time facing the aftermath of surgery because it can change one's self-perception. Even more difficult can be how the husband's (or wife's) views change. I know of women who lost their husbands or significant others after a mastectomy. That can be worse than the uncertainty of not knowing whether one will live long enough to see children or grandchildren grow up. Many younger women are especially traumatized by the surgery. I can understand why some women choose to have reconstructive surgery.

Unbelievably, and unfortunately, there are still women who won't seek a doctor's advice because they and their husbands don't believe women should expose their breasts to a male physician. These men and women are embarrassed to even discuss that part of the body. This attitude prevents women from seeking the necessary physical examinations needed for early detection and the best prognosis.

While my husband, George, was frightened for me and concerned about our family, he was supportive in every way. If I wanted to rest, he arranged it. If I wanted to go out, he agreed willingly. All in all, he was a great help and a rock of strength. George never seemed to feel that I was disfigured in any way. He willingly talked with other husbands about cancer and just seemed to instinctively know the right way to handle the situation. As always, he was my biggest supporter.

In the more than twenty years since my diagnosis, I have talked personally with thousands of women across the country and in Nevada, from all walks of life, who are breast cancer survivors. Among the hundreds of women to whom I have sent notes upon learning of their diagnosis was Supreme Court justice Sandra Day O'Connor. State senator Bernice Martin-Mathews and I were co-honorees at an event for breast cancer survivors in October 2000. Bernice is generous with her time and also talks frequently about her breast cancer, and she walks in the races. More commonly my contacts have been with women who are out of the public eye. Breast cancer doesn't recognize income level or position in life. It is a great equalizer and something all too many women share. Every woman who finds out she has breast cancer has the same questions and needs the same support. That's why I can't stress enough how important it to talk with someone who has been there. When Mary Gojack, my opponent in the 1982 campaign, was diagnosed with breast cancer, she and I communicated by telephone a great deal. Facing the same problems, we became friendly, as women do who share this disease. We had warm conversations on the phone and sent notes to each other. She ultimately passed away at age forty-nine in November 1985.

The biggest lesson I learned about breast cancer, which I try to pass on to everyone, is that early detection saves lives. A positive attitude is a plus, too, of course. And it helps immeasurably to have a supportive husband and family.

Of course, breast cancer changed my life. But the time of diagnosis, treatment, and recovery was short. Once I was past the initial uncertainties, the impact of having breast cancer has been almost entirely positive. It had a major influence on my legislative agenda in Washington. And it brought me into contact with so many people of courage and faith who are doing so much to help others deal with this disease.

And, of course, after surviving breast cancer, I found that the little irritants in life become less important. Each day is a blessing.

CHAPTER THIRTEEN

A Woman's Place in the House

When I think of my granddaughters—Elisa, Farrell, Nora, Jennifer, Maggie, Casey and Heather, and Janaya—and my great-granddaughters—Morgan, Kelley, Philomena, Madelein, Elizabeth, and Amelia—I think of the issues that will influence their futures. I believe that all legislative matters affect women, not just "women's issues" such as the Equal Rights Amendment (ERA) or abortion. Some of these "women's issues" were settled while I was in Congress, while others continue to be the subject of ongoing battles.

There were only about two dozen women in the House of Representatives when I was first elected in 1982. Over the years a great deal of attention was paid to my gender, partly because I didn't fit the stereotype of what some expected from women legislators. As far as critics were concerned, I was on the "wrong" side of any number of issues. Those with a more liberal perspective would have been happier if I had supported what they defined as "women's" issues—since I was a woman, after all. I refused to be put in that kind of a box because many issues deserve a much broader perspective.

Personally, I considered myself a feminist, if that meant believing in equal treatment under the law and equal pay for equal work, regardless of gender. I was pleased and proud when women were elected to office or appointed to positions of power. Women brought a perspective, based on their experiences, that was different from that of men. During my lifetime, I'd seen numerous changes in the way women were treated in society, in the business world, and in politics. I'd raised my daughters to be independent women, and I like to think that I had an influence on my granddaughters because of the role models with which they have been provided in their own family.

As I first took office, I was older and more conservative than most of the other women in Congress, even my fellow Republicans. We disagreed on many issues, but our gender brought us together on others, such as breast cancer, that cut across all political philosophies.

With very few exceptions I was never treated differently by male colleagues because I was a woman. I was viewed first as a Republican, second as a westerner, and last as a woman. Party membership and political philosophy were far more significant than gender. Disagreements with Democrat male members, such as Jim Weaver, Nick Rahall, and George Miller, were based on issues, not gender. That doesn't mean I didn't have to assert myself occasionally.

In any organization with 435 members, there were bound to be people you got along with better than others, people you respected more or less than others, and people with whom you simply had personality differences. In general I got along with all the women, just as I did the men. Everyone made an effort to make sure differences of opinion didn't get personal. I worked with conservative and pro-life Democrat women on many social issues and with the Democrat women in committees, such as Carrie Meek when she needed help because of the damage Hurricane Andrew did in 1992 in her district.

I felt that the Democrats in Congress took their women members for granted and did not treat them fairly. They seldom got good committee assignments, and some Democrat women rightfully complained that they never had any party leadership positions. The Democrats finally opened up a little more, and some women took advantage of it, notably liberal Nancy Pelosi, who became minority leader in 2003. On the other hand, during my years in Congress it appeared that Republican women were better able to work their way up through the ranks of the leadership positions. There were plenty of opportunities for women in the Republican Party, and we received good committee assignments.

In many ways, for both men and women in Congress, advancement depended on the individual's attitude. Those women—and men—who were difficult, who didn't vote with leadership or the party, and who constantly and openly argued against the leadership were kept from advancing. Male or female, in order to succeed, you had to be a team player and not defy the leaders.

Bob Michel, our Republican leader when I arrived in the House, had served his whole career in Congress as a member of the minority party. He naturally appointed those members who approached things like he did, those who were more conciliatory, not bomb throwers. I was fortunate that Michel appointed me to many important committees and caucuses, even though I was frequently aligned with the more outspoken conservative groups. I think his trust reflected my ability to get along with members on both sides of the aisle.

Although I resisted using the phrase "women's issues," the general public and the press did not. In addition to my work on breast cancer prevention and research, I also got involved in the debates over comparable worth, parental leave, gender discrimination, and, of course, abortion rights.

My toughest votes in the House were always on the pro-life issues. Most of my staff, some of my family members, many of my friends, and a majority of Nevadans disagreed with my position. But I was a Roman Catholic, and my views on abortion were naturally colored by my upbringing. I have always believed abortion is the taking of a life. I voted that way as a member of Congress, and I would vote that way again today. I realized early on that you had to be true to your convictions, even if it meant you might not win the next election.

In my mind, every child is entitled to a chance at life. When my son Mike spoke on the campaign trail for me and was asked about my views on the subject, he always replied, "I'm glad my mother didn't believe in abortion, or I might not be here today."

During the 1994 U.S. Senate and House–sponsored nondenominational National Prayer Breakfast when Clinton was president, guest speaker Mother Teresa said, "If there are any children you don't want, give them to me."

Her speech was well received by most of the audience. Pro-choice Bill and Hillary Clinton sat, polite and respectful, at the head table, but at Mother Teresa's comments they became stone-faced. For me, it was a very moving experience. I thought she was saintly.

I can't think of an issue as emotionally charged as abortion. When I arrived in Congress, only three Republican women were pro-life: Virginia Smith, Marjorie Holt, and myself. The rest of the Republican women, and almost all of the Democrat women, were pro-choice. That changed somewhat over the years, and there were several Democrat women with whom I worked in the Pro-Life Caucus, most of whom were Roman Catholics or members of conservative Christian churches. The Democrat women were Beverly Byron, Marcy Kaptur, Lindy Boggs, Marilyn Lloyd, and Mary Rose Oakar. The Republican women who were most active in the pro-choice movement were Marge Roukema and Nancy Johnson, both married to ob-gyn physicians.

After Virginia and Marjorie retired, I didn't have a Republican ally until Ileana Ros-Lehtinin arrived in 1989. Ileana was also Roman Catholic and had actually used her pro-life stand in her campaign, something not many candidates do. Once she was elected, she was reluctant to speak out on the issue, although her vote could still be counted on. That surprised me a little.

The most vigorous discussions were over funding of abortions for women in the military and in the foreign aid bills allowing the United States to fund abortions in other countries. I worked closely with Republican Henry Hyde to pass the Hyde Amendment, which prohibited the use of federal tax funds for abortions. That prohibition would have gone away if the ERA had been approved. I argued that we could not call this an Equal Rights Amendment when it allowed—even mandated—that the rights of one individual may cost another, the unborn, his or her life. In my opinion, there could be no "equality" in such a situation.

The Equal Rights Amendment was a major ongoing debate across the nation and in Congress throughout much of the 1970s and into the 1980s. The amendment, both originally and as revived in 1983, stated that equality of rights under the law shall not be denied or abridged on account of sex. Under the amendment, a woman could sue if she believed she was discriminated against because of her gender. While I supported equal rights, I was opposed to amending the Constitution in a way that would have opened up numerous opportunities for filing lawsuits. The legislation was vague, without any limits or definitions.

The original proposed amendment to the U.S. Constitution, a highly divisive measure in many states, died in 1982 when not enough states had ratified it within ten years of its original passage in Congress. That didn't stop the liberals from making another effort. It was my handling of the ERA fight in the House that was the first step to propel me into a leadership role with the Republicans in Congress.

During my first term in Congress, ERA supporters attempted to put the amendment up for a vote under a suspension of the rules, which meant that there could be no debate or amendments added to the ERA language. A number of meritorious changes were proposed, for instance to restrict the use of public funds for abortions or to keep women out of direct combat, but none of them could be considered under a suspension of the rules.

I believed that stifling debate on a constitutional amendment was unacceptable, so I organized a coalition that ultimately sent ERA back to committee. I worked with Democrat Marilyn Lloyd, and we sent letters to all the members of Congress urging them to vote against the legislation unless amendments were allowed. Without amendments, we argued, the bill would die in the Senate or in the ratification process.

We also distributed floor statements in opposition to the passage of the ERA under the suspended rules, and I spoke against the procedure in our Republican Conference. Through our efforts, the proposed legislation was defeated on November 15, 1983, a final nail in the coffin of the ERA.

I was exposed to the legislative concept of "comparable worth" during my first term, when I worked with Republican Dick Armey to defeat a proposal that would have forced businesses to pay employees on the basis of job descriptions, not on that of productivity or skills. We felt that the bill was anti-business, almost a socialist proposal, and we appeared at forums to speak against the issue to various business and professional groups. The legislation finally died when it failed to pass the House. As a small businesswoman, although I supported equal pay for equal work, I was opposed to comparable worth because it was not a fair way to reward a worker. Lumping all employees together, rather than allowing employers to deal with each individual's abilities and talents, seemed like an ineffective practice and an unnecessary burden on businesses to address problems that did not exist.

One of the people who helped us during the comparable-worth debate was Virginia "Ginny" Lamp, an outstanding lawyer who later married Clarence Thomas. Newt Gingrich, his wife, Marianne, and George and I were the only ones from Congress at their wedding on June 3, 1987, in a small meeting room at the Omni Shoreham Hotel in Washington. I think only about thirty people were present for their subdued civil ceremony. During Clarence's confirmation hearings in 1991, at the height of the Anita Hill attacks, I often spoke to the press on his behalf because of Ginny's friendship and what she told me about Clarence.

While we saw Ginny and Clarence occasionally in restaurants in the District and at social events, I did not know Clarence well. My impressions were that he was a solid citizen, quiet and reserved but friendly with people. His young son was often with them, and I felt he was a strong family man. After his confirmation, I attended public forums when he spoke and was impressed with his conservative values and court decisions. He reflected my beliefs, and I had no regrets that I spoke out on his behalf.

In 1984 Mary Rose Oakar and I teamed up on the House Administration Committee to challenge the Democrat leadership on gender discrimination. We publicly questioned why the full committee chairmen—all Democrats—had no women in their highest-paid staff positions. The reaction we received from the Democrats ranged across the board—from Morris "Mo" Udall, who made changes, to Peter Rodino, who ignored us. Chairman Gus Hawkins, an African American and an old-fashioned, kind guy, felt that as chair anything he did was okay. He never seemed to relate the issue to his own situation. Our actions changed some of the committees, but I'm not sure it changed much in House Administration because all the subcommittee chairs were men.

Interestingly, while Mary Rose Oakar and I were being criticized because we didn't go along with liberal "women's" issues, we worked together to implement the first child care center on Capitol Hill for staff and members. For many reasons, few members and staffers live in the District of Columbia, where Capitol Hill is located, so most of them commute at least an hour each way from home to work and back to home. We were concerned not only about the parents' long commutes but also about the late hours worked. Congressional staffers rarely leave the office at 5:00 P.M. or even 6:00 P.M.. It was usually much later at night when they headed for home, and anyone who has had small children in day care knows how difficult it is to find a facility willing to put up with such erratic and late hours.

Bill Frenzel, the ranking Republican on the House Administration Committee, helped us push the legislation through. We wanted the center to be staffed properly without being too expensive. We even found a building to use. The Senate later established a child care center for its staff. Later on, the child care centers were opened to all parents who worked on "the Hill."

In 1987 the Republicans pushed through a parental leave bill that we felt fairly balanced the needs of parents against the rights of businesses. It allowed women and men to take a leave of absence without pay for a reasonable period of time and to retain their jobs. Democrats and most women's organizations objected that it didn't go far enough, but I felt it was fair to everyone.

Before I arrived in the House, the Republican women formed an informal group that got together for dinner on Tuesday or Wednesday nights once a month to discuss how we could help one other and to get to know each other better. This group was our answer to the groups the men had, such as the long-standing Chowder and Marching Society. While we women talked about going to those gatherings, we weren't invited and we did not want to "crash the party."

One of the major differences between men and women in Congress was that the men usually had only one life, that of being a congressman. That was all that was required of them. Women were expected to pay as much attention to family concerns and outside responsibilities as they were to their positions in Congress. That was our common bond and our basis for friendship.

Congresswoman Bobbie Fiedler introduced me to the Republican women's group in my first term. Not all of us could attend every dinner, but the regulars over the years were Jan Meyers, Nancy Johnson, Marjorie Holt, Susan Molinari, Jennifer Dunn, Deborah Pryce, Helen Bentley, Tillie Fowler, Ileana Ros-Lehtinin, Virginia Smith, and Lynn Martin.

Lynn was a vital part of our group and its informal leader, often hosting the meals at her house. Otherwise, our gatherings were either a Dutch treat affair or we "brown-bagged it." Occasionally we invited women lobbyists who were friendly to our side of the aisle to join us for dinner, and they usually paid for the meal. As women and as Republicans, we had a lot of issues in common. We exchanged ideas about how to deal with serving in the House while keeping our home life together. Many had husbands who did not move to Washington when they were elected, and some had children at home or in college.

Our age differences were a factor in my relationship with the women in the House. In any gathering of Republican women in Congress, I was the oldest or next to oldest; Virginia Smith was older than I was, and she retired before I did. I had come to adulthood in a different era and had many life experiences to which the others could not relate, just as I had trouble relating to some of theirs.

The meals and company were pleasant, but when the conversation turned to abortion issues, I knew it was time to excuse myself, since most of the women were pro-choice. Deb Pryce once asked me why I usually left when the subject came up. I told her, "I'm not going to change anyone's mind or my own."

Most of the time, however, we would just look at each other, shake our heads, and laugh about our differences. We managed to get along because we made it our business to do so. As a result, I developed not only a friendship with many of the women with whom I served but also a great deal of respect for the positions they held and the way they represented their constituents. Five congresswomen in particular stand out.

My classmate Nancy Johnson became chair of the ethics committee, officially known as the Standards and Official Conduct Committee, when Republicans took control of the House. Nancy eventually found herself in the middle of controversy when her committee investigated an ethical question over Speaker Newt Gingrich's receipt of a $4.5 million book advance from the Rupert Murdoch News Corporation. At the end of the investigation, the committee fined him an unbelievable $300,000, payable to the House. Newt's acceptance of the advance was considered insensitive because he took advantage of his political position; yet Senator Hillary Clinton's book advance wasn't criticized by anyone, much less was she sanctioned.

Newt's fine made the Republicans uncomfortable and the Democrats ecstatic. Despite what seemed like a hefty fine, Democrats argued that Nancy had not done enough to punish Gingrich. I thought the whole thing was an effort by the Democrats to bring Newt down. As soon as the decision was made, Nancy demanded to be let off the committee, and the Republicans relieved her of this assignment. At her next election, she lost the endorsement of some women's groups and barely won.

Jennifer Dunn was ambitious, articulate, and represented the Republican Party well, especially among women. When she first arrived in the House, she was active in the liberal-leaning Women's Caucus. When she realized that wouldn't help her, she changed her tune. I felt that she changed on a lot of those issues, although she stressed the need for women in leadership. She was elected secretary of the Republican Conference when I retired, and then elected vice chair when Susan Molinari retired. Jennifer ran for majority leader against Dick Armey in 1998, stressing the need for women in leadership. She finished third out of three because the moderate and liberal Republicans did not support her.

Helen Delich Bentley was a natural ally because she was born and raised in Ely, Nevada, and was Serbian. She knew many of George's friends and had relatives who lived in Nevada. She helped me on issues important to Nevada, and I assisted her on issues important to Maryland and the Baltimore Harbor, which was in her district. A former head of the U.S. Maritime Commission under President Nixon, Helen ran three times before she was finally elected to Congress. Her main issue was the dredging of the harbor, important for trade and jobs in her district. In her first term she obtained federal money for the dredging. She was one of the most fearless women I know, extremely competitive. She was maybe all of five feet tall, but she would be right in anyone's face if she or he disagreed with her. The men seemed amused by her, but she got what she wanted. She would probably still be in Congress if she hadn't decided to run unsuccessfully for governor. Today, she lobbies on trade issues, although she ran again for her old seat in 2002 when Congressman Bob Erlich successfully ran for governor. Unfortunately, she lost that race.

Pat Saiki was a good friend. She was congenial but assertive, without being a nuisance. We played golf together, but she wasn't on any of my committees. She was the first Republican to represent Hawaii in the

House. I met her before her first campaign, helped her during her first election, and contributed to her campaign. After Pat was elected in 1986, George and I were vacationing in Hawaii, and I telephoned her to invite her and her husband, Stanley, a doctor, to lunch. I asked if her husband was going to Washington, D.C., with her.

She replied, "Oh, yes." She paused. "But he doesn't know it yet."

What to do about your spouse (if you had one) was always an issue for elected women.

One of the younger women, Susan Molinari, was a refreshing change. I admit I was startled the first time she appeared in the chambers dressed in casual pants and an attractive blouse, her usual attire. In contrast, most of the other women members, including myself, traditionally wore suits with jackets and skirts every day. As I recall, the press made quite a story of Susan's appearance because she was the first woman member to wear pants on the floor of the House.

Susan came from a prominent political family in Staten Island, New York. She was elected in a special election when her father, Guy Molinari, was elected Staten Island borough president and left Congress. She had been a member of the New York City Council before her election to the House. Susan fought hard during her first year to get Staten Island designated as a navy home port. She had strong opposition from powerful committee people, but she won in a remarkable vote. Freshmen in the minority don't usually have much clout.

Susan married a fellow New York State member, Bill Paxton, and they had their first child while she was in the House. They were a popular couple, touring the country on behalf of the Republican Party to campaign for House challengers and incumbents.

Congressional facilities weren't set up for the growing number of congresswomen. For instance, the men and women each had a gym in the House. They were separate but certainly not equal. The women's gym was rather small and filled with castoff equipment from the men's gym. The men were frequent users of their gym, which included basketball and handball courts, but the women I served with were not overly interested in athletics or physical activity. Occasionally an aerobics class would begin, but it never lasted for long. We were all too busy with other activities.

There was a swimming pool available for use by both men and women, although during one period some of the men took to swimming in the nude in an overt effort to keep the women out of the pool. It wasn't long before the male members were wearing bathing suits again.

We made a major gain in October 1990 when we held a reception in the newly redecorated Lindy Claiborne Boggs Congressional Women's Reading Room, the congressional women's suite off Statuary Hall. Democrat Lindy was retiring, and the rooms obviously were named after her. The suite included a huge portrait of her, and we had our pictures taken with her. All the women were supportive of the project because it was quite a boon to get our own suite of rooms.

While the women's rooms existed before 1990, the suite didn't really have a name before that. It was always difficult to get to these rooms before and after the dedication. In fact, Tom Foley's wife took over the hallway when he was Speaker, so you couldn't just walk into the suite from the corridor. Later, you had to go through Dick Gephardt's office for access, by dialing a certain number to get in, or through another door with a key. Yet it was great to have a place, finally, where we could relax and kick off our shoes. The men didn't have a suite; they just used all the rooms off the floor.

I will admit that being one of the "oldest" women in Congress helped differentiate me from many of my colleagues, whether I liked it or not. For example, in 1985 the Capitol Hill publication *Roll Call* did a Mother's Day story on female members of Congress with children. Of the twenty-four women in Congress, seventeen were mothers. I led the list of mothers, with five children, while three had four children, four had three, six had two, and two had one.

At that time I had seventeen grandchildren, and in 1991 the "Battle of the Great-grandmothers" took place. Lindy Boggs announced that she was the first great-grandmother to serve in Congress. I hadn't realized that we were having a contest, but I made it clear that I had been a great-grandmother since 1987, when my great-grandson Brendan Manuel Cafferata Erquiaga was born to my oldest granddaughter, Elisa Piper Cafferata Erquiaga. (Strangely enough, this story was picked up by newspapers as far away as Rome, Italy.)

One of the things all Republican House members were expected to do occasionally, at the request of the National Republican Congressional Committee, was to meet with potential candidates for the House. That was especially important for women, who looked forward to exchanging ideas about issues and campaigning. We tried to offer our advice when asked. It might seem superficial, but we were often asked about appearance. For example, at a meeting in October 1989, one woman candidate from Utah was wearing a very dark, almost black, navy suit. She asked me if I thought it was appropriate for campaigning, and I told her it wasn't. She was tiny, and the suit overwhelmed her.

Women candidates have a difficult time striking a balance between looking attractive and looking competent. Their clothes should not be so memorable that they detract from their message. Male candidates rarely have to worry about their clothes on the campaign trail, but women don't have that luxury. Men's clothes get noticed only when they are overdressed or underdressed—for instance, if they show up in black tie when everyone else is wearing jeans—or when they are wearing clothes that they don't normally wear. An example would be seeing a candidate in cowboy clothes, knowing full well that he isn't comfortable in such an outfit. They stand out like rhinestone cowboys. But women usually have a much finer line to walk than men when it comes to how they dress on the campaign trail, and it is unfortunate but true that this affects their ability to get elected.

One of my last activities before I left the Congress was to organize the Women's Leadership Summit, held in May 1996, with the help of RENEW, a Republican women's organization based in Washington, and some political consultants. I felt at the time, and still do, that Republicans were not getting their message out to women in America that there was room in the Republican Party for women from all walks of life and with varying philosophies.

The summit was an opportunity to showcase Republican women and our ideals. We invited several hundred women, not necessarily Republicans, in the professions, in business, with foundations, serving in elected positions, and working as community activists from every state. The speakers at the summit included Republican leaders like Newt

Gingrich and women senators and congresswomen, plus other men and women in the administration. Most of our Republican congresswomen expressed support for this summit.

When I arrived in Congress after the election of 1982, it was pretty much a male place. When I left it in 1996, it was still pretty much a male place. Oh, there were some women who won leadership positions when the Republicans became the majority party in Congress in 1994, but women in the House have a long way to go before they will have an equal voice in setting and controlling the agenda. A woman's place in the House is still a challenge, although few, if any of them, are willing to take a backseat to any male congressman, and they have worked hard to achieve equality and, frankly, to be taken seriously.

Those who have been the most successful, in my opinion, are those who recognized that gender was secondary to getting the job done for their constituents. No one should be identified simply as a congresswoman. Certainly, there are issues that, as women, we feel obligated to speak out on, such as breast cancer research. But to suggest that breast cancer is a "woman's issue" would be much like suggesting that prostrate cancer is a "man's issue." Those issues affect all of us, our families, our friends, and certainly our constituents.

As a woman in the House, you find yourself walking a tightrope between what needs to be done and what is expected of you. As in the business world, a woman who is aggressive and speaks her mind often finds herself stereotyped in ways that would never happen to a man. Women have to be careful, more than men do, to avoid the stereotypes if they hope to remain effective.

I was a member of Congress; I was a woman. I managed to succeed by being consistent and by not picking unnecessary fights. I made it a point not to become identified with any one issue. I always represented my district and state on the issues that were most important to the folks at home.

CHAPTER FOURTEEN

Nevada on My Mind

My congressional responsibilities were usually never far from my thoughts, but my family was also on my mind. My first great-grandchild arrived on Thanksgiving Day in 1987. Brendan Manuel Cafferata Erquiaga was actually born before the last of my seventeen grandchildren, David Anderson, joined the family. Brendan's parents were my oldest granddaughter, Elisa, and her husband, Dale Erquiaga. George and I celebrated Brendan's arrival with the family at the Thanksgiving dinner table. Neither Washington, D.C., nor Nevada was on my mind that day.

"Nevada on My Mind" was a theme I used frequently for radio advertising during my later campaigns. Each sixty-second radio spot allowed me to talk informally about an issue that was of concern to Nevadans, without being overtly political. While issues are important, I would not be considered a "policy wonk" or activist for a cause. No one else in the Nevada delegation would fit that description either. Yes, there were members who focused on a particular policy or who were passionate, devoting all their time to a single policy, but they were in the minority.

For example, during all his terms in the House, Republican Jack Kemp of New York zealously championed reforming America's economic and tax policy. He advocated the flat tax and other tax simplification proposals. There were others like Republican Chris Smith, who came to Congress as a former executive director of the New Jersey Right to Life. A sincere, dedicated opponent of abortion, he founded the bipartisan Pro-Life

Caucus. He rallied his supporters whenever abortion was being debated. Another single-issue activist who comes to mind was elected in 1996, the year I retired. Democrat Carolyn McCarthy was elected on the issue of gun control. Her husband had been murdered by a gunman who opened fire on a Long Island Railroad train. To this day, gun control is her main focus.

There were other activists in Congress, but the "average" member was usually a generalist on the diverse legislation with which he or she was confronted. I was considered a generalist not only on Nevada and western issues but also on women's health issues.

Having said that, I must add that politicians everywhere talk about "issue-oriented campaigning," and it is a necessity in Nevada. Voters expected their officeholders to stay away from personalities and focus on issues, and I am proud to say that I tried to run my campaigns that way. Of course, there was never a shortage of "Nevada" issues. Some of them were on the table before I arrived in Congress, and many continued to be debated after I left. For the most part, the issues that directly concerned my congressional district were—and still are—resource issues related to the public lands, such as mining, ranching, and grazing. I spent a lot of time on these issues because they were important to my largely rural geographical district. My seats on the Interior Committee and later on the Appropriations Committee gave me an ideal position from which to be effective for Nevada on those issues.

In addition, I was involved in a number of issues that reached beyond the Second Congressional District and had an impact on all of Nevada, such as gaming and tourism, which were the state's primary industries and so were vitally important to our economy. The Nevada delegation continually fought to protect gaming from federal intervention and from federal taxation. Mostly we were successful because of our willingness to set aside party differences and work together.

Because of Nevada's small population and limited representation in Congress, we often faced an uphill battle in dealing with issues like public lands and legalized gambling. Senators and congressmen outside of the West had little experience with gaming or federal land ownership, so we tried to educate them about our issues. Believe me, it was a challenge to educate congressmen from New York City or Alabama about Nevada, let alone get them to care about the rancher trying to squeeze out a living on sagebrush-covered rangeland. Similarly, it was hard to get them to move past stereotypical images of the gambling industry and be concerned about such problems as blackjack dealers being harassed by the Internal Revenue Service.

Nevada was an easy target for many. To be successful in protecting our state, our delegation needed to work together and use our seniority and our relationships with non-westerners to promote Nevada and our issues.

Yucca Mountain

One issue that left a trail through my years in Congress was nuclear waste and proposals to put a national storage facility in Yucca Mountain in my district. Yucca Mountain, of course, is located on the old Nevada Test Site, which in turn was part of the old Las Vegas Bombing and Gunnery Range from the post–World War II era. In 1951 the U.S. Atomic Energy Commission began using the site for "routine" testing of atomic bombs, a concept hard to imagine today. Before testing was halted in 1992, there were more than nine hundred atomic explosions at the Nevada Test Site. In the 1950s a number of tests were conducted aboveground. Longtime Nevadans can still remember family outings to watch the mushroom clouds that resulted from atmospheric tests. Common sense, not to mention political and environmental concerns, would not allow such testing today.

Yucca Mountain became a big issue in the 1980s. Originally, Democrat Mo Udall's Nuclear Waste Policy Act passed in 1982 directed the Department of Energy to study nine sites around the country for storing nuclear waste and ultimately to select one site in the East and one in the West. By 1986 the department had reduced its study to three sites in the West—Washington State, Texas, and Nevada—with the intent to select an eastern site later.

Then Democrat senator Bennett Johnston got a bill passed through the U.S. Senate that reduced the study to one site—Nevada. This bill was popularly dubbed the "Screw Nevada" bill, and twenty years later the fight is still ongoing. I met with Senator Johnston, who invariably listened politely but gave no sign that he would back away from his position, or with other federal officials. And I met with Secretary of Energy James Watkins in 1989 in Senator Reid's office to discuss Yucca Mountain. Watkins was unwavering in his support for storing nuclear waste in Nevada.

Johnston made it impossible for the Nevada delegation to stop this bill. He cut a deal as part of the Budget Reconciliation Act of 1987 in conference committee. Since conferees on major bills are usually the most senior members of the House and Senate, Nevada didn't have a member on the committee. Senators Hecht and Reid were too new to the Senate, and I was only in my third term, while Jim Bilbray was a House freshman. The Democrat majority in the conference gave Johnston what he requested. There was nothing we could do to stop Johnston at the time. Over the years, I introduced numerous bills to slow down the nuclear waste process and to try to prevent it from coming to Nevada.

I toured the Nevada Test Site and Yucca Mountain numerous times, visiting with workers and learning about past testing and about current activities taking place. I visited the building where they used robotics to handle nuclear materials and, of course, the Yucca Mountain tunnel, the proposed storage area. There are some technologically marvelous things being done at the Nevada Test Site, but I have remained convinced that the Yucca Mountain site was not—and is not—appropriate for nuclear waste storage.

Of course, public opinion in Nevada was strongly against locating the repository in the Silver State, but that was only part of the reason I worked so hard against it. In my mind, I didn't believe that the scientific community had ever made a solid case for the safety of storing nuclear waste in the Nevada desert.

For years, there have been popular bumper stickers in Nevada proclaiming NEVADA IS NOT A WASTELAND. Those of us who appreciated the wide-open splendor of Nevada's backcountry agree with that sentiment, but this issue is a classic case of how difficult it can be to convince Eastern legislators and bureaucrats that public land doesn't mean public nuclear waste dump. Having the waste storage facility in Nevada would be harmful to our tourism industry, and there have been real questions about transporting the waste from locations around the country to Nevada, whether by rail or by highway. Nevada would not be the only state at risk. One of my priorities in Congress was to encourage research into recycling of nuclear waste or developing disposal technologies. These processes continue to be viable alternatives to simply sticking it in the ground in Nevada.

Water

Water was the lifeblood of Nevada, a truly precious resource that has resulted in some of the biggest public policy debates in our history. Easterners, especially, had little concept of the importance of water in the relatively arid Great Basin. In the early years, people shot one another over water rights, and emotions ran strong. A classic example—although without gunfire—was the debate over allocation of Truckee River waters. At one point, rights to water of the Truckee were central to the longest pending federal court case in the nation.

The Truckee begins at Lake Tahoe, travels out of the Sierras, flows through Reno, and empties into Pyramid Lake. In the early 1900s, creation of the Newlands Reclamation Project in the Fallon area resulted in river water being diverted from the river for agricultural purposes. Later, the building of water storage and flood control dams upstream from Reno also changed historic stream flows. Ultimately, the fight over who had what right to how much water resulted in lawsuits involving, at various times, the Pyramid Lake Paiute Tribe, the City of Reno, the Sierra Pacific Power Company, the Truckee-Carson Irrigation District (representing Fallon-area farmers), and various federal agencies, including the U.S. Bureau of Reclamation and the Army Corps of Engineers.

Finally, in order to end the litigation and rancor, serious efforts were made to bring all of the parties together. Ultimately, most parties signed off on the Truckee River Negotiated Water Settlement, although some, particularly Fallon farmers, were not happy. Senator Reid introduced the Negotiated Water Settlement bill in the Senate in 1990, while I introduced a similar bill in the House. The Senate passed the legislation, but the House did not take action until the final hours of the session. It was only after I got George Miller, the powerful California member of the House Interior Committee, to sign off on the bill that I was able to convince Speaker Tom Foley to bring the bill up for a vote. To this day, Harry Reid gives me credit for getting the legislation passed. The Negotiated Water Settlement, although not perfect, was a compromise that I believe was the right answer.

The other big water issue I dealt with in Congress involved the Colorado River, on the southernmost boundary of Nevada. I worked with Arizona Democrat Mo Udall, chair of the Interior Committee, on Colorado River water allocations for Southern Nevada that required reappropriation by Congress every ten years. Some of the states on the river don't fully use their allocations, but they were reluctant to give their water to other states. Discussions were difficult, with California always wanting more water. I worked with Pat Mulroy, general manager of the Las Vegas Southern Nevada Water Authority, and the Southern Nevada business community and elected officials, to protect Nevada's interest in Colorado River water allocations and to find ways to borrow and/or store water.

Great Basin National Park

In the mid-1980s, Nevada was one of the few states in the nation without a national park, although 87 percent of the state's lands are federally owned. Years earlier, it had been proposed that a park be established near Ely in eastern Nevada, to be known as the Great Basin National Park. Offering the scenic beauty of Mount Wheeler and other natural attractions, the park made sense for tourism. My concern was balancing and protecting the existing rights of ranchers and miners against the tourism interests.

When we decided to move ahead with legislation to create Nevada's first national park, the biggest dispute was over the size of the park. Harry Reid wanted the park to be 430,000 acres, while I supported what I felt was more than adequate—a park of 137,000 acres. I thought his proposal was too large and would have a damaging effect on existing ranching and mining permits held by people whose livelihoods depended on their ability to have access to these public lands. After a spirited debate, the Democrat majority in the House agreed to the Reid proposal, and Great Basin National Park was dedicated on August 15, 1987. Although I still think it is too big, it is an asset to Nevada.

Wilderness

Another long-standing debate in Nevada has been over wilderness. Keep in mind, Nevada's public lands were already protected by federal law and were managed by the Bureau of Land Management and the U.S. Forest Service. That will never change. At the same time, as someone who has enjoyed camping and fishing on our public lands for almost as long as I've been in Nevada, I am a strong believer in "multiple use" of the public lands.

These lands should be managed for public benefit, with appropriate safeguards. If that means allowing mining for essential minerals, so be it. If it means development of some unpaved roads to improve public access to some areas, so be it. All of those uses—mining, ranching, travel and more—were already governed by existing federal laws, rules, and regulations.

In my opinion, the restrictions that come with a wilderness area designation were almost elitist because they would have prevented all but a tiny minority of the people from ever enjoying the public lands that are part of the Nevada lifestyle. In fact, I believed much of the push for additional wilderness area designations in Nevada was coming from environmental activist organizations. As Nevadans, we certainly understood the emotional appeal of wild and scenic lands. But to most westerners, these were working landscapes, vital to our livelihoods. We couldn't afford to have them locked up and made off-limits. It was easy for congressmen and senators from the East to push for wilderness designations here because they had no concept of how Nevadans use the vast open spaces and federal lands.

I'm not sure when the federal Wilderness Act was passed originally, but no one ever took advantage of it until the 1980s, when wilderness supporters discovered how to use the law. Democrat congressman John Seiberling, chair of the National Parks and Recreation subcommittee of the Interior Committee, began pushing for more wilderness in all the western states, including Alaska. He wasn't interested in more wilderness in his home state of Ohio, which contained probably about one percent public land, or in any of the other eastern states, all of which had little public land. But, in a scenario with which Nevadans are all too familiar, non-western legislators felt they could dictate what we should do with public lands within our state borders.

Seiberling arranged a weeklong tour of some of the proposed Nevada wilderness sites in 1989. I went along, as did Senator Reid, Congressman Jim Bilbray, and some employees of the National Park Service and the Forest Service. We flew in helicopters to Tonopah, to the Grant and Quinn areas, and to the beautiful Arc Dome in the Toiyabe National Forest in central Nevada. When we weren't flying, we rode horseback into some areas and camped overnight in tents. We also visited Ely, Elko, Jarbidge, and the Santa Rosa area, and ended the tour at Maya Miller's home in Franktown for a Sierra Club barbecue.

It was a trip through some of the most beautiful parts of Nevada, but it was probably too successful, from my point of view. Partly as a result of what he saw on this trip, Congressman Seiberling, with Senator Reid's support, successfully pushed through the Nevada Wilderness Act in 1989, despite my opposition. I felt the bill went too far in restricting land use and land access, and I unsuccessfully tried to get it modified. Once again, a Democrat majority made the difference, just as it did later in a subsequent proposal to create additional wilderness on Mount Rose in Washoe County.

Mining

Nevada was known as the "Silver State" for good reason. Our state was brought into the Union in 1864 because President Lincoln needed additional votes in Congress. Later the Comstock Lode bullion helped finance the Civil War. There have been other major silver strikes in Nevada through the years, and the Nevada landscape is dotted with "ghost towns" in testimony to short-lived mining boomtowns. In recent years, with improvements in mining technologies, Nevada had become the nation's largest gold producer.

The battles over mining usually revolved around revising the Mining Law of 1872, one of the oldest federal laws in existence. Democrat congressman Nick Rahall tried to restrict mining in the West every way he could, aided by a very diligent staffer who was a strong environmentalist and to whom Nick gave a free hand. Because the changes he was seeking would have hampered development of Nevada's mining industry and would have created economic hardships in the state, I held off the opponents many times with amendments and prolonged debate. This battle continued during most of my tenure in Congress; it seemed we were always on the defensive. We were also mostly successful.

Ranching

On the agriculture side, while our crop production may be small compared to that of most states, we had a significant cattle ranching industry and there were pockets throughout the state where agriculture was a major local industry. The issues involving Nevada ranchers offered a classic example of the challenge of explaining Nevada's unique lifestyle to non-westerners. Because there was so much public land in Nevada, ranchers had to graze their cattle on land that was managed by the U.S. Forest Service or the Bureau of Land Management. Without access to that land, ranchers couldn't succeed in their businesses. And because of the sparse vegetation on our state's arid public lands, it took a lot of land to feed the cattle.

The federal government would frequently try to raise the fees that ranchers paid for grazing rights, usually under pressure from environmentalists. The increases often were impossibly high, given the economic realities of public-land ranching. This federal attitude gave rise to the Sagebrush Rebellion in the 1970s. The arguments involving environmentalists on one side, ranchers on the other, and public-land managers in the middle continued throughout my years in Congress.

My job was to try to negotiate with all sides to achieve some balance, and it was not easy. Trying to explain the concept of fees based on animal unit months to an eastern congressman whose closest association with cattle was what showed up on his dinner plate was difficult. The fight was not always a success for the ranchers and farmers.

Indian Gaming

It wasn't all that long ago that if you wanted to enjoy the fun of casino-style gaming, you had two choices: Nevada or Atlantic City. That changed rapidly in the 1980s and 1990s with the presence of gambling on many

Indian reservations. The Interior Committee dealt with Indian affairs and was chaired by Democrat Mo Udall, who believed that tribal economies would be helped by legalized gambling. Mo and I were friendly, but we disagreed mightily on this issue. I saw the expansion of Indian gaming as a threat to our tourism-based economy. If people in Chicago could drive to a casino within 100 miles of their home, there would be less incentive for them to fly to Reno or Las Vegas.

When the issue was debated in the late 1980s in the Interior Committee, I threw up as many roadblocks as I could to protect Nevada gaming. At the time, I was especially pleased to secure an amendment to the Indian Gaming Act that provided that no tribe could have gaming unless the governor in the state in which the casino was to be located approved a specific compact with the tribe. I thought that most governors would be reluctant to sign such a compact, but I later found that a number of them were more than willing to sign, for political as well as economic reasons. As a result, today there is gambling on Indian reservations in several states, including Oregon, California, and Arizona, all bordering Nevada.

In my opinion, there are a couple of major problems with Indian gaming, aside from the negative impact on Nevada tourism. First of all, unlike Nevada casinos, the Indian establishments do not pay any federal or state taxes on their gaming income. The tribes are considered sovereign states, so the federal government and state governments have no control over their activities. Also, while Nevada has an internationally respected Gaming Commission and Gaming Control Board, controls over tribal gaming are considerably looser. All Indian casinos are supervised by a five-member federal gaming commission that reports to the secretary of the interior. One member of the commission must be a Native American. The commission simply doesn't have the experience or the ability to have day-to-day control over Indian gaming operations. At the same time, there is no protection for the consumer (the gambler).

Unquestionably, the expansion of gambling has been a mixed blessing for Nevada. We are no longer the only game in town for gamblers. Many people live within a few hours' drive of casinos located on reservations. There's no doubt that this is a hindrance to our tourism industry, especially outside of Las Vegas. On the other hand, many Nevada casino operators and equipment manufacturers are heavily involved in Indian gaming, with management contracts and Nevada-manufactured equipment. The challenge for Nevada, particularly in smaller markets like Reno, has been to offer people something more than simply a gambling experience.

Taxing of Tips

For a generation, Nevada's service and tourism industry workers have been fighting with the Internal Revenue Service over the taxing of tips—"tokes" in the Nevada vernacular. The IRS accused dealers and others of underreporting tip income. On the other hand, there was a strong feeling that Nevadans were too often singled out for audits and other IRS enforcement. With tens of thousands of tip earners in Nevada, it was an issue I was involved in frequently.

I joined Senators Paul Laxalt and Chic Hecht in trying to get the IRS to adopt a more reasonable attitude. Taken to an extreme, some felt that the IRS was stereotyping Nevadans as tax cheats who regularly failed to report income. Our position was that Nevada wage earners were willing to pay their fair share, but shouldn't be targeted for over-aggressive audit policies and should always be given the benefit of the doubt.

The fact is that many tip earners were paid a low salary, which employers justified because the workers received tips. The IRS proposed setting an arbitrary amount as tip income, on which all employees would be required to pay taxes. The agency also wanted employers to withhold an arbitrary amount from the employees' paychecks. It was an unfair idea because there is no way to measure tip income with any certainty. Some people tip generously, others not at all. A waitress in Goldfield is not tipped like a waitress in a major casino in Las Vegas. A gambler may hit a hot streak at a blackjack table and tip extravagantly, but not always. A gambler who wins a $25,000 slot machine jackpot may tip $1,000 or $5. The IRS, apparently feeling clairvoyant, believed that its industrywide, one-size-fits-all standards would work. We didn't.

This proposal hit the restaurant association and the casino industry hard, as well as the Culinary Union workers and other union members. Because of this issue, I met lots of people in the restaurant business that I wouldn't ordinarily have met, as well as people who worked as bellhops, luggage handlers at airports, car valets, and taxicab drivers. We organized some of the opposition and staged protests for the many hearings held on the proposal. As a result, the IRS proposal was scuttled. Later, the IRS and the gaming industry negotiated an agreement on how tips would be taxed, although the IRS continues to try to increase the amount subject to taxation.

Thinking about tips, I remember the press criticizing me for submitting my tips for reimbursement from the House for my travel between Reno and Washington. Since my tips were higher on the average than those declared by other congressmen, I was referred to as the "Big Tipper." The response from my constituents was overwhelmingly positive because so many of them relied on their tip income.

Source Income Tax

If you don't live in a particular state, why should you have to pay state income taxes there? That very logical question was at the heart of the long discussion of the "source income tax," one of my successes of which I am most proud. Nevada has many retirees, particularly from California and from the military, who were being forced to pay income taxes on their pension incomes to the state where they had lived while they were working (the "source" of the pension), even if they no longer lived or worked there.

While the logic of repealing the source income tax made sense for a lot of people, it was opposed by a number of heavily populated—and thus well represented in Congress—northern states and California, places where retirees once lived and worked and states that liked having the tax income from former residents without having to provide services to them.

I was the primary sponsor of the bill to repeal the tax. I got the idea from some of my constituents, particularly in the Carson City area. This piece of legislation was the most important single bill I sponsored during my fourteen years in the House. I cosponsored other bills, but this one was mine. It took six years to get the bill passed. But the result, preventing any state from imposing an income tax on the retirement income of nonresident individuals, was well worth the effort.

Defense Issues

Because of my family's background, I have always been a strong supporter of our nation's need for military preparedness and for the welfare of our enlisted personnel. My personal interest was compounded by a significant military presence in Nevada, especially the Fallon Naval Air Station and Nellis Air Force Base.

I was able to help these two bases in a number of ways. I worked to get additional lands for military air exercises near Fallon and to prevent removal of the Tactical Fighter Wings Unit from Nellis. I also sat on the Military Construction (MIL CON) subcommittee of the House Appropriations Committee, so I could help secure money for numerous improvements at both Nellis and Fallon.

55-Miles-per-Hour Speed Limit

The 55-miles-per-hour speed limit was put into effect by the federal government in the late 1970s in response to a national energy crisis. If you have ever driven across hundreds of miles on wide-open Nevada highways, you know how nonsensical the speed limit was in our state. Working together with other westerners, we eventually achieved a bipartisan solution that made sense, despite opposition from easterners. With no understanding of the vast lands in the West, they just couldn't comprehend how speeds in excess of 55 miles per hour were part of our way of life. We finally convinced enough other members and won the fight. Repeal of the 55-miles-per-hour speed limit was a happy day for those who drive in rural Nevada.

Notch Babies

During my time in Congress, I fought an annual battle to correct a problem with Social Security benefits that affected so-called notch babies, those born between 1917 and 1926. Years ago, Congressman Claude Pepper pushed a bill through Congress that changed the formula on payments to seniors, the effect of which was to reduce payments to those born in the "notch."

On a great day for Nevada, I am addressing the news media at a press conference outside the Capitol after we passed the repeal of the 55-miles-per-hour law in 1995. *Behind me, left to right:* Senator Steven Symms (Idaho), Representative Richard Stallings (Idaho), Senator Phil Gramm (Texas), Senator Chic Hecht (Nevada), Congressman Jim Hansen (Utah), and Congressman Dave McCurdy (Oklahoma).
Collection of Barbara F. Vucanovich

Every year, not because I was born in the notch but at the request of seniors' organizations in Nevada, I would try to change the formula to correct this unfair inequity in the law. I was never successful. As the years pass and fewer "notch babies" are still alive, it is becoming less of an issue. But it should still be fixed.

USS *Nevada*

Sometimes I had the opportunity to represent Nevada at events that were spectacularly meaningful. In 1991 I was one of seventeen members of

Congress flown by the navy to Hawaii for the fiftieth anniversary of the bombing of Pearl Harbor. The event included presenting a plaque at a wreath-laying ceremony for the USS *Nevada*.

On December 5, we toured the USS *Arizona* Visitors Center for an emotional Survivors Day program. I gave an impromptu speech on behalf of Nevada because Governor Bob Miller at the last minute could not make the trip. He sent as his official representative state senator Lawrence Jacobsen. Jake is a Pearl Harbor survivor, although he was not on the USS *Nevada*. All of the states that lost ships were represented: Arizona, California, Maryland, Nevada, Oklahoma, Pennsylvania, Tennessee, Utah, and West Virginia. In my speech I gave a brief history of the USS *Nevada* and remarked on the bravery of those serving aboard the only ship to get under way the morning that Pearl Harbor was attacked.

The Nevada was a 583-foot, 27,500-ton battleship, the first oil-burning battleship, and the oldest in the U.S. fleet at that time. Commissioned in 1916, she was the third USS *Nevada* and had seen action in World War I. (The first *Nevada* was a screw steamer built in 1863. The second was a harbor defense monitor built in 1898.)

On December 7, 1941, the *Nevada* was damaged by a torpedo to the forward section, which killed 50 men and wounded 109 others. As the ship pulled away from her dock, enemy planes diverted from other targets began dive-bombing the vessel. The bombs caused the water to erupt in huge geysers around the ship, which emerged with its superstructure afire and riddled with gaping holes. To avoid the risk of the ship's sinking and blocking the channel, the Nevada was deliberately run aground in the shallow waters off Hospital Point. After the attack, she was repaired and modernized and went on to participate in the Normandy invasion and the invasion of southern France in 1944 and then returned to the Pacific theater to provide fire support for the capture and occupation of Iwo Jima. The USS *Nevada* earned seven battle stars for her service in World War II. She was later used at Bikini as a target ship for atomic bombing tests, but she did not sink until navy dive-bombers sank her in 1948.

In 1986 I was in Groton, Connecticut, when the latest USS *Nevada*, an OHIO class nuclear-power fleet ballistic missile submarine, was commissioned. The next time I saw this new USS *Nevada* submarine was when it pulled into Pearl Harbor in 1991. We were standing on the deck of the

USS *Chosin,* an Aegis cruiser at the time. Later, we toured the *Nevada* and met the crew. I was pleased to see the famous Nevada Mackay silver service on display in one of the glassed-in showcases on board. (John Mackay was a well-known miner who made a fortune during the Virginia City mining boom of the 1870s.)

The trip wrapped up on December 7, 1991, an emotion-filled morning. Secretary of Defense Dick Cheney gave commemorative remarks, and President George Bush was the keynote speaker. The president was introduced by Captain Don Ross, a Congressional Medal of Honor recipient who practically single-handedly kept the boilers going after the USS *Nevada* was hit. The president's voice was choked with emotion when he said, "Praise the Lord and pass the ammunition." I had not known before that that frequently heard quote came from Pearl Harbor.

When Assemblyman Jim Gibbons and I participated in the wreath laying for the *Nevada,* Jim introduced Captain Ross, who led the singing of "God Bless America" and got so excited that he threw his cane away.

Judges

In 1992 I had the unique opportunity to recommend to the president a federal judicial nominee for a vacancy in the federal district court of Nevada. Ordinarily, that responsibility is given to the ranking U.S. senator of the president's political party. However, both of Nevada's senators, Harry Reid and Dick Bryan, were Democrats, of course, and I was the only Nevada Republican in the House. As a result, I was able to recommend three attorneys to the president for his consideration.

In order to be fair about the process, I invited everyone who was interested to apply, regardless of party affiliation. I established a review committee, chaired by my old friend Dick Horton, to screen potential candidates for the nomination. To the best of my recollection, other members of the committee included Dr. John Fred Burgess, businessman Remo Fratini, public relations consultant Bill Martin, and community and political leader Edwina Prior. The committee interviewed about a dozen applicants, and I ended up sending the names of George Allison of Carson City and Larry Hicks and Jay Sourwine of Reno, all highly respected attorneys, to the president with my endorsement.

As it turned out, all three were interviewed by the presidential selection/ nominating committee, and Larry Hicks was ultimately nominated by President Bush. Unfortunately, the Democrats in the Senate stalled the approval of his nomination until after President Bush was defeated and Bill Clinton was elected president, effectively killing the nomination. I was delighted when the second President Bush nominated Larry again in 2001. It was an honor to be on hand to watch Larry Hicks be sworn in as the newest member of the federal bench in Nevada on January 10, 2002.

It is interesting to me that many of the issues we were dealing with in the 1970s and 1980s in Nevada were still around in the new millennium. That's particularly true of public land and resource issues. Activist environmentalists know how to use the media, and they know how to generate support from the public. As a result, even as administrations change in Washington, grassroots support for multiple use of Nevada's public lands will be an issue.

Nevada, with its abundance of public lands and its gaming heritage, is a unique state in many ways. Its residents—and its elected officials—are proud of what the state has to offer and can get protective about defending her against outside forces who don't appreciate our state's one-of-a-kind charms.

Because Nevada's representatives in the House and the Senate are few in number, they will always have an uphill battle in protecting Nevada's interests. Representatives from states with few or no public lands—or with little interest in gaming issues or the challenges of nuclear waste disposal—will never share Nevada's perspective. That makes our ability to use seniority, committee assignments, and our relationships with other members of Congress more important than ever.

CHAPTER FIFTEEN

House Mates

*In 1993, Taylor George Cafferata, the first son of my oldest grandson, Reynolds
Cafferata, was born. Taylor joined the other men in the family: my husband,
George; my sons, Mike, Kenny, and Tommy; my other grandsons, Mike Jr.,
Trevor, Patrick, Scott, and David; and my great-grandson, Brendan. He
was born in Altadena in Southern California—ironically, not far from my
original Shorb and Yorba ancestors' family homes. I sometimes wonder what
José Antonio Yorba, who arrived in California in 1769, might think about the
family. I spent time with all of my grandsons and great-grandsons during my
time in the House, especially on holidays, birthdays, camping, and at sporting
events and other activities. Family functions always took priority over the
many social activities in the House.*

The House of Representatives was not an easy place to make close friends,
for several reasons. First of all, we weren't there to socialize; it simply
wasn't a priority. Second, except for the fact that we were elected members
of Congress, we had little in common. Third, because I was back home
in Nevada so often, like most members who took advantage of breaks to
return to their districts, there were few opportunities to get together on
weekends. Finally, even those occasions when we were brought together
away from work—the almost nightly receptions when we were in session,
for example—were more of an opportunity to grab something to eat
before going back into session than they were to make friends. Mostly,
I got to know other congressmen through my committee assignments,

classmate meetings, Republican organizations, and occasional trips. The congressmen I came to know best were those with whom I served on committees. My major committee for several terms was Interior, and the Republicans were in the minority the whole time I was on this committee. When I first arrived, there were twenty-eight Democrats and fourteen Republicans on the committee.

Our first chairman was Democrat Morris "Mo" Udall, while Republican Manuel Lujan was the ranking minority leader. As was the case in most committees, our battles usually split along party lines. The Interior Committee, because of the nature of its work, tended to attract Democrats who were more conservative than their leadership. My occasional allies included Democrats like Chic Kazen; Phil Sharp (who told me I reminded him of his mother); Austin Murphy, who represented a coal mining constituency; Ray Kogovsek; Beverly Byron, and Alan Mollohan, who had worked for Consolidated Coal before being elected to Congress. Western Republican members included Jim Hansen and Dan Marriott, Don Young, Larry Craig, Ron Marlenee, Dick Cheney, Bob Lagomarsino, Chip Pashayan, Hank Brown, Denny Smith, John McCain, and me. We worked together to present a united front on natural resource issues important to the West. Republican Bill Emerson was not truly a westerner, but he was helpful. He stands out in my mind because he chain-smoked in committee; he ultimately died from lung cancer. Meetings, meetings, meetings. . . . Jim Hansen held meetings to coordinate Republican efforts before major votes. When Don Hodel, an outgoing, friendly man and a strong conservative, was secretary of the interior, he often held breakfast meetings at his office with us. Dick Cheney, while he was in Congress, also held small meetings to help individual congressmen. Cheney became an important ally of mine because we had similar views, being westerners from small states. Later, of course, he became secretary of defense under the first President Bush and vice president under the second President Bush. Neither president could have chosen a better person. Dick is tough, knowledgeable, and a great American.

Interior subcommittees met three days a week, with full committee hearings on Tuesdays. Full committee meetings usually lasted five to six hours. The first hearings during any session involved budget matters; administration officials, led by the secretary of the interior, presented their

At a Republican Policy Committee meeting at the Capitol in 1993, I am greeting
Secretary of Defense Dick Cheney. Dick and I were political allies from the time we
served together on the Interior Committee. President George W. Bush could not have
selected a better person to serve as his vice president.
Collection of Barbara F. Vucanovich

budgets for our approval. Each secretary was treated differently by the
committee. Republicans Jim Watt and Don Hodel were given a hard time
by the Democrats. Manuel Lujan, who succeeded Hodel, was well received
by both sides mainly because he was a former member of the committee.
Democrat Bruce Babbitt, although from Arizona, made most everyone
from the West upset by his views on western issues.

Don Young and Ron Marlenee were hard-boiled and tough when
dealing with equally hard-nosed Democrats like George Miller, John
Seiberling, Jim Florio, Ed Markey, Bruce Vento, Pete DeFazio, Jim
Weaver, Sam Gejdenson, and Jerry Huckabee. Nick Rahall was always
difficult to deal with on mining issues because the mining in his district
was not like mining in Nevada. Ironically, some of the toughest fights I
had in the House came from a fellow Republican—Ralph Regula—who
was constantly trying to reform the Mining Law of 1872 in a way that was
not in Nevada's best interests. We served together on the Appropriations
Committee's Interior subcommittee. Since he was a moderate and a strong
environmentalist, we were on opposite sides of most issues. Ralph was

one of the senior Republicans in the House, having been elected in 1972. He liked to work with Democrats to craft legislation and tried to avoid ideological confrontations. In floor debates on Interior issues, he controlled the time allowed for Republican members to speak. Very often, he kept my time short and seldom spoke in support of my positions on mining and other resource issues. I never felt his treatment of me was personal; it just reflected the fact that he was more moderate than I was.

The second group of members I had the most contact with were my Republican classmates, from the Class of 1982. There were Democrat members of the class, too, but we didn't have a lot in common. There is no assigned seating on the floor of the House of Representatives, so during the floor sessions I often sat with fellow Republican classmates Herb Bateman, Steve Bartlett, and Bob Smith. Bob's wife, Kay, was active in the Congressional Wives Club. George attended their meetings too, because there was no "Congressional Husbands Club," and Kay took him under her wing. (As more women were elected to the House, the name of the organization was changed to "Congressional Spouses.") Shared interests also brought me together with other Republicans. Often George and I attended ball games and harness racing events with Mike Bilirakis and his wife, Evelyn. Other Republicans I got to know well were Tom Lewis and Connie Mack. Both of their wives were breast cancer survivors, too.

And I got to know the members who shared the same office building. The more senior members of Congress had offices in the Rayburn Building. The Cannon and Longworth buildings, where the freshman and sophomore offices were located, were next to Rayburn on the House side of the Capitol. Consequently, I saw my classmates and those close in seniority in the elevators and walking back and forth to the Capitol for votes. It was an easy time to strike up a conversation with members of both parties.

One might think it was common to join fellow members of Congress for lunch during the workday, but it usually wasn't convenient. Our work hours were very odd, and we frequently had meetings with constituents. It wasn't unusual for me to grab a sandwich at my desk in the office. Sometimes I ate lunch in the official dining room in the Capitol, but that was a partisan experience, believe it or not. There was one table set aside for Republicans and one for Democrats. When we ate alone, we sat at our party's table. The dining rooms were open to the public, but were reserved exclusively for members from noon to one o'clock. There were also private dining rooms where special meetings were hosted, often with members of the administration or with other dignitaries.

Another place to get food was in the cloakrooms. Each party had a cloakroom with a snack bar. The menu wasn't imaginative, but the service was unique. We sat in overstuffed chairs while our food was served on a wooden board that rested on our laps. Later in my tenure, a cafeteria opened in the Capitol, where the food was served buffet style. It was a place to get a quick bite to eat before going back to vote. This restaurant was more bipartisan and closed to the public. We could sit down in any open seat whether we knew the others at the table or not. Even there, if we had a choice we gravitated toward members of our own party and people we knew.

Nevada Mates

When I arrived in Congress in 1983, the senior member of the Nevada delegation was Senator Paul Laxalt; the other members were all newly elected, including Republican senator Chic Hecht, Democrat congressman Harry Reid, and me. That gave us three Republicans and one Democrat. Because we were a small state, greatly outnumbered in voting strength, it was important that we have a united front on issues important to Nevada, so we worked together. Paul was, of course, our leader and usually our spokesman, and we met and discussed the issues before we talked to the press.

All of that changed when Paul retired in 1986 and Harry Reid succeeded him in the Senate. Harry was replaced in the House by Democrat Jim Bilbray and for that one term the delegation was evenly split, with one Republican and one Democrat in each house. In 1988 Dick Bryan defeated Chic in his reelection effort, and I became the lone Republican in the delegation. A member of the news media asked me if I was concerned about serving with these three Democrat men. I replied something along the lines that I'd raised three boys, so I was confident that I could handle these three Democrats too.

Things certainly were different, however, and I sometimes found myself

In January 1983, shortly after I was sworn in as a member of the House, I met with other Nevada officeholders, past and present. We are standing in Paul Laxalt's Senate Office. *Left to right:* Governor Dick Bryan, Senator Chic Hecht, former member of Congress Jim Santini, and Senator Paul Laxalt. Missing from the photograph is Congressman Harry Reid. Collection of Barbara F. Vucanovich

the odd woman out. We still met as a delegation on Nevada issues, but it was not as bipartisan as it had been. Often I was not even included in the Wednesday luncheons that Harry arranged, especially when an issue that he considered partisan was going to be discussed. In 1994 John Ensign defeated Bilbray, and that left our delegation as all Republican in the House and all Democratic in the Senate. We still caucused as a state, but usually only on issues upon which we agreed.

During all the years I was in Congress, our entire delegation would join to testify before House and Senate committees on Nevada issues. For these occasions, our staffs worked together so we wouldn't repeat the same testimony. We were united on our issues, and for the most part the issues are not partisan. Since we were such a small state, our delegation, when testifying, included not only the senators and the congressmen but often the governor as well. In the larger states, depending on the issue, the governor and only a few of the congressmen and senators testified together.

In describing my Nevada colleagues, I have no reason to be critical of any of them. We may have had different opinions on policy, but we were collegial. All of them were courteous and cordial to me. Every member of the Nevada delegation I served with had a distinct personality, style, strengths, and shortcomings, including myself. Let's face it, there are few saints in this world, much less in Congress.

There were no political mavericks in the Nevada delegation, and everyone pretty much supported his or her respective party's agenda. We had one thing in common, however: We cared about Nevada and Nevadans. That was number one on all of our agendas. That was not to say that we agreed on all issues; we didn't.

Chic, John, and I were the non-lawyers in our delegation, while Paul, Harry, Dick, and Jim were attorneys. Except for John and me, all had served in elected offices before they were elected to Congress.

John never told me about any of his difficulties in adjusting to congressional life, but early in my first session, a funny incident happened to me that showed me how much I had to learn. One evening I was sitting on the floor listening to the debate, when the Speaker said, "The committee rises," and everyone left the chamber except me because at that time I didn't understand all of the legislative procedures. Another member finally explained to me that the debate was over for the night with nothing resolved. Gradually, I learned the rules.

Paul Laxalt

Paul Laxalt continued his active interest in the Republican Party from his early days in Carson City to his time in Washington. During Ronald Reagan's presidency, Paul was general chairman of the Republican National Committee, with Frank Fahrenkopf of Reno running the day-to-day operations. With Paul's close friend Ronald Reagan in the White House, naturally the delegation strongly supported the president's conservative agenda. The Democrats controlled the House, so it was difficult going on some issues.

When Paul was in the Senate, he helped Reagan get his programs through Congress. It helped that Paul was friendly with both Republicans and Democrats, including Teddy Kennedy, and that he played tennis with Bennett Johnson and Patrick Leahy. Even with the people who opposed him on issues, he forged good personal relationships. That was helpful to all of us and to Nevada.

Paul's personality was the foundation of his success. Charismatic, handsome, warm, and outgoing, often with a twinkle in his eye, he loved to tease his friends and supporters. What impressed me most was that he included everyone who was affected by a decision in meetings of the Nevada delegation and the Republican Party. He may have had an idea of the outcome he sought, but he solicited and listened to everyone's opinions before arriving at a conclusion. He made everyone feel like part of his team. Paul is comfortable with who he is, as evidenced by the fact he was one of the few to wear cowboy boots in Washington, D.C., and not be concerned that they weren't regular apparel on "the Hill."

Chic Hecht

Chic Hecht was and is a great friend. He owned a western apparel store in Las Vegas, and I first got to know him when he was in the state senate while Paul was governor. Small in stature, Chic has a big capacity to be a loyal friend, and he truly enjoyed public service. He had strong family ties and kept in close touch with his father, who lived to be almost a hundred years old. He was Chic's role model. Chic was also a hands-on father and very involved in raising his two daughters.

When Chic ran for the U.S. Senate in 1982 against Howard Cannon, most people didn't give him much of a chance. George and I supported him with the maximum campaign contributions allowed, and Chic never forgot it. Chic was a humble man, and he felt that the odds were always against him, so he worked doubly hard to make a difference for Nevada. While he was in the Senate, we worked together on all kinds of issues.

He was particularly proud of his association with Ronald Reagan and almost always voted with the president. Although Chic was proud of his Jewish heritage, one of the things that hurt his reelection effort was his support of the president on issues that some claimed were against the national interests of Israel. For example, he was never forgiven for his vote to sell planes to the Saudis, who were considered enemies of Israel.

Another thing that hurt his reelection campaign was that he wasn't a good speaker, and the media blew some of his comments completely out of proportion. He certainly was not a born politician, and when Dick Bryan ran against him, Chic was no match for Dick's second nature as a politician. I don't mean that in a negative way. Dick remembers names and was genuinely interested in people. Chic was interested in people, but he just didn't have the knack for names and faces that Dick did. Dick was one of the best campaigners in the state and did not miss many events. On the other hand, Chic didn't like to fly in small planes, so he had volunteers drive him around the state to events. As a result, he missed some gatherings that might have made the difference in the election results. (In a statewide race, flying in small planes is a given if you expect to attend all the events.) Finally, I think Chic received some bad advice in the campaign and made a mistake in Washoe County by not sending his volunteers door-to-door with his literature the week before the election. As a result, he lost in Reno and lost the race.

After he left office, President Bush appointed him ambassador to the Bahamas, where he served until Clinton became president. Chic continues to work on behalf of others and is an unbelievably generous person. He financed a synagogue in Israel after he retired. Without a doubt, Chic's strengths are his loyalty and his work ethic.

Harry Reid

I first remember Harry Reid from his losing campaign against Paul Laxalt in 1974, but his political history in Nevada goes back to the 1960s, when he and Dick Bryan, both young men then, served in the state legislature. In fact, in Las Vegas they were known as the "Gold Dust Twins." Harry's future seemed bright when he was elected lieutenant governor under Mike O'Callaghan in 1970. After his narrow defeat for the Senate by Laxalt in 1974, he returned home to Las Vegas and ran for mayor. He lost again, and after that I think most people figured he wouldn't continue to pursue a political future. But after serving as chair of the Nevada Gaming Commission, he was elected to Congress when Nevada was given a second congressional seat in 1982, the same year I was elected. Four years later he was elected to an open seat in the Senate.

While our relationship during the difficult 1974 Laxalt-Reid race was awkward at best, when we served in Washington things improved as we worked together on Nevada issues. Harry was particularly responsive on the mining and water issues that are important to the state. He was aware of his constituents' concerns and was usually successful in prodding his fellow Democrats to pass his legislation. An exception was Yucca Mountain— Nevada's four votes can't compete with the votes from the numerous states that want to get rid of their nuclear waste. Fair-complexioned Harry is not a big man, but he is a former amateur boxer. He stays physically active, running and working out regularly. Harry is not as outgoing as Dick Bryan. Probably because he is a Mormon, he is more conservative on social issues than Dick, although not as conservative as I was. I would not describe Harry as a particularly aggressive personality, but he was a student of the political process and the congressional system. He was successful in the House and later in the Senate. He figured out early in his service how to get appointed to serve on the committees that made a difference in advancing up the Democrat hierarchy in leadership. He was generous with his power in helping others, who in turn helped him.

When he was the leader of the Nevada delegation, he tried to control and influence conclusions, a change from Paul's open discussions. On the other hand, if the Nevada newspapers are to be believed, Harry also tries to control the Democrat Party in Nevada, something Paul did with the Republican Party.

One of the biggest problems between us occurred in 1986, when he was running for the Senate. I filed a complaint accusing him of misusing his congressional "franking" privilege by mailing a letter from his Washington office to all the voters in Nevada, including those in my district, outside his Southern Nevada district, which is against House Rules. Needless to say, Harry wasn't happy with me. He may have finally forgiven me, however, because when legislation was proposed to name the federal post office in Reno after me, he supported it.

As the Democrat whip in the Senate and now minority leader, he is in a position to influence a great deal of legislation, and he may be Nevada's most influential senator after Paul Laxalt. Of course, because of the positions he held, that meant he had to be a lot more partisan. Harry's strength was his understanding of the congressional process and how to use it to gain power for himself and Nevada.

Dick Bryan

Dick Bryan was the attorney general of Nevada when I first met him. Although he was the state's attorney, he rarely wore the lawyer's "uniform" of dark suit, white shirt, and conservative tie, preferring light-colored suits or sport jackets. He has sandy hair and is of average build, but I'm not aware of his being particularly athletic. After his election to the Senate in 1988, he was cordial to me and others, seldom partisan. We worked together for the good of the state.

Dick staked out issues that were different from those of the rest of our delegation. For instance, he served on the Banking, Housing, and Urban Affairs Committee and the Commerce, Science, and Transportation Committee—not traditional committees sought by Nevada legislators. The biggest issue Dick pushed was the CAFÉ (Corporate Average Fuel Economy) standards to increase the fuel efficiency of American-made automobiles. I'm not sure how that benefited Nevada, but he sure made the senators from Michigan and other states that manufactured automobiles mad. Although he was unquestionably of a Democrat philosophy, he voted for the Gulf War resolution and supported a balanced budget constitutional amendment, both of which were popular issues in Nevada.

Although Dick never discussed it with me, I thought it must have been a difficult transition from being governor and in charge of the political agenda to being the freshman in the Nevada delegation with someone else calling the shots. I don't know what he expected to accomplish in Washington, but he didn't move up the Democrat leadership ladder like Harry had.

What made Dick a successful politician was not his stands on the issues but how he related to people. He impressed me as an exceptionally good campaigner who kept in touch with Nevadans. Whenever he saw me, he was friendly and interested in my family, asking about them by name. He was just as interested in the families of everyone else in Nevada that he met. The people couldn't help but like him and vote for him.

Jim Bilbray

Jim Bilbray served two terms in the House with me, representing Southern Nevada. We worked together on the Nevada issues that were important to his district, but he wasn't much interested in my natural resources issues. Once, at a meeting with about fifty mining lobbyists, speaking after I did, he told them without any shame that he didn't care about them or their concerns because he didn't have any mines or miners in his district. Every person in the audience looked like he'd been slapped in the face. I suppose he was trying to be honest, but I don't think he realized how insensitive he sounded. Jim was always in the majority party when he was in the state senate and in the House, so he was comfortable being extremely partisan.

Outspoken, abrasive, and opinionated, Jim was the most partisan of the members of the Nevada delegation with whom I served. He made no effort to be cordial and struck me as a Democrat political activist who made no effort to work with Republicans, unlike Harry and Dick.

John Ensign

I first met veterinarian John Ensign and his wife, Darlene, when he was exploring a possible candidacy for Congress. George and I encouraged him to run and offered our assistance in any way they needed. Darlene was reluctant to move to Washington, and we talked about the pressures on one's family and marriage that come with serving in Washington. We discussed the merits of moving the family to Washington, rather than having them stay in Las Vegas. George told them about the life of the spouse of a representative. There are demands on your personal life that people don't realize when they first run, such as the loss of personal time and the lack of privacy that are the nature of the job. Everything you say or do has the potential of being covered by the media—not to mention the times they misquote you.

John was handsome and well dressed. Whether by his selection or Darlene's, his suits, shirts, and ties were always color-coordinated. He had a flair for dressing well that the lawyers in the delegation did not possess.

I made my Washington office available to him when he was first elected, before he moved into his own office. My staff assisted him in setting up his office and "learning the ropes" on the Hill. I remember one night we were working late again after several late nights already because the Republicans were under a lot of pressure to pass the Contract with America. I asked him how he was doing, was he eating properly and was he getting enough rest. He looked at me, rather surprised; after all, he was about half my age. He couldn't believe I was concerned about the pressure on him. He said he was fine and then asked, "What about you?"

John was a thoughtful young man. Before he came to Congress, he taught Bible classes and often read from the Bible. I saw him maybe ten to twelve times a day when I was in Congress. We discussed our positions before voting on Nevada issues, but he had an independent streak and often voted with his 1994 conservative classmates against the Republican leadership. John had an advantage that I didn't have when I started my terms in the House: He arrived when the Republicans were in the majority. He had strong support from groups across the country, so he got a seat on the important Ways and Means Committee his first year, an unheard-of honor for a freshman.

John narrowly lost to Harry Reid when he tried to move up to the Senate in 1998, but he was not discouraged by the experience. When Dick Bryan retired, John ran again in 2000 and was elected to the Senate. He was successful because he is energetic, enthusiastic, and a quick study in learning the legislative process and staying knowledgeable about the issues that are important to Nevada.

California Mates

Nevada House members, because they are few in number, frequently look to larger states for allies on issues that are important to our state. During the 1983–84 session, since I was the only Republican in the House from Nevada, I was invited by Dave Dreier and Jerry Lewis to join the California Republican Caucus. It was nice to be included, but more importantly it gave me some needed help in the House on issues that mattered at home.

Carlos Moorhead, chair of the California Caucus, had one idiosyncrasy. He allowed conservative congressman Bob Dornan to drone on at every meeting, a time referred to as the "Dornan Hour." The caucus met a couple of times a month, or called special meetings on important issues. We met on the floor or in the Republican whip's office, right off the floor. I met with the California delegation throughout the time I was in Congress, even after John Ensign replaced Jim Bilbray and I was no longer the only Nevada Republican in the House.

The issues common to California and Nevada were the border problems, such as development at Lake Tahoe and protection of the unique environment in Death Valley. The two members that were helpful on agricultural issues were Gene Chappie and Norm Shumway, who represented agricultural districts. Bob Lagomarsino and Chip Pashayan were my allies on the Interior Committee.

Jerry Lewis was one of my strongest supporters in the House. When he became the chair of the subcommittee on the Veterans Administration, Housing and Urban Development, and Independent Agencies (Space) of the Appropriations Committee, he arranged for me to be his vice chair. A strong conservative on economic issues, he was a moderate on social issues. That didn't stop him from helping me advance in Congress.

House Leadership

Seniority is no longer as important in the House as it once was, but it is still extremely important that you have a good relationship with House leadership. I enjoyed working with Massachusetts congressman Tip O'Neill when he was Speaker of the House. He was a typical friendly Irish politician (although unable to remember anyone's name).

One of his successors as Speaker was much more difficult to work with. Jim Wright of Texas was extremely partisan and ran roughshod over everyone. If there was a nice way to do something, he didn't do it that way. Most members I dealt with were pleasant in their manner even though they might differ with you. When ethics violations caused him to be dethroned by Newt Gingrich, he was very bitter, but I didn't feel sorry for him.

From Washington State, Tom Foley, the most thoughtful of the Democrat speakers, was a gentleman, pleasant and articulate. He was forced by his own members to be partisan, however. I think if he had been left to his own devices he would have been more bipartisan. His wife, who ran his office as a volunteer, was more partisan than Tom, and she controlled a lot of the agenda.

The Democrat Speakers were rarely on the floor, except for ceremonial times, such as at the opening and closing sessions. Their Capitol offices were right next door to the floor, so if they were needed they could be there.

Republican Newt Gingrich was the brightest of all the Speakers with whom I served, and I knew him well. He was more active in the day-to-day operations of the House and more accessible than the Democrat Speakers. The goal that Newt pursued for more than twenty years was to be Speaker of the House. I'm sure no one ever expected it to happen, but it did. In hindsight, Newt didn't seem surprised when Republicans gained a majority in the House that year. In my mind, he changed the direction of American politics and was instrumental in shaping American political thought for many years.

Bob Michel was the minority leader during my time in Congress when the Republicans were in the minority. A dignified man, he was personally offended if people got ugly in their disagreements. He tried to help everyone and was accessible. He had a good staff, especially Billy Pitts, who helped him challenge the majority from time to time. Bob was conservative, but he had been in the minority for so long that he spent years compromising to get things done. He believed that if we were going to work with the other side, we could not be confrontational. In his efforts to get along, he often played golf with Speaker Tip O'Neill.

Trent Lott, while he was in the House, was not happy to be serving in Bob Michel's shadow. He was ambitious and hardworking, and he did his job on the floor. He was a typical Southern gentleman, a "young" good old boy. He did a good job as the Republican whip and never pressured me or anyone else unless he had to do it to get the votes.

In general, my House mates were usually friendly and knowledgeable. Most members of the House had a tendency to be provincial and concerned with the needs of their own districts, as was appropriate. A successful member of the House, regardless of party, was one who was willing to listen, even while standing firm on personal convictions. Party politics were extremely important, and most members of Congress respected you for your political philosophy, even if they didn't agree with it. But it was also important to have the ability to find solutions for problems without trampling upon other members of Congress. Those who succeeded were the ones who built consensus, who worked hard to earn the respect of their peers, and who kept their word when they dealt with their colleagues. The quickest way to fail in Congress was not to do your homework and to earn a reputation as two-faced or unable to keep a commitment.

PART IV

Back in the Great State of Nebraska

CHAPTER SIXTEEN

In the Other House
(The White House)

Few Americans meet a president, much less spend any time with one. I met eight, some before I was elected to Congress and some when I was in the House. Although I didn't necessarily introduce them, some of my children and grandchildren met a few of the presidents, too. Patty met Richard Nixon, Jerry Ford, Ronald Reagan, the first George Bush, and Bill Clinton. Tommy and Susie met Richard Nixon, and Susie also met Ronald Reagan. Grandchildren Elisa and Reynolds met the first George Bush, and Reynolds and Mike Jr. attended his first inauguration. My grandson Patrick escorted me to a White House dinner when Bill Clinton was president. I'm not sure which presidents my family members liked the most, but my favorite was President Ronald Reagan. I served with him the longest and knew him the best.

Because of my position in public life during the 1980s and 1990s, and because I was active in politics before that, I met many of the presidents since Franklin D. Roosevelt, all except Truman, Kennedy, and Johnson. Although candidates don't often come to Nevada, which has only a few electoral votes, I met a surprising number of presidents (and those who wanted to be president) while they were campaigning in our state.

I've often heard the argument that if Nevada held a presidential primary election, candidates would visit the state more often. I'm not sure that is true, but the fact is they do visit Nevada, though admittedly mostly on their way to and from California. It happens more and more often now that Las Vegas is a major population center and the source of considerable campaign contributions. Still, my path frequently crossed those of presidents and candidates.

I met Franklin Roosevelt, Dwight David Eisenhower, and Jimmy Carter before they became president. The meeting with Carter was very brief, when he was campaigning in Reno in 1976. It was just a handshake, but I count him on the list of presidents I've met. My contacts with the others were more substantial.

I met both Roosevelt and Eisenhower when I was a child in New York State. My parents were Roosevelt supporters, and he was governor of New York when I met him. That would have been about 1930, after he appointed my father chief engineer of the New York State Department of Public Works. So, of course, I knew he was a very important man.

I knew Eisenhower as an army general and a friend of my family. We would see him often at West Point reunions or social gatherings. I would later meet Ike when he was president, during the Republican National Convention in San Francisco in 1956. When we were introduced, he remembered me when I told him I was Tom Farrell's daughter. Ike was always regarded as a national hero because of his World War II leadership.

The presidents I had the closest working relationships with were Richard Nixon, Ronald Reagan, and George H. W. Bush. I am proud to consider them friends, as well as political allies.

Richard Nixon

I also met Richard Nixon during the 1956 Republican National Convention at the San Francisco Civic Center, when he was vice president. Over the years I would see him at conventions, on the campaign trail, and when I was in Congress, after he had left the White House. I found him much different in person than his rather aloof public image suggested. He was always warm and pleasant to talk to and invariably well versed in Nevada issues, candidates, and campaigns. Part of that may have been because his wife, Pat, was a Nevada native, born in White Pine County near Ely.

When Nixon ran for president in 1960, I saw him at the huge Nevada Republican Party rally for him in Reno. Considering that Nevada Democrats outnumbered Republicans by a two-to-one margin at that

Gy Bush   *Ronald Reagan*   *Jimmy Carter*   *Gerald R. Ford*   *Richard Nixon*

In this photo, taken at the Ronald Reagan Presidential Library in California, are some of the presidents I knew or met. *Left to right:* George H. W. Bush, Ronald Reagan, Jimmy Carter, Gerald Ford, and Richard Nixon. I also knew Franklin Delano Roosevelt and Dwight David Eisenhower, and I have met George W. Bush. While I was in Congress, I served with Presidents Ronald Reagan, the first George Bush, and Bill Clinton. Collection of Barbara F. Vucanovich

time, it was astonishing to me that he lost Nevada to John F. Kennedy by fewer than 2,500 votes.

He also visited Reno when he was campaigning for president in 1968. We held a rally for him at the new Centennial Coliseum (now the Reno-Sparks Convention Center). I took my daughter Susie to meet him, and I still have a picture of Nixon down on his knees talking to my eight-year-old. He would go on to win Nevada's three electoral votes that year, at that time the only Republican other than Eisenhower to carry Nevada since 1928. I believe that helped set the stage for Republican successes in future years.

At his peak, before Watergate, Nixon was popular with the Republicans, and I felt comfortable with him. He always remembered me when we met. He was attentive when he spoke with a person, and I never ceased to be amazed by his knowledge of Nevada politics. He treated Nevada as if it was important, even with its small population and Democrat majority in those days. Of all the presidents and vice presidents I met, only Ronald Reagan understood Nevada better.

The first presidential inauguration George and I attended was Nixon's, on January 20, 1969. It was the first of several we would attend, although at the time we had no idea what the future held. It was an exciting time for Republicans because it marked a return of the GOP (Grand Old Party) to the White House after eight years of Kennedy and Johnson. There were huge crowds, and George and I attended one of the inaugural balls, in a downtown hotel, where we saw the new president and the first lady standing in a private box, shaking hands with the people.

Before, during, and after his presidency, Richard Nixon loved politics and national and international affairs. When I was in Congress, Newt Gingrich arranged for members of the Conservative Opportunity Society to meet with Nixon at a New York hotel. We talked for almost two hours about his views of what was happening in the country and the world. He was well informed, and his insights were helpful to an understanding of the entire political scene.

In March 1993, Nixon visited Washington and spoke to the Republicans in the Ways and Means Committee room. When he met me, he said, "Oh, yes, Barbara, you are from Pat's home state." He talked about Nevada politics and politicians and, as usual, grasped what was happening in our state.

After Nixon died on April 22, 1994, I attended his funeral in Whittier, California, at his presidential library. Congress canceled its sessions, and travel arrangements were made for any members of Congress who wished to go to the funeral, although I don't recall that many members attended. Although Nixon will be most remembered for Watergate, I believe history will record that he was a good president, especially in the area of international relations.

Gerald Ford

Gerald Ford was a frequent visitor to Nevada for Lincoln Day dinners and other events while he was a member of the House of Representatives from Michigan, long before national developments propelled him into the White House. I first met him when he spoke at a Lincoln Day dinner in Carson City in the 1950s. Ford always gave the traditional Republican speech, supporting lower taxes and government spending and states' rights, and urging people to vote for the candidates who wanted to keep the people's money in their own pockets.

Later on, Ford took his position as House minority leader seriously, traveling all over the country to assist Republicans in their campaigns, sometimes appearing in several states in a single day. He would fly into town on a regularly scheduled airline, most often traveling by himself.

Because of his hectic travel schedule (and because it was easy to do), he sometimes got mixed up about where he was. I remember two occasions when he made that mistake. Once he said, "It is great to be back in the great state of Nebraska." Another time he said, "It is great to be back in the great state of Montana." In both instances he repeated the slip of the tongue four or five more times in his speech, never aware that he had made a mistake. On one of these occasions I had taken my father, a Democrat, to meet Ford and listen to his speech. Dad thought Ford's blunders were hilarious.

After I was elected to Congress, I understood how Ford could have been confused about where he was. As I traveled the state campaigning, I learned that one banquet room looked like any other after I'd given five speeches that day. Your notes must be in perfect order for local references, or you'd better not make any. I've seen politicians make these mistakes often on the campaign trail. Gerald Ford wasn't alone.

A big man, more than six feet tall, Ford was friendly, outgoing, wholesome, and warm. He was a master politician and went out of his way to recognize people. He was even well respected by the media until he pardoned Richard Nixon after the Watergate scandal. Most analysts now think it was the right thing for the country, but it hurt his political career.

I don't remember if Ford came to Reno when he was running for president in 1976. Nevada was pretty much Ronald Reagan country because of Reagan's friendship with Paul Laxalt. In Nevada's Presidential Preference Primary Election that year, Reagan carried the state by more than a two-to-one margin. All the Nevada delegates to the Republican National Convention were committed to Ronald Reagan, except Attorney General Bob List and state Republican chairman Frank Fahrenkopf.

Ronald Reagan

A case can be made for Ronald Reagan as one of the greatest leaders of the twentieth century. Undoubtedly he was one of our greatest presidents. A consummate politician, tall, slender, and athletically built, he looked and acted like a president. His sense of humor was always apparent, and he could charm anyone he met, even Democrats like Congressman Tip O'Neill, Dan Rostenkowski, and others. From Ronald Reagan, I learned to be true to my beliefs and that it isn't necessary to be disagreeable in order to disagree with others. Personally, what I liked most about him was his sunny disposition, his good nature, and his sense of humor. What surprised me about him was his youthfulness.

The first time I met Reagan was in 1976, when he ran unsuccessfully for president. Paul Laxalt was his national campaign chairman and included George and me in many campaign activities, among them social events and intimate gatherings in Paul's hotel suite during the Republican National Convention. In 1980 we were also heavily involved in helping to organize Nevada for both Reagan's and Laxalt's reelection.

I attended both of Ronald Reagan's inaugurations, in 1981 and 1985. During the first I was working for Laxalt, and my responsibilities included finding tickets for Nevadans to attend events. There were far more requests for tickets than could be filled. We were able to secure 70 inaugural ball tickets, but we had requests for 280. For the inaugural gala, we had 13 tickets and 200 requests. Unfortunately, George and I were not among the lucky 13 who attended the gala, although we did attend an inaugural ball at the Kennedy Center.

It was a high honor when President Reagan invited me to fly on *Air Force One* from Andrews Air Force Base to Las Vegas to campaign for U.S. Senate candidate Jim Santini on June 24, 1986. The plane was a

Boeing 707, with impressive service provided by members of the military. Mementos were given out with the Air Force One emblem on them— agendas, matches, plastic glasses, napkins, and jelly beans. The president had a suite in the front of the plane with a bedroom, an office, and a galley. There was a "changing" art gallery in the presidential section of the plane, with pictures updated to reflect current events. The Secret Service members were seated just in front of the president's suite, behind the pilot and other crew. The second section of the plane was where the visitors sat, in huge, plush airline seats. Some of the seats faced one another with a table between them. The next section was for staff; it contained office equipment, work stations, fax machines, and computers. There were two other galleys, one midship and one at the far back end of the plane. The back of the plane was reserved for members of the press corps.

In my opinion, Ronald Reagan turned our country around, using his great communication skills to raise and exceed my expectations for America. I'm sure the story told about him digging through a manure pile and exclaiming, "I'm sure there's a pony in here somewhere" had more than a little truth to it. He was optimistic and upbeat even in the most challenging times. Ronald Reagan was an inspiration to most Americans after four years of "malaise" during Carter's presidency.

Unfortunately, Reagan suffered from Alzheimer's disease in his later years and had no memory of his life and times. Both Nancy and Ron were brave and open about his illness, with Nancy especially dealing with her sadness in a heartwarming way, continuing her involvement with the Reagan Library. I was privileged to attend the congressional ceremony in Washington that awarded the Congressional Gold Medal to both Nancy and Ron in 2002. She accepted the medal with grace and emotion. Unfortunately, I had a previous commitment and was unable to attend his funeral in June 2004.

George H. W. Bush

Taller than Ronald Reagan, the elder George Bush is friendly and outgoing, interested in other people. He has a great ability to remember names and faces and is comfortable meeting and talking with new people as well. He is known for keeping up with his friends and acquaintances with personal notes. I have received several such notes myself. Once I was eating lunch in the House dining room with a liberal Democrat visitor from Nevada. Bush, who was vice president at the time, was dining at the next table with several Republicans. He made it a point to come over to our table and say, "Barbara, so good to see you." My lunch guest was suitably impressed.

The first time I met George Bush was in the 1970s, when he was chairman of the Republican National Committee and he spoke to the Washoe County Republican County Convention. He visited Nevada many times over his political career, including when he was vice president and president.

When he was vice president, he and his wife, Barbara, lived on the grounds of the U.S. Naval Observatory in Washington. The house sat on a hill off a busy public street in northwest Washington, so it was gated, with tight security. It was a lovely, gracious home, with beautifully maintained grounds. When I was there, many of Barbara Bush's needlepoint projects were on display in the public rooms. Barbara is a relaxed, outgoing woman with a knack for making people feel at ease.

On September 18, 1987, I was invited to the vice president's house for a small, intimate lunch with six or eight others. It was a social event, but designed to reinforce our relationship in preparation for Bush's upcoming presidential campaign. The timing was very good from my standpoint, because up until then I had been committed to the presidential candidacy of Paul Laxalt. Paul, who had announced his candidacy the previous April, dropped out of the race just after Labor Day of 1987, so I was free to endorse Vice President Bush.

A month later I had the honor of introducing the vice president at the Western States Republican Leadership Conference in Seattle, Washington.

Bush was exceptionally well qualified, of course, and had earned the respect and loyalty of most Republicans because of his allegiance to President Reagan. That didn't mean he had no opposition; Senator Bob Dole was also running. In February 1988 I campaigned for Bush in New Hampshire, with other members of Congress. Several of us spoke at rallies, walked the streets with him shaking hands with people, and attended events in gyms, fire stations, and town halls in several small towns. The Bush victories in the primaries of 1988, and subsequently in the general election, were deserved. In February 1992, we campaigned in New Hampshire with him again in the snow and the cold, although he lost the general election that time.

Shortly after the presidential election in 1988, I learned that I was under consideration for appointment as secretary of the interior. I found out about this honor from the members of the media. I even made the "short list" of people to be considered, but I never had any direct contact with White House personnel or the president about the position. I suppose the reasons I was on the list were because I was fifth in Republican seniority on the Interior Committee and, of course, because I had supported President Bush in his successful campaign.

Naturally, when I heard I was under consideration, I gave some thought to what the appointment would mean to me. First, I would have to give up my seat in Congress, but I was relatively sure it could be held by another Republican. Second, it would be an enormous honor for Nevada, as well as for me. The appointment would recognize the importance of issues that I had championed during my years in Congress. Although I didn't do any research on the matter, I believe that up until that time no woman had held the position of secretary of the interior. In any event, I didn't spend a great deal of time thinking about this opportunity because the president soon selected another westerner.

At some point before the final recommendation was made, the president decided he didn't want to appoint sitting congressmen to his Cabinet because he needed as many "friends" as he could get in the Democrat-controlled House. I was thrilled when my friend and colleague Manuel "Manny" Lujan from New Mexico was sworn in as the new secretary on February 3, 1989. I attended Senator Bob Dole's reception for Manny in Dole's office in the Capitol. Manny had just retired from Congress and had been mentioned for the post before but had been passed over twice by President Reagan, who appointed James Watt and then William Clark in his first administration. It was flattering to be considered for the post, but I thought the president made the right choice when he nominated Manny.

One of the most unpleasant moments of my congressional career occurred in July 1989 when I broke my arm two days before I was scheduled to fly on *Air Force One* with President Bush to attend a Disabled Veterans

Aboard *Air Force One*. President George H. W. Bush and I are flying to Las Vegas,
Nevada, to attend a Disabled Veterans of America meeting in 1989.
Collection of Barbara F. Vucanovich

of America event in Las Vegas. I had been walking in the rough off the
fairway of a Washington-area golf course (looking for my brother's ball,
not mine!) when I fell and broke my humerus. It was not humorous,
however, when I had to board *Air Force One* with my arm in a sling. I took
quite a bit of good-natured kidding from the president on that trip.

Former president Bush currently serves on the Barrick Mining Company
board of directors, so he occasionally visits northeastern Nevada. I learned
from George Bush that it is wise to nurture friends and acquaintances
whose paths may cross mine many times in my life and career, as ours
have. What I liked most about him was his lack of pretense. He never
appeared to think he was better than anyone else. What impressed me the
most about him was his intelligence and also his interest in international
affairs.

George Bush was particularly interested in international affairs, and
consequently the media were able to imply that he didn't care about
domestic affairs, which contributed to his defeat by Bill Clinton in 1992.

His success in Desert Storm, driving Iraq out of Kuwait, was not enough to carry him to victory over Clinton (and Bush's campaign was hurt by the candidacy of Ross Perot as well).

George W. Bush

I may have met George W. briefly at the presidential debate in Los Angeles in 1992, but I definitely remember meeting him at a luncheon at the Republican National Convention in San Diego in 1996. We sat together at a table for eight people. I was struck by the fact that George W. has his father's mannerisms but his mother's personality. It was almost a foregone conclusion that the media would underestimate Republicans running for president, and George W. was no exception. Before September 11, 2001, the national press and many Democrats were calling George W. a buffoon, implying that he was not up to the job of being president. He proved them wrong.

It is often said that great events create great leaders, and I am sure that is the case with George W. and the events of September 11. The entire nation, if not the entire world, looked to the president and to First Lady Laura Bush for comfort and leadership—and faith—after that day. As this is written, it is too early to assess the overall George W. presidency, although he certainly will go down as one of our great leaders. I expect his second term will be as successful as his first. And, the nation will owe George W. a debt of gratitude for his ability to unite the nation after September 11.

Dan Quayle

Dan Quayle was never president, of course, but in my opinion he was qualified to serve in the White House. I was—and still am—a fan of Dan Quayle's, although the liberal media demonized him. Despite all the bad things written about him, I found just the opposite to be true. We first met when he was in the Senate, and we would see each other often at Republican functions. He was always well informed, articulate, and extremely intelligent.

I also worked with Dan and Marilyn Quayle on several cancer events. I found them both to be very friendly and informal. Marilyn was a serious

Vice President Dan Quayle and me, at the House of Representatives in our Republican Conference Room. Dan was another of my political allies in Congress, serving in the House from 1976 until 1980, when he was elected to the Senate. Dan was an outstanding conservative, and I was dismayed over the treatment he received from the liberal members of the media. Collection of Barbara F. Vucanovich

but likable woman who did her best to keep things in perspective. She was a lawyer who spoke skillfully and always seemed well informed. What I liked most about her was her ability to relate to other women as both a mother and a friend.

Vice President Quayle visited Nevada several times when he was in office. I remember that he toured a housing development in Las Vegas and afterward attended an event at the MGM Hotel and Casino. When he was running for president in 1999, I arranged a small coffee for him with local political leaders, including former governor Bob List, former attorney general Brian McKay, former state treasurer (and my daughter) Patty Cafferata, and a few other political activists. I also hosted a fund-raising reception at my home for him, on June 24, 2000, which raised more than $10,000 for his presidential bid.

I was disappointed when he withdrew from the 2000 presidential race, but the prospect of having to contest sixteen or eighteen primaries and raise millions of dollars was just too much for him. He knew he couldn't get the money. Dan called me on October 29, 2000, to thank me for my help. He recognized that even though people didn't know Texas governor George W. Bush or what he stood for, they had jumped on his bandwagon. It is still hard to understand why some campaigns take off and others don't, but if a candidate doesn't try, he or she will never know what kind of support to expect.

I learned by watching Dan Quayle how vicious and relentless the national press can be in dealing with conservatives. What I liked most about him was that he never complained about the media and continued to speak out for his beliefs and convictions.

Jimmy Carter

As I said before, I met Jimmy Carter when he visited Nevada during his quest for the presidency in 1976. He came to Reno for a rally at Idlewild Park, and George and I went to hear him because it wasn't often that you had the opportunity to see a presidential nominee. He was very upbeat, and his blue eyes sparkled when he looked you in the eye while shaking your hand. Congressman Jim Santini, then a Democrat, introduced Carter. I don't remember much of Carter's speech, but Santini's introduction was almost as long as Carter's talk.

I admit I was surprised that Carter came to Nevada, because he was too much of a southerner to appeal to Nevadans. No one gave him much of a chance in the general election, especially since the Nevada Presidential Preference Primary that year had been won easily by former California governor Jerry Brown, with Carter a distant, distant second. Voter registration in 1976 favored the Democrats by almost two to one, but Ford carried Nevada by an 8,000-vote margin, even in that post-Watergate year.

When Carter won the election, I was working for Senator Laxalt in his Reno district office and had little opportunity to get to know Carter. My impression of him was that he was insensitive to western issues. He seemed to have surrounded himself with advisors who either didn't understand or didn't care much about mining, grazing, or other resource issues important to Nevada and the West.

During Carter's term, people across the West often referred to his policies as "the War on the West," started by his criticism of the construction of the dams in the West. Carter was the catalyst for the "Sagebrush Rebellion" that swept the West in the late 1970s. Westerners in the states, with a large percentage of their lands controlled by the federal government, were tired of the "feds" dictating and controlling their wide-open spaces. The miners and ranchers led the rebellion seeking more state control of their destiny.

Among other things that Carter did, when he insisted on carrying his own suitcase I thought he tried to be too much like a "regular guy" and didn't project himself as a leader. He failed to live up to the aura of the presidency projected by so many of our presidents. It was a small point, but an indication of many of the image problems he had.

Bill Clinton

Needless to say, President Bill Clinton was not one of my favorites, although I met him several times. He was charming and charismatic, and it was easy to see why he appealed to people. Of course, we disagreed on most substantive issues, and since he is of the opposite political party, we did not spend much time together. The times I saw him or heard him speak, I thought that he didn't have any strong political or public policy beliefs. He stood in stark contrast to Ronald Reagan, who had strong convictions and never changed his positions. What Reagan said when he was governor of California in the 1960s, he said when he was president twenty years later.

Clinton, on the other hand, espoused the positions that his polls indicated were popular with the people. In early March of his first term in 1993, President Clinton and Vice President Al Gore came to the Hill and met with congressional Republicans in Statuary Hall. Clinton spoke about his agenda and how he wanted to work with Congress. I had the opportunity to say, "Mr. President, I represent a district that has a lot of mining in it. I hope you will give some consideration to mining." The president turned to Gore and said, "The vice president will be sure to help you with that."

It was the last I ever heard from the Clinton administration on mining.

The other event I participated in during Clinton's administration occurred on September 13, 1993. I was among the members of Congress sitting on the White House lawn to watch Clinton's historic attempt at the peace process between Yitzhak Rabin of Israel and Yasser Arafat of Palestine.

Al Gore

When I arrived in the House, Al Gore was a member of Congress from Tennessee. His Democrat colleagues had already nicknamed him "Prince Albert." I thought of him as self-confident and aggressive. When he was in the Senate, before he became vice president, I testified before one of his committees about nuclear waste being sent to Nevada. As I remember, he was supportive of nuclear waste coming here.

Barry Goldwater

I met Senator Barry Goldwater of Arizona in 1964 when he ran for president and was campaigning in Nevada, as I previously mentioned. Goldwater was a handsome man who wore black horn-rimmed glasses that didn't detract from his brilliant blue eyes. Of course, he was a conservative; many of us who supported him still have elephant pins with black horn-rimmed glasses as souvenirs.

Bob Dole

I don't really remember the first time I met Bob Dole, although it may have been when he ran for vice president with Gerald Ford in 1976. I specifically remember that he came to Nevada to campaign for Senator Chic Hecht in 1982. He always wore dark navy suits and usually looked rather glum. Although he had a sharp sense of humor, it hurt him because it so often was viewed as biting and sarcastic rather than warm. Nonetheless, I was fond of Dole. From him I learned that a candidate can win on matters of importance if he or she is willing to give a little on things that are less important. I liked his honesty and sincerity and that he wasn't afraid to be himself—very different from the average politician.

Jack Kemp

I met Jack Kemp when I was elected to the House and Jack was our Republican Conference chair. He was well known for his support of supply-side economics and tax cuts, but the Reagan people were suspicious of him because he sometimes voted against the president's policies. As Bob Dole's vice-presidential running mate in 1996, Jack was a contrast to the more reserved senator. Jack was an extremely outgoing, gregarious, glad-handing, backslapping, arm-around-you politician. Although he was sometimes typecast as a lightweight because he had played professional football, Jack really was an intellectual. On the podium he was intense and earnest, sometimes too much so, with a tendency to talk too long and turn people off. What I liked most about him was his easy manner and his open mind. I was surprised by his support for women in the House and his willingness to listen to our ideas and concerns.

First Lady's Luncheons

One of the best perks of being a member of Congress was the opportunity to attend social events involving the White House. The First Lady's Luncheon, held in the spring, was one example. Invited guests are members of the Congressional Club, originally wives of senators and congressmen, although now membership includes women members of Congress.

I joined in 1986, and the luncheon that year honored Nancy Reagan. I attended later luncheons honoring Barbara Bush and Hillary Clinton. The first ladies had, as expected, different speaking styles. Nancy Reagan gave a simple, pleasant speech; Barbara Bush gave a wonderful, humorous talk;

and Hillary Clinton gave a professional and businesslike performance. Each club member was allocated four tickets, and I usually took my sister Patsy and my daughters-in-law Sandra and Cathy Dillon or sometimes my women staff members.

In the White House

Occasionally, presidents held receptions at the White House to thank congressmen and senators for their support of legislation and programs. I attended one such reception held by Ronald Reagan on July 22, 1986, for those who had voted for aid to the Contras in Nicaragua. The event was held in the State Dining Room with a generous buffet supper, and everyone ate standing up. I think the idea behind this was that no one would get too comfortable and stay too long.

Among the most memorable events were the White House Christmas parties, held in early December. Every member of Congress and his or her spouse were invited. The White House was decked out with lovely Christmas decorations, and it was an opportunity to have your picture taken with the president and first lady. I attended almost every White House Christmas party during my time in Congress under the Republican presidents, but not many while Bill Clinton was in office. Ronald Reagan's parties were formal compared to George Bush's. The Christmas decorations of Barbara's needlepoint ornaments showed her interest in literacy.

Presidential Debate Commission

In 1987 I was honored to be appointed as one of the Republican members of the newly established Presidential Debate Commission. The purposes of the commission were to guarantee that there would be debates during each presidential election, to eliminate a lot of the jockeying and negotiating that usually preceded such debates, and to bring some bipartisan perspective to the process. The commission was established by an agreement between the two major parties, not by Congress.

The commission included five members each from the two major political parties, including the chairs of the parties. Besides me, the initial Republican members were Frank Fahrenkopf, a Nevadan who was the chair of the Republican National Committee; Nebraska governor Kay Orr; California senator Pete Wilson; and political activist David Norcross of New Jersey. Democrat members were Charles Mannatt, chair of the Democratic National Committee (soon replaced by Paul Kirk); Vernon Jordan; Pamela Harriman; former Senator John Culver of Iowa; and Richard Moe, a political activist. Our executive director was Janet Brown, a capable and respected woman, a hard worker who was extremely efficient.

The commission met in 1987 and early 1988 to decide which cities would host debates before the coming election, and over the next several years we held a series of meetings discussing the debate process from all perspectives. We talked about the number of debates, their length, and the schedule. We decided the selection process for the moderators and the format of each debate. We reviewed topics and questions to be asked, considering the debates from the perspective of the candidates, the media, and the public.

In 1992, after researching the format, we learned that a single moderator was more successful than a panel of people questioning the candidates. We also discussed the site-selection process and considered how to raise money to sponsor the debates.

I tried to attend at least one presidential and one vice-presidential debate each election cycle while I was on the commission, but it was difficult because I was always campaigning for my own reelection. I think that the most exciting debate was on October 13, 1988, in Los Angeles, when George Bush clearly and overwhelming won the debate over Michael Dukakis. Dukakis's answer to the first question offended many people, when he was asked if he would believe in capital punishment if his wife, Kitty, had been raped, tortured, and murdered. He never recovered from that mistake.

Serving on the commission was a wonderful experience and a great honor. It was an educational process, not a political process. Few people get to make decisions on who the moderator will be and where the presidential debates will be held or have the opportunity to see history being made firsthand.

I also believe the commission made a difference in presidential campaigns. The debates are watched by millions of Americans. The candidates don't try to dodge them anymore, although they and their consultants naturally try to control the agenda, the format, and the locations. The biggest contribution of the Presidential Debate Commission was to create an even playing field for the candidates.

I was still on the commission in 1997, after my retirement, but I soon resigned because I felt that a sitting member of Congress should be representing the House.

CHAPTER SEVENTEEN

A World Beyond the House

No matter where my travels took me as a congressman, my family continued to expand with new births and marriages. Even though I traveled beyond Washington, I still attended the family events, such as Reynolds and Becky Cafferata's wedding the same year I visited the American Territories in the South Pacific and France, 1989. Scott Anderson was born in 1986, the year I first went to Nicaragua, while his younger brother, David Anderson, was born in 1988, the year I returned to Nicaragua and also visited Bikini. Great-granddaughter Morgan Erquiaga was born just before my trip to visit the troops in Desert Storm in 1991.

My life as a congressman wasn't limited to Washington and Nevada. My position also gave me the opportunity to travel to different parts of the world, representing the United States and Nevada. It was not a major part of my life in the House, but I participated in nineteen trips over fourteen years. Of my 5,110 days in Congress, I spent fewer than 140 out of the country.

Congressional travel was an easy target for criticism by the media, and a few members may have abused the system. Most people don't understand that the vacation-style foreign "junket" had virtually disappeared by the time I arrived in Congress, the result of close scrutiny by the media and, most important, the ethics reforms pushed by Republicans in Congress in the 1980s. The reasons for travel had to meet high standards and had to be justified as appropriate to a member's duties and responsibilities. Every trip in which I participated while I was in Congress was directly related to either Nevada issues or my positions on the Interior or Appropriations Committee.

A Congressional Delegation trip—usually known by the informal designation "CODEL"—had to be approved by the House leadership. Members were invited to participate by the person managing the trip. Before departing, we received a thick binder of briefing materials on the history of each country to be visited and its relationship to the United States. Our packets included the current issues of concern; lists of the government leaders, U.S. officials, and businesspeople (American and local) we would be meeting; information on the weather, money, and customs; local maps; and a daily schedule of activities. Most trips were fully scheduled, from early-morning breakfast meetings to evening dinners, with lots of meetings, briefings, and site visits in between meals. There was very little downtime for "playing tourist." Sometimes spouses were permitted to travel with us, but they were responsible for all of their own expenses and normally kept the same schedule we did.

I traveled quite a bit before entering Congress, so I didn't feel a need to explore foreign soil just to sightsee. But as the world has grown much smaller, what happens in other countries frequently has an impact on our country. Since America does not exist in isolation, it was important to interact with and establish bridges to the leaders of other countries. Trips can be important fact-finding missions; learning about the problems of other countries and how they solve them is very helpful. The United States doesn't have a monopoly on good ideas or developing technology. I never took a trip on which I didn't learn something that helped me as a member of Congress.

The Marshall Islands and the South Pacific

From Nevada's perspective, the most important trips for me were the ones to learn about nuclear waste management and storage because of the constant debates about nuclear waste storage at the Nevada Test Site. Because of that interest, the first CODEL I arranged was to the Bikini Atoll and the Marshall Islands in the Pacific Ocean for six days in April 1988. This was a fact-finding trip arranged because the government officials in the islands had expressed an interest in storing nuclear waste, believing it would be an economic benefit to their area.

As far as I could tell, I was the first member of Congress to visit Bikini, and certainly I was the only one interested in taking this trip. George accompanied me, along with Pam Whitaker Robinson, my legislative director. The Department of the Interior and the Department of Defense have interests on these islands, so they sent staff along, as did the State Department and the House Appropriations Committee's Interior subcommittee.

In addition to my official duties, I was interested in seeing the Bikini Atoll because of my father's involvement with the testing of atomic and hydrogen bombs nearby during and after World War II. I took my father's journal with me and read his observations about the effects of the bombs that were detonated on several battleships, including the uss *Nevada,* in July 1946. It was moving to visit the same area my father had seen four decades before.

Bikini, an atoll of no more than two square miles in size, is covered by a rain forest where fruit grows wild. It was still uninhabited and no one stayed for long or ate the fruit because of the remaining contamination from the bomb testing. All meals, water, and other foods were brought in from elsewhere. We stayed on a boat provided by the Department of the Interior for the two days we were on Bikini, wading to land each day. (A picture of me wading ashore at Bikini appeared in some of the newspapers in Nevada, drawing good-natured comparisons to MacArthur returning to the Philippines.) The boat was fairly small, with an upper deck for daily activities and a lower level with about half a dozen small staterooms. We rode atvs around the island to visit the buildings, which were mainly lean-to shacks.

During our stay in the Marshall Islands, part of the U.S. Trust Territories, I was briefed on the status of the economy and the governing body and met with local officials. En route home from this trip, we stopped in Maui and met with Marshall Islands president Amato Kabua to discuss a feasibility study he wanted on locating nuclear waste on some of his islands. The islands he was interested in were environmentally stable and remote from human populations, and some were already contaminated with radioactive materials from the previous nuclear weapons tests. Yet, because of environmental, transportation, and other concerns, it was doubtful that nuclear waste would ever find a home in the Marshall Islands. As a result of my trip, I was able to advise the Interior Committee on the needs and concerns of the islanders.

I had an opportunity to return to the islands the following February as part of a ten-day Interior Committee trip to the South Pacific led by Democrat congressman Mo Udall. The Interior Committee had oversight for the U.S. Territories and some of the islanders were concerned about how Congress dealt with local industries and environmental concerns.

We traveled to Guam, Saipan, Palau, American Samoa, and the Marshall Islands, then visited New Zealand and Australia, meeting with government officials to discuss issues of mutual concern. Each location had different needs, but generally looked to America for help in solving their problems. For example, American Samoa wanted $7.5 million to improve the petroleum storage facilities built by the United States during World War II, the only source of petroleum in the South Pacific for our military. Guam was seeking federal funds of approximately $75 million to improve its port and $4 million to improve its hospital.

Congressional delegates Ben Blaz of Guam and Eni Faleomavaega of American Samoa were with us on the trip. Both were members of Congress and sat on the Interior Committee, although, as with other delegates (such as the representative of the District of Columbia), they were allowed to vote only in committee and not on the floor. Secretary of the Interior Manuel Lujan and his wife, Jean, also joined us on the trip.

On Guam, I was surprised to learn of strong disagreement among residents about their governing status. Some wanted to remain a commonwealth, and others wanted more involvement with the United States, including possible statehood.

The Republic of Palau, made up of about two hundred islands and islets, was the home of a major Japanese naval base in World War II that was captured by American forces. One of the highlights of the visit there was a boat trip to the tuna "farms" on the Rock Islands. The water was so clear you could look down and see boats that had sunk many years ago.

After Palau, we flew to Australia, where we discussed proposals for

George and I are talking to Secretary of the Interior Manuel Lujan on a Bureau of Land Management congressional fishing trip on the Potomac River in 1991. Manny was another ally of mine when we served together on the Interior Committee. I attended Senator Bob Dole's reception for Manny after he was sworn in as George Bush's secretary of the interior. Collection of Barbara F. Vucanovich

nuclear free zones at sea and in their ports and the implications of visits by our reactor-powered U.S. Navy ships. In New Zealand we studied its sheep industry and the country's national parks system and were briefed on research programs in the Antarctic.

Nuclear Waste

In August 1995 I took part in a trip to visit nuclear power facilities in Russia, the Ukraine, and France. The trip, to study how these countries dealt with nuclear waste, was organized by Congressman John Myers, a Republican and chair of the Appropriations Energy and Water Development subcommittee. (Russia was particularly memorable, for a number of reasons, discussed in the next chapter.)

On this trip, we visited the Super Phoenix Reactor near Lyon, France, and the Marcoule Spent Storage Site operated at Avignon and owned

In 1989, on one of my CODELS to study nuclear waste storage, I visited the Central Interim Storage Facility at Oskarshamn, Sweden. Sam Fowler, Interior Committee staff, is second from the left; George is standing behind me; Pam Robinson, my legislative director, is to my left; and the others are unidentified.
Collection of Barbara F. Vucanovich

by COGEMA, a private French company. At the time, France had fifty-five nuclear reactors, and the COGEMA site had five thousand full-time employees reprocessing spent fuel from gas-cooled reactors, fast breeder reactors, and light water reactors. France reuses 95 to 96 percent of its uranium waste to power reactors, resulting in less waste for disposal.

This was actually my second visit to Avignon; I had also been there in 1989 as part of a trip to Sweden and France to study their approaches to nuclear waste. At that time, we visited the Central Interim Storage Facility in Oskarsham, Sweden, for spent fuel and the facilities in Forsmark, where waste is stored in the sea beds. In France, we visited La Manche Repository near Maupertus and the Cadarache facility near Avignon. At Cadarache, nuclear waste was turned into black glass through a process known as vitrification; it was still radioactive, but much more stable.

After each of these trips to study nuclear waste disposal, we reported our findings to the appropriate congressional committees, including the

Interior Energy and Environment subcommittee. Unfortunately, although other countries were making headway in research efforts to recycle nuclear waste, there was still no federal plan under way for alternative storage in the United States, other than Yucca Mountain in Nevada.

Nicaragua

I made three separate trips to Nicaragua, two involving fact-finding efforts during Ronald Reagan's presidency and one, a largely ceremonial visit, with Vice President Dan Quayle. I supported the Freedom Fighters (the Contras) and felt I needed to learn as much as I could about Nicaragua, its leaders, and how the United States could support democracy there. At the time of my first visit, in 1986, the president of Nicaragua was Daniel Ortega, supported by the leftist Sandinistas. The Soviet Union and Fidel Castro were looking for a foothold in Latin America, and I believed it was important to our nation's interests to ensure that Central America was under democratic, not communist, control.

Just before a March 1986 vote on supplying aid to the Contras, Dan Quayle, then a senator, invited me to fly to Nicaragua on a trip he arranged. Quayle was on the Armed Services Committee and chair of the Defense Acquisition Policy Committee. He supported aid to the Contras as I did and organized a group of about twelve senators and congressmen to make the trip. This visit to Nicaragua was to determine whether defense spending was appropriate. We met with the publishers of *La Prensa* and many of its executives. The newspaper was heavily censored by the Ortega government, by simply cutting out of the paper any articles that criticized Ortega.

Surprisingly, we were allowed to move around and meet some of the opposition leaders, although we were always watched by the military. We always traveled in cars equipped with bulletproof windows and doors and with armed security personnel. We visited with some of the mothers whose sons had been pressed into service in President Ortega's army. The mothers, although quite subdued and anxious, seemed thrilled to be able to speak with women members of Congress, because they could relate to us as mothers. As in many of the foreign nations that I visited, in Nicaragua I was struck by the poverty, ranging from unpaved streets to "houses" that were open to the elements on several sides.

Two years later, in July 1988, just before another House vote on Contra funding, I made a second trip, along with Republican Tom DeLay and Democrats Robin Tallon Jr. and Beverly Byron of Maryland. We were briefed by Ambassador Richard Melton and met with both government representatives and opposition leaders to discuss human rights. The Sandinistas had expanded their prison system to house political prisoners. We toured one of their prisons, which was so primitive that the prisoners were held in cages.

Unfortunately, our two-day trip created something of an international incident. Several members of our delegation, including DeLay, Tallon, and some staffers, went out into the streets to watch the demonstrations, although the ambassador had advised us against it. A member of my legislative staff, Jim Kameen, ended up on Nicaraguan television gesturing to another staffer to cross the street. His gesture was interpreted by the local media as obscene, although it was not. Our visit, and that incident, I believe, resulted in Ambassador Melton's being expelled from the country the day after we left for home.

There was one thrilling surprise during the trip. Mother Teresa was visiting Nicaragua at the time, and George and I, along with Beverly Byron and her husband, a former Catholic priest, attended Mass and sat in the front row with her. I met her briefly. I was impressed with the power of her presence, although she was incredibly tiny. I'm only five feet three and a half inches tall, and I towered over her.

When we returned to Washington, Beverly Byron and I briefed Colin Powell, who was then the national security advisor to the president, on the human rights abuses in Nicaragua. The House passed a resolution condemning Nicaragua, protesting the expulsion of our diplomats. We also urged President Ortega to change his policy on human rights and civil liberties, especially on the freedom of the press.

My final trip to Nicaragua was with Vice President Dan Quayle and Marilyn Quayle on April 25–26, 1990, as part of an official delegation to participate in the inauguration of Violeta Chamorro as president of Nicaragua. The delegation included nine senators, among them Harry Reid; eleven congressmen; Jeb Bush, one of the president's sons and now governor of Florida; and United Nations ambassador Jeane Kirkpatrick.

Chamorro, supported by the Contras and the United States, had

In a church in Nicaragua. *Left to right:* George Vucanovich, an unidentified boy, me, Congresswoman Bev Byron (Maryland), two unidentified nuns, and Mother Teresa, whom we met after the church services. I first heard Mother Teresa speak at the National Prayer Breakfast in Washington. I couldn't help but think she was a saintly woman. Collection of Barbara F. Vucanovich

defeated Daniel Ortega in the presidential elections. The daughter of a wealthy Nicaraguan rancher and landowner, she had been educated in the United States, and her husband, Pedro Chamorro, had been the publisher of *La Prensa* until he was assassinated during the Somoza regime in 1978. The Chamorros were the parents of four children, two of whom joined the communists; the other two remained loyal to their mother. Her daughter Christina edited the newspaper after her father's death.

I thought Violetta was an elegant and strong-willed woman, appearing confident and well aware of her opportunities and difficulties. The Sandinistas and Daniel Ortega made her presidency a challenge. They schemed to make sure she did not do well, although she served diligently until the end of her term in 1996.

China, Taiwan, and Korea

I made three trips to the Far East during my time in Congress. American relations with China and Korea are important because both countries trade with America, and many Americans, including many Nevada companies, do business in these countries. There are also significant security risks during these trips because of the nature of the government in China and the friction between North and South Korea.

My first trip, in August 1987, was by invitation of Republican congressman Jerry Lewis. The delegation was small, with only seven members of Congress, our spouses (including George), and a few committee staff as participants. We visited Beijing, China, and Taiwan to explore opportunities for American and (from my perspective) Nevada businesses. We met with important officials and leading industrialists, including Chinese premier H. D. Yu, who spoke no English, and Taiwanese vice minister John Chang, who spoke English well. We toured the China Steel Corporation, and while on Taiwan we met with the secretary general of the China Nationalist Association of Industry and Commerce. We met informally with legislators to discuss trade deficits, alleged labor rights abuses in Taiwan, and the pros and cons of protectionism. We also visited Kinman, where you can look out across the water to the Republic of China, and toured the underground tunnels built during the days of Chiang Kai-shek to help defend the small island.

In China, we stayed in American-style hotels, including the Sheraton in Beijing. The rooms were plain and sparsely furnished, with formal furniture and high ceilings. The small twin beds were always uncomfortable for six-foot-four George. The meals were "fancy," meaning that a small portion of food was dressed up to look good even though it wasn't. All the menus were printed in Chinese, and at one dinner we each received a diagram of the large square dinner table with a picture of a hand with a finger pointing to the assigned seat. The hotels had separate dining rooms for the Americans, with English-speaking waiters and waitresses, so you tended to see the same people at every meal.

From Taiwan, George and I flew on to Seoul, Korea, as part of a separate CODEL led by Senators Ernest "Fritz" Hollings and Charles Grassley. We met at the Ilhae Institute and Center for Strategic and International

Studies in Seoul, where representatives from both countries spoke about politics, bilateral trade, and economic issues. We also toured the facilities for the Summer Olympics, set for the following year, but I went off on my own to visit the day care centers set up by the military for our armed forces personnel stationed there.

This was George's first trip back to Korea since the Korean War. Spouses were not allowed to accompany the delegation on its trip to the Demilitarized Zone, so while we went there, George arranged to fly to Pusan, where he had been stationed. It was a nostalgic trip for him. He had served as an MP (military policeman) and had many memories of his service. He commented on how "citified" Pusan had become since he had last seen it.

In January 1988, on my second trip to the Far East, we visited Beijing, Xian, and Shanghai in China and returned once again to Seoul. The trip was led by Congressman Gerald Solomon. Seven members made the trip, as did George. We met with economic experts on trade, economic reform, monetary policy, and a special economic zone. In a meeting with Chai Zemin, chairman of the Chinese People's Institute of Foreign Affairs, our discussions ranged across topics such as Sino-American relations, human rights, sale of Chinese Silkworm missiles to Iran, Soviet aggression in Asia, bilateral trade, U.S. investment in China, Chinese economic/political reform programs, and Chinese-Korean relations. We also met with representatives of the extensive American business community in China and toured the McDonnell Douglas airplane factory in Shanghai.

In Korea, we attended a state dinner hosted by newly elected president Roh Tae Woo. I thought that he was very formal and that he did not particularly care for America and the visiting congressmen. We didn't have direct discussions with him, for he did not speak English. Later, we were briefed by our military leaders on the central command facility for the joint U.S. and Korea military forces.

My last trip to China and Hong Kong, in August 1991, was sponsored by the American Chambers of Commerce in Hong Kong and Shanghai and by Ross Engineering Corporation, which had manufacturing and trade operations in numerous countries. It was a large delegation led by Republican senator Hank Brown and including eleven Republican and

Democrat members, sixteen family members, and four congressional staffers.

My Nevada Democrat colleague, Congressman Jim Bilbray, was accompanied on the trip by his daughter, Erin. He was aggressive with the Chinese in discussing human rights, political prisoners, and the treatment of Catholics. He demanded information on a specific dissident being held in prison, asking about his release and his treatment and implying that he felt the man was being mistreated. I thought Bilbray was not very diplomatic, though perhaps justified in his attitude. Another congressman, Arthur Ravenel, a Republican, went so far as to threaten the Chinese with loss of Most Favored Nation status if a certain dissident died in prison. Ravenel said the prisoner's name so quickly that I couldn't tell if he was talking about the same man that Bilbray had mentioned. The whole scene surprised me because it was confrontational and we were on a diplomatic mission.

Despite the questions asked by my colleagues, the purpose of the trip was to achieve better understanding and to strengthen the relationships between the leaders of China and America. We wanted to encourage long-term improvements on political, economic, and cultural issues. We met with Jiang Zemin, the Communist Party general secretary in China, who spoke English and surprised us by proudly reciting the Gettysburg Address. While in Hong Kong, Beijing, and Shanghai, we also met with the consulate generals, economic trade officers, and the leaders of the American chambers of commerce.

My overall impression of China, on the basis of my three trips, was that there were large contrasts between the people we met with and the people we saw on the streets, between the rich and the poor. Bicycles, the main source of transportation, were everywhere; they were simply everywhere. Outside the towns, there were few trees or people, except in the shopping areas. The women all dressed the same, in colorless gray tunics and pants, and there seemed to be no distinction of status of any kind. There may have been a few women leaders, but I never met with any women in China.

The biggest change I noticed in China between 1987 and 1991 was the increased number of individual entrepreneurs on the wide city streets. There were little booths everywhere, with men and women selling their wares. By the time of my last visit, I was surprised to see the masses of people on the city streets. Modern hotels overlooked the homes of the poor, where the smell of coal oil used for heating and cooking was heavy in the air.

Korea seemed to be more "westernized" than China, probably reflecting the fact that trade with the United States opened up so much earlier. The homes were usually one story, constructed of plain stucco. The women's dress was rather sophisticated in the shopping areas but more informal in the countryside. I don't remember meeting any women leaders in Korea, either. Like China, there were huge contrasts between the rich and the poor. Poverty was a major problem. You constantly saw hand-pushed wagons with elderly men, women, and children moving along the streets, as well as three-wheeled motor vehicles and bicycles everywhere. The changes in Korea I noted over the years were that there were even more businesses and activities going on in the streets and fewer military people were in evidence. At that time everyone was being encouraged to welcome visitors in anticipation of the Olympics.

Eastern Europe

One of my more memorable trips was in January 1990, to Eastern Europe. The trip, led by Democrat congressman John LaFalce, chair of the Small Business Committee, was to Belgrade, Budapest, Prague, Krakow, Auschwitz, Birkenau, and Warsaw to learn about the business communities in the post–cold war era. All of the countries were struggling with the transition from the failure of communism and governmental control to privatization and a free-market economy.

The meetings with government officials and private-sector representatives were diverse and informative. For example, in Hungary we met with the government ministers of finance, trade and industry, and foreign affairs and with bankers and other businesspeople. They seemed a bit intimidated to be meeting with members of the U.S. Congress, but they still were eager to hear from us and interested in opportunities for doing business with the United States. (I was struck by how many people chain-smoked throughout our meetings.)

In Poland, we visited Krakow, where Karol Wojtyla was cardinal and archbishop for eleven years before he became Pope John Paul in 1978. I attended Mass held at a side altar in a dark, dreary, and solemn cathedral with few pews and no kneeling benches at all. There were some statues, but not many. Those in attendance were mostly older people, all wearing dark, warm clothes. I did not see any children.

In Czechoslovakia, we met the newly elected president of the Czech Republic, Vaclav Havel. In my opinion, he was a typical European man, wearing rumpled tweeds and chain-smoking. He had gone directly from prison to the presidency. One of the reporters we met told of Havel holding a news conference, after which, as he picked up his briefcase, the catch popped open and his papers fell out, including a roll of toilet paper. As Havel bent down, scooped everything up, and returned it to his briefcase, he explained, "You never know when you are going to be arrested. It is intolerable to be in prison without toilet paper, a basic necessity." We also met with the U.S. ambassador to Czechoslovakia, Shirley Temple Black, at a reception she held for us at the embassy.

I made a number of other trips that helped me understand other countries and cultures and, on some occasions, reinforced my pride in our military forces overseas. In December 1995 I participated in a trip arranged by Congressman Susan Molinari to Bosnia, Croatia, and Sarajevo, parts of the world so often preceded by the adjective "war torn" because of the constant unrest there. In Yugoslavia, the Serbs, Croats, Slovenians, and Muslims are of different religions, customs, and beliefs. Their hatred for one another is long-standing, going back for centuries.

It wasn't really scheduled, but we had an opportunity to meet Sloban Milosevic, the Serbian leader, during the trip. Most of the delegation was anti-Serbian because Milosevic was suspected of tyranny and oppression of non-Serbians in Yugoslavia. Although George was not with me, "Vucanovich" is a familiar Serbian name in that part of the world, so Milosevic was exceptionally friendly to me. He didn't speak English, but he seemed pleasant and harmless in my brief encounter with him. When our United Nations ambassador, Richard Holbrook, provided us with post-visit briefings, however, he revealed the details of the true situation in the country, and I was horrified by the extent of Milosevic's atrocities against his enemies.

Elsewhere in the World

One of the most moving trips involved the forty-fifth anniversary of the Normandy invasion in 1989. We visited the D-day landing beach sites, the cemeteries, and the underground bunkers. The French countryside is best described as picturesque, with narrow cobblestone and brick streets. The homes were two to three stories high, all attached to each other, ancient but durable. Both men and women dressed in simple clothes. Many of the men wore black or navy berets. American flags flew in welcome everywhere in the town. The French cheered, as if it were the first liberation. It was an emotional event; we all cried unashamedly. It was especially moving for me because my brother Tommy had died during World War II in Italy.

George and I were part of a delegation that went to Israel, located at the eastern end of the Mediterranean Sea. Israel was a relatively new country, created after Jews began to pour into the area in the 1930s when Adolf Hitler was persecuting them in Germany and elsewhere. The League of Nations carved Israel out of Palestine in 1947. This November 1988 trip was sponsored by the Anti-Defamation League of B'nai B'rith, with my expenses underwritten by the Kantor Foundation and the Eugene R. Warner Fund of Las Vegas.

An ancient land, the territory that included Israel and Palestine had been ruled by the Muslims for centuries, yet the area was considered a holy land by the Jews, Muslims, and Christians. I was amazed by how small and geographically close Palestine and Israel were, literally only a "stone's throw" from one another. It was no wonder that both sides were always on alert. Israel was a fraction over 8,000 square miles, while Palestine is much smaller—2,200 square miles on the West Bank of the Jordan River, with 139 miles on the Gaza Strip.

The area wasn't much larger than Washoe County, so it was hard to comprehend the impact of these tiny entities on the rest of the world. There is no simple answer to resolve their conflicts. A primary sticking point is the status of Jerusalem, located on the border of the two countries. President Arafat insisted that Jerusalem must be the capital of his country, and the Israelis also laid claim to Jerusalem. Because this area is sacred to both Muslims and Jews, it was no surprise that clashes between these religious groups continue to this day.

We met with U.S. ambassador Tom Pickering and such well-known Israeli leaders as Yitzhak Rabin, Yitzhak Shamir, and Simon Peres. Peres was a peacemaker, and to this day he continues to urge finding a way to peace. My informal notes taken while talking with Shamir and Peres reflect that I thought Peres was interested in a peaceful solution, while Shamir was more confrontational. U.S. consul general Phil Wilcox arranged a meeting with representatives of the Palestinian community, including newspaper editors, a hospital director, and the president of the Jericho Fruit and Vegetable Co-op. They seemed uncomfortable discussing the problems between Israel and Palestine while they were guests in Israel.

We visited the Golan Heights, the Northern Border, the Holy Sites, and the Sea of Galilee. On the rocky and narrow streets, we saw Hasidic boys and men wearing yarmulkes and modestly dressed women everywhere. The most emotional visit we made was to the Holocaust Memorial and Research Center. The place was an exact replica of Auschwitz, Germany. We walked down the stairs to see the ovens and graphic displays showing exactly how the Nazis killed the Jews. The procedures were explained in detail, with shocking displays of skeletons, stacks of baby shoes, and piles of shoes from the people who had been executed. It was horrific and gave me nightmares after the visit. I still shudder when I think of what the Nazis did to the Jews.

We also toured a church used by three different religions and a Jewish settlement in Bethlehem, southeast of Jerusalem in Palestine, where we met many of the settlers. We visited a kibbutz as well, meeting families in their homes, and we stayed overnight in a guesthouse. One aspect of our visit to the kibbutz that unnerved me was the presence of Uzis and other weapons carried by the people. Civilians, as well as soldiers, were armed with some kind of weapon. When any of them came in to eat a meal, they casually placed their weapons on the floor by their seats while they ate.

During Desert Shield and Desert Storm, I visited the Nevada troops in Saudi Arabia and Kuwait, where I received reports on the troops and on the performance of the National Guard and selected reserves. With miles of sand and no grass or trees, it was not usual to see camels as we traveled

Riyadh, Saudi Arabia, 1990, during Desert Storm. I am visiting with General Norman
Schwarzkopf at his headquarters. He struck me as a plainspoken, no-nonsense U.S.
commander in chief of our armed forces. Collection of Barbara F. Vucanovich

throughout the countryside. All the men wore turbans and flowing robes.
Women, even the little girls, were covered from head to toe in black robes,
and many had their faces covered with a veil. A separate government force
had the unconditional power to enforce the women's dress code. It was
difficult for the women in our military to conform, but they did their best
by wearing a black gauzy cover over their uniforms. I was asked to cover
my clothes when we traveled throughout the towns. Alcohol is forbidden,
and none of our group challenged the rule.

In December 1990 I visited Desert Shield, where our troops were
defending Saudi Arabia against possible attacks by Iraq. A nineteen-
member CODEL headed by Democrat congressman Anthony Beilenson,
flew to Riyadh, Saudi Arabia, and met with the imposing, no-nonsense
U.S. commander in chief, General H. Norman Schwarzkopf. He was
plainspoken and to the point, which was evident when he got into a verbal
confrontation with liberal Democrat congressman Tom Lantos. Lantos
interrupted the general's presentation, apparently without listening to

what was being said. Born in Hungary and a Holocaust survivor, he was a strong supporter of Israel. I believed that he was simply showing off his credentials by interrupting Schwarzkopf, who handled the situation with aplomb. We also visited air bases in Riyadh and Jabail, where we were briefed by local commanders. We ate lunch with the troops and inspected their living facilities and a mobile hospital with fifty beds and a full operating room.

From Saudi Arabia, we flew to Israel, where we met with the foreign minister, the defense minister, and other leaders, including Benjamin Netanyahu, in separate meetings. Netanyahu was an imposing man with a good command of the English language, a natural leader who exuded self-confidence. In Jerusalem, we visited the Wailing Wall, which was not as large as I had imagined. When you arrived at the site, you stepped down to a lower level. It was a solemn place where people wearing yarmulkes were standing in prayer. We journeyed to Bethlehem, also a tiny place, with stones everywhere in the streets. At one of the churches, we saw many women in worship; remarkably, there were no men present.

In April 1991 I was privileged to visit our troops during Desert Storm in Kuwait, Saudi Arabia, Southern Iraq, and Bahrain. I met about a dozen soldiers from Nevada. I had my picture taken with each of them and sent them a copy of the photo. When I got back to Washington, I called each of their families and sent them a copy of the photos, too.

We were briefed about the problems the troops were having during the withdrawal process. More than 274,000 soldiers had gone home by the time of our visit, but there were more than 200,000 remaining in the Persian Gulf region. There was some friction about who should be deployed first because many active-duty personnel were going home before the reservists and the National Guardsmen. The reservists wanted to return home to their jobs, while the regular military personnel didn't have such demands. Deployment was being slowed by a Department of Agriculture requirement that military equipment be dismantled and thoroughly sanitized to eliminate any dirt, debris, insects, or diseases before being returned to the United States. All the vehicles—including planes, helicopters, and Jeeps—were reassembled and shrink-wrapped before being shipped home.

Among the responsibilities of the MIL CON subcommittee was the oversight of expenditures for military housing. As chair of the subcommittee, I arranged an inspection trip to the North Atlantic Treaty Organization (NATO) in Brussels. The seven members of the subcommittee who made the trip were briefed at NATO on our nation's financial support of the organization. Our budget was split fifty-fifty between construction and procurement for our 100,000 troops. President Clinton had requested $179 million for the coming years, but I left the briefing convinced that the United States was giving too much money and control to NATO.

From Brussels, we flew to Italy and our air base at Aviano, which provided air combat support for the United States in Europe and NATO. We were particularly interested in the quality of living conditions on the base, so we evaluated housing, support facilities, schools, child care accommodations, and hospitals. The Italian construction was scandalous, and the shoddy workmanship on the housing units was obvious to the naked eye. For example, the new porches on the buildings were unstable, crumbling and falling down. In subsequent appropriations discussions, I introduced legislation to increase funding to improve this housing. I also arranged for an investigation of the Italian firms responsible for the housing problems.

Not all of the travel was international. I made two trips to Alaska as part of my Interior Committee responsibilities on natural resource issues, in 1985 and 1991. In 1985 I was part of a group that studied the opening of a portion of the Alaska National Wildlife Refuge to exploration and eventual drilling for oil. (Interestingly, this debate continues nearly two decades later.) The second trip was primarily to visit the Offshore Seawater Treatment Plant and the Waterflood Project at the Prudhoe Bay Oil Field.

In Alaska we traveled by helicopter, bus, or small float planes, with almost daily briefings by either the Department of the Interior, the U.S. Forest Service, or the National Park Service. At different times, we visited Juneau, Deadhorse, Sitka, Barter Island on the Arctic Ocean, Fairbanks, Beetles Field, Anaktuvuk, and other locations. We flew over the Gates of the Arctic National Park and Preserve, the Portage and Mendanhall glaciers, and Denali National Park. We visited underground gold mines and the Kennecott Greens Creek Mine and Millsite on Admiralty Island, at that time the largest silver mine in America. In the small village of Nondalton, we held a town hall meeting to discuss Alaskan Native American issues. The tribes we met with included the Athabaskan, the Aleuts (Eskimos), and the Tlingit.

The two things that impressed me the most about Alaska were its sheer size and the wildlife. I was used to the wide-open spaces of Nevada, but in Alaska it was common for people to fly small planes in and out of the communities because they were so far apart. Float planes were parked in harbors in most of the towns. We saw bald eagles everywhere, as well as caribou, moose, and other wildlife. Frequently we saw teams of sled dogs around people's homes, usually in outdoor pens.

The people we met were friendly and outgoing and seemed healthy and active. Most of the women I came in contact with were fairly young employees of the Interior Department or the Park Service. No one seemed to have "cabin fever," and no one expressed a desire to leave, although it appeared that almost everyone planned a trip to the "Lower Forty-eight" at least once a year.

I felt fortunate to have traveled while I was in Congress. I took the work seriously, prepared myself before I left Washington, and tried to put what I had learned to good use when I returned. As I noted earlier, the world is growing smaller, and members of Congress have a responsibility to understand foreign countries almost as well as they understand their own districts. In addition, both the Interior and the Appropriations committees had oversight responsibilities, and it was useful to see things firsthand rather than having to depend solely on staff analysis. Frequently, with trips that involved nuclear waste or trade promotion with other nations, I was able to directly benefit Nevada because of my participation. Ultimately, the nineteen CODELs I participated in made me a better representative for the people who elected me.

CHAPTER EIGHTEEN

Twenty-Seven Years and
One Revolution Later...

In 1968, when I made my first trip to Russia, my grandson Reynolds Cafferata was two years old. The last time I visited there, in 1995, his first son, Taylor, was two years old. In this twenty-seven-year period Russia changed less than my family had. My children Kenny, Tommy, and Susie, and my oldest grandchildren, Elisa and Farrell, graduated from high school before I was elected to the House. During my time in Congress, my grandchildren Reynolds, Mike Jr., Trevor, Nora, and Jennifer graduated from high school, and my son Kenny and my daughter Susie, along with my grandchildren Elisa, Farrell, Reynolds, and Mike Jr., graduated from college. Susie received her CPA certificate, and Patty and her son Reynolds also graduated from law school, while Elisa received her MBA degree. Russia was not nearly as dynamic.

My 1995 visit to Russia was not my first trip behind what used to be called the Iron Curtain, but it was certainly one of the most chilling trips I ever took and one of the most poignant, for a number of reasons.

At the time, nuclear power was a major component of Russia's energy supply, with twenty-nine reactor units at nine different nuclear power plants, and still more units were under construction. This made Russia a natural stop on our nuclear waste CODEL. After meeting government and private nuclear energy officials in Moscow, we flew to Kiev, which had fourteen reactor units at five sites supplying 30 to 40 percent of the country's electrical power. From there, we flew in a small plane 700 miles north to Chernobyl.

Chernobyl, of course, is where a nuclear reactor disaster occurred on April 26, 1986, releasing into the air an estimated hundred times more radiation than Hiroshima. The disaster contaminated areas of the Ukraine, Russia, and Belarus. It is estimated that thousands died and the health of millions was affected, but the true extent of the disaster may never be known. At the time of my visit, the United States, Russia, and other countries had entered into a joint effort to clean up the contamination and install safety measures at Chernobyl, and the United States was spending $11 million for improvements at the plant.

The scene was eerie. More than nine years after the disaster, a complete town remained standing, but no one lived there. Workers were bused in and out of the facility daily. They told us they had not been paid for a year, but they had no place else to go. I have a picture of me dressed in a paper suit standing next to the plant. Undoubtedly, the paper suit offered little protection from any remaining radiation.

Later we visited Novosibirsk, home of the Siberian branch of the Russian Academy of Sciences. When we were sitting on the plane ready to fly out of the city, the cabin suddenly filled with smoke. The pilot and copilot got up and walked off the plane, leaving us behind, paralyzed by fear. Here we were, in this nuclear wasteland, in a plane filled with smoke. Luckily, the plane didn't catch on fire and all twenty of us were able to get off it. It took several hours for our CODEL leaders to find us another plane.

While we were in Moscow, we were given carefully guided tours of the walled-in Kremlin grounds and the Russian Armory. In the walls we saw burial markers for former leaders. The Romanov crown jewels—huge, ostentatious stones in antique gold settings—were also on display.

We attended religious services at Yelokhovsky Cathedral, a Russian Orthodox church famous for its icons, relics, tombs, and music. The largest operating church in Moscow, it had high ceilings, was not well heated, and was lighted almost exclusively with candles. There were no pews; people stood or knelt on the stone floor.

Moments of quiet and solitude in the church gave me an opportunity to reflect on my first visit to Moscow, nearly three decades earlier, and the tiny, almost secretive church I visited then. A lot had changed about Russia, and much remained the same.

Congressman John Myers (Indiana) led a CODEL to Russia and Chernobyl in 1995. He is on my left, and an unidentified congressional staffer is on my right. The others are unidentified Chernobyl employees. We are dressed in paper suits and hats. At the time I did not think the paper suits offered us much protection from radiation.
Collection of Barbara F. Vucanovich

Russia 1968

In 1968 Nevada governor Paul Laxalt nominated me to represent the state in a delegation of "Outstanding Representative American Women." Our mission was to meet with women in the Soviet Union to improve goodwill and relations between our two countries. This was at the height of the cold war, of course, and not many Americans traveled to the Soviet Union. We were not overly concerned for our safety, but we had no idea what to expect.

Each participant was required to pay her own way on the trip; the cost was about $5,000, as I recall. All of us brought mementos from our respective states to give to the Russian women we would be meeting. White Pine County's Kennecott Mining gave me copper medallions. Sea and Ski, which had a plant near Reno, donated some of its products, probably hand cream or lotion of some kind. (I don't think suntan lotion, Sea and Ski's best-known product, would have been too useful to women in the Soviet Union.)

The group included about sixty women from all across the country and from a variety of backgrounds. There were doctors, businesswomen, housewives, and teachers. We flew out of New York on September 17, 1968, bound for London, Moscow, Leningrad, Kiev, Budapest, and Prague. We stopped in London for a dinner with the women members of the British Parliament. According to a program I still have from the dinner, the group included the future prime minister Margaret Thatcher, although I don't remember meeting her at the time.

The Iron Curtain was in full effect in those days, and when we landed in Moscow all of our baggage was opened and searched in a back room. While we waited, they fed us, but not much. Throughout our trip, nearly all of our travel was closely restricted, if not guarded. Our hotel rooms and our sightseeing, if it can be called that, had been prearranged by Intourist (the Soviet travel office) and a branch of the Russian government. The arrangements ensured that we had "guides" everywhere we went. On every bus or train we took, there were guards, but no other passengers—just the women from our group and the soldiers.

In 1968 Moscow was a city with only a few buses and a few official-looking cars, so there was not much traffic on the wide, bumpy streets. The people walked wherever they went, carrying string bags. There was, however, a metro underground used by the residents who commuted. People recognized us as Americans, and children often ran up to us, asking for gum and ballpoint pens. The armed guards who accompanied us chased them away. There were lines everywhere, even to buy just one banana. There was no refrigeration in their homes, so women shopped every day. We also saw lots of men on the streets drinking directly out of vodka bottles. After seeing how they lived, I could almost understand why.

The Volga River ran through the city, which was fairly hilly, with lots of ugly two- and four-story buildings. All the buildings looked the same, mostly drab in design and with dull colors. I do remember that some, clearly influenced by the Eastern cultures, had the famous onion-top roofs. The best example of this type of architecture was St. Basil's Cathedral, built by Ivan the Terrible in the 1550s to commemorate his victory over the Tartars. When we were there, it was surrounded with scaffolding, allegedly to restore the exterior. I thought it was to keep people out.

All the Russians shopped at GUMS, the huge government-run department store. It was the only place in Russia where I saw escalators. We did not find much of anything to buy there. The clothing being sold was mostly drab and of poor quality, some men's, women's, and children's clothing, but not much of it; there was very little else you would expect to find in a department store. The "black market," where you could buy almost anything, from cigarettes to blue jeans, operated in private buildings. Well-connected or high-level Soviets could buy any luxury item there—including clothes, jewelry, crystal, and china.

At the Lucia, the "modern" hotel in Moscow where we stayed, one of the women looked at the floor and said, "I wonder when they are going to put the carpet down." I said, "I hate to tell you, but that is the carpet." In fact, it looked like carpet padding. The hotel had twelve floors but only one elevator. The rooms were very sparse, with beds that were more like cots with sheets and thin, thin blankets. Many nights I slept in my coat to keep warm. Every room had a radio built into the wall. I was—and still am—convinced that we were being bugged the entire time we were there. The bathroom was down the hall, but we had a sink in our room. These were "deluxe" Russian accommodations of the day.

It wasn't a friendly tourist environment. I don't suppose they had learned much about guest services. A matron on each floor kept your room key when you left. We didn't mind too much, since the keys were about a foot long, and that discouraged us from taking them out of the hotel anyway. There was a coffee shop on the second or third floor that stayed open late. The food was not something to write home about, but we could get a sandwich or a glass of wine. The coffee shop had no windows, and the barren walls were decorated only with the obligatory radios.

Everywhere we went, we were fed in isolation, always separate from the general Russian population. They made sure our tables had bottles of water, as well as wine. I couldn't help but wonder what the people thought of us. We went to a museum where we had to leave our coats and umbrellas with the coat check attendant. When it was time to leave the museum, I couldn't find my coat claim check. Mine was the only coat left in the cloakroom, but the attendant refused to give it to me without the claim check. I finally had to dump out my entire purse to find the claim check and recover my coat.

Despite the security, I managed a couple of unplanned and unescorted visits in Moscow. Each time, I simply took the elevator downstairs in the hotel and walked through the lobby and out onto the street. I kept expecting to be stopped at any moment, but no one bothered me, so I just kept going. I had a rudimentary map of the city and used it surreptitiously.

On one such "escape," I went to a beauty school—the closest thing I could find to a hair salon—to get my hair done. I had to stand up and lean over the sink while the beautician used a bar of yellow soap to scrub my scalp and hair. Believe me, I had second thoughts about my vanity at that point.

I also attended Mass at the Church of St. Louis of the French, the only Catholic church allowed to remain open in Moscow during the Soviet era. This was mostly for propaganda purposes, since it allowed the Soviets to point to it as an example of supposed "religious freedom." I learned about it when I asked at the hotel desk for the name and address of the nearest Catholic church. I walked outside to where the taxis were lined up, but as I approached, the cabbies rolled up their windows so I couldn't talk to them. Finally, one did talk to me, but when I told him I wanted to go to the church, he said, "No, I can't take you there. There is no church by that name." When I insisted that I had the address, he reluctantly drove me to the church.

It was surrounded on three sides by the buildings of the infamous Lubyanka prison, an execution and torture facility and headquarters of the KGB. (I learned later that cameras were constantly trained on the entrances to the church to keep track of those attending services.) I found the entrance totally deserted, with high weeds all around the walkway. The church itself was set 150 to 200 feet back from the street. Inside, there were only a few women, with babushkas over their hair, not one of them younger than sixty years of age. There were not very many benches, so most of the women stood or knelt on the wooden floor for the service. Despite the humble setting, the women responded to the priest with beautiful singing voices. The women handed out rice and salt at the door—whether to supplement the diets of churchgoers or for some other purpose, I don't know.

Lenin was everywhere in Moscow in 1968. In the factories, the workers had handouts with his picture on them and the words "Who is the Boss of the Factory? One Man Management." Even the playgrounds had his statue. We visited Lenin's tomb in Red Square, a huge monument with guards all around it. I hadn't read up on it, so I didn't know what to expect. As I walked down the steps inside, the atmosphere got very quiet and very cold. For a long time, Lenin had been buried somewhere else. Later, his body was dug up and taken to Red Square. I still remember the guards standing vigil, with Lenin's body laid out under glass. Most of his face was decayed, so it was filled in with wax. I was so surprised that I laughed out loud. One of the guards swung his bayonet at me and held it within inches of me. I left there in a hurry.

Eventually we met with the Russian women, the purpose of the trip. Since I was there as a teacher (of Evelyn Wood Reading Dynamics), I met with the women who took care of children and with schoolteachers. I visited schools and day care centers, although the day care was more like an orphanage or a boarding school. The children were there from Sunday evening until Friday night so their parents could work through the week. I was shocked to see all the lines of little cribs with babies inside. It was sad that these children not only had so little time with their parents but also had minimal human contact.

In the schools we visited, most of the children recited their English lessons like little robots. The girls, perhaps dressed up for our visit, looked uncomfortable with the big, fancy, stiff bows in their hair. The older children were schooled in "pioneer palaces," huge buildings where martial music played so loudly that we could hear it for what seemed like miles away. Most were being trained for compulsory military service. The Russians claimed they had no juvenile problems.

A few members of our delegation were medical doctors, and after they visited Moscow schools and clinics, they reported that the health care provided in Russia was comparable to 1920s care in our country.

While we were there, the Russian delegation of women asked the American women to put on a fashion show with the clothes we had brought with us. We were surprised at this; we didn't think our clothes were suitable for a fashion show. We modeled for them, however, and they modeled their clothes for us. They even had a runway for us to parade down. They handed out a style or fashion magazine full of European fashions, but I thought it was propaganda since it was printed in English. We never saw anyone dressed in European styles anywhere.

We left Moscow in the middle of the night on a train bound for Leningrad. The train was grim and the accommodations were rather basic. The windows were covered with black paint, so we couldn't see out. Soldiers marched up and down the aisle continuously, and one soldier stood guard at the end of each railroad car.

In Leningrad, I visited the Kazansky Cathedral, which housed the Museum of Religion and Atheism, containing revolting and gruesome displays of the Spanish Inquisition. I was shocked. The graphic exhibits were meant to get a reaction and instill revulsion against Catholicism. The Russian Orthodox cathedral had been built in 1811 in the image of St. Peter's Basilica in Rome. (As an example of how things have changed, the museum today includes a small section on the history of Catholicism and a larger section on Orthodoxy, with church art, historical paintings, and various religious articles. Church services are once again being held in the building.)

Next we flew to Kiev to catch a flight to Budapest, Hungary. As soon as we were airborne, everybody on the plane spontaneously began clapping. I imagine that was a common response for people traveling out of the Soviet Union in those days. We were giddy with relief to be out of Russia. We spent a couple of days in the beautiful cities of Budapest and Prague, Czechoslovakia, before returning home. The trip gave me some understanding of the people, the climate, the landscape, and the politics. It reinforced my belief in democracy—I wouldn't want government control from the cradle to the grave. Still, there were many people in the Soviet Union in 1968 who seemed to like the system.

The Soviets touted their equality between men and women. The men ran the elevators, while women swept the streets. There were women construction workers, who dressed and looked like men and climbed scaffolding. In government there were women on all the committees with fancy titles, but that was all they were—titles. The equality was superficial because the women had no actual power. Although there were women doctors and other professionals, they didn't make the decisions. Years after my visit to Russia, Raisa Gorbachev brought style to the professional women, but she was disliked by Russian women in general. They saw her as an "uppity dame."

Because travel to the Soviet Union was so unusual in those days, when

I came home I was asked to give a number of speeches to different civic groups on what I'd seen. It was an honor to have been selected and to have represented Nevada, and the trip gave me insights into world politics and a foundation that I found invaluable when I served in Congress. When I read newspaper accounts of Russian events or when Russian leaders visited Congress, I had a better understanding of how they operated and the status of their women.

When I returned to Russia almost thirty years later, the security was a lot less visible. We were able to move freely around the towns we visited, and there were no soldiers with guns in evidence. I was able to see Russia's progress toward a more democratic form of government from the 1960s to the 1990s, although some of the changes were small. Everyone was very poor, not many people had jobs, and men were still standing around drinking vodka, but there were more cars and activity in the streets. Red Square was still walled, as it was when I visited in the 1960s. Lenin's tomb was guarded but no longer open to the public.

The scaffolding was gone from St. Basil's. The church was open to visitors, but I saw only a few people inside. I would have liked to revisit St. Louis of the French, the little church I had attended in 1968, but because of time constraints I was unable to do so.

PART V

Home Means Nevada

CHAPTER NINETEEN

Coming Home, Looking Back

I can't believe how quickly those fourteen years in the House went by. The family still hasn't stopped growing. The first great-grandchild, born right after I retired from the House, was Henry Wilson Cafferata in January 1997. Since then, Elisa Cafferata Erquiaga married Richard Maser, and their son, Kenton, and Richard's daughter, Kelley, joined the family in 1998. Nora Dillon Golden and her husband, Chris, became the parents of Philomena and Elizabeth, while Maggie Dillon Cranmer and her husband, Toby, became the parents of Patrick, Madelein, and Amelia. And Farrell Cafferata and Caren Jenkins brought the newest members into the family, Dean and Quinn. I continue to fill my days with family. And they remind me that as a grandmother I'm not really that tough.

I decided not to run for an eighth term in November 1995. It was not really a hard decision, and I was comfortable with retiring. George had been battling leukemia for some time, and I wanted to spend more time with him. On November 30, 1995, I told my staff about my decision. I had hoped to keep it quiet for a while, but that was not to be. The next day I flew to Bosnia on a congressional trip and when I returned, the media met me at Andrews Air Force Base when we touched down.

Before I told the staff, I invited my daughter, Patty, to lunch and suggested she run for my seat. I encouraged her because I felt she was qualified. A former state treasurer and Republican nominee for governor, she was a capable woman. She was interested, of course, and we discussed when I would officially make my plans known and when it would be appropriate for her to announce her candidacy.

Patty made a series of trips to Washington early in 1996 to raise money and meet people for her campaign. I held a couple of fund-raisers for her and introduced her to lobbyists and others who were helpful. I was present when she announced her candidacy on March 4 at Bishop Manogue High School, and I participated in as many of her events as I could fit into my schedule, including a rural campaign swing from Tonopah to Ely via Rachel, Alamo, and Caliente in our motor home. Patty ran a good campaign, but lost in the Republican primary to Jim Gibbons. I was disappointed for her, but Jim has been a fine representative for the district.

Once I decided to retire, I was eager to leave Washington. We put our condominium on the market in September 1996. Congress adjourned early in September, and the movers arrived the next month to collect our furniture from the condo for the move to Reno. The end of the month was tragic. As previously mentioned, my son Mike died suddenly, only days after we moved home.

While I was still grieving, I closed my offices in Elko and Las Vegas on December 1, then flew to Washington to attend a seminar for retiring members to assist them with the transition from Congress and to explain what activities were available for former members. I joined the U.S. Association of Former Members of Congress.

George and I also attended the White House Christmas party. It was rather nostalgic to realize the next time it would be held I would be retired. Each year since, I have been invited to attend the party, but I have not gone.

I flew home to Reno the next day, with mixed feelings, of course. I would soon be a regular citizen again, but it was nice to contemplate no more weekend flights across the country, and I looked forward to controlling my own schedule.

On the downside, naturally I would miss many things about Congress. I would miss being informed of the issues that affect us all, the camaraderie I shared with other members, and being involved with the big issues that affect our country and my state. Washington is an interesting, exciting, mentally stimulating town. But I knew I would not miss the days of rushing to answer the bells for votes, the long commutes back and forth across the country every week, or the partisan bickering. On the plane coming home it was hard not to think about the fourteen years that were coming to an end.

Being a member of Congress was actually a small part of my life. I had a full and vibrant life before I ever went to Washington. I was elected at age sixty-one and served until age seventy-five. I ran for Congress because it was an opportunity for me to contribute to Nevada. I admit that when I first ran, I wondered if I could do the job. I wasn't a lawyer or even a college graduate. I was not a great public speaker. I didn't how I would measure up against the other officeholders. But I learned quickly that a lot of things that people think are qualifications really aren't. Most of all, I believed that I could do the job because I understood the issues and loved Nevada and the greatness of America. I was just a person with common sense. A tough grandmother, I suppose.

During my time in Congress, I was proud to represent a conservative woman's point of view. I supported legislation that I believed would help families and lessen the burden on women who were wage earners and small business owners. I did my best to represent all Nevadans, including the people in the rural counties, and was a voice in the House for safeguarding Nevada's mining from alleged reforms that would have destroyed the gold mining industry and for protecting the mining jobs that contribute to the Nevada economy. For example, it was barely noticed at the time, but I blocked Nick Rahall from securing changes in the mining laws that would have hurt Nevada mining. I introduced some 150 amendments to a bill he had proposed. Fortunately, the bill never became law.

I also fought to protect the gaming industry, particularly from the spread of Indian gaming. We were able to obtain legislation that limited Indian gaming to those states where the governor approved such activity. I did not expect governors, for the most part, to welcome Indian gaming to their states. Ultimately, the spread of Indian gaming has been a mixed blessing for Nevada.

And I vigorously fought to prevent the storage of nuclear waste at Yucca

Mountain in every one of my seven terms. I was not, however, surprised when Nevada lost the vote in 2002 to stop nuclear waste from being shipped to and stored here. Other states, particularly those that generate nuclear waste, do not want to store it close to home. They have more votes than Nevada does.

When I first went to Washington, I thought that storage of nuclear waste at Yucca Mountain was a reasonable plan. In fact, there was support for the idea from some people in Nevada, especially Southern Nevada businessmen who saw it as having some economic benefit for the state. But after I learned more about the government's proposal, I changed my mind and opposed the storage of nuclear waste in Nevada. On a positive note, I was able to arrange for the direct payment of funds from the federal government to local governments that might be affected by the waste storage project, without requiring them to go through a grant application process.

I still believe there is a lot of misunderstanding about Congress and the role a member plays. Most congressmen and congresswomen are genuinely hardworking, sincere, and trying to do a good job for their district, state, and country. I believe the media play a large role in portraying the worst, rather than the best, picture of Congress.

I did not originally run for the House with any particular agenda in mind. I believed in good government and wanted to make a difference for Nevada. It was an honor to serve, and I learned a great deal about the country and the rest of the globe. It was an opportunity to see the whole picture rather than just my own slice of the world. By getting to know other members, I could understand why they voted as they did—because of their backgrounds and their districts. Similarly, I worked hard for Nevada, especially the rural interests that were so severely underrepresented in the House.

I am proud that I stood up for my pro-life beliefs every time proposed legislation threatened the lives of unborn babies, even when I took heat from the media and from members of my staff who did not agree with my position. For instance, I assisted in defeating the Equal Rights Amendment once and for all, in large part because it would not protect the unborn. With my leadership, we were successful in preventing a two-thirds vote that would have sent the amendment to the states for ratification for a second time.

I supported equal pay for equal work, but I helped lead the fight to defeat the comparable-worth legislation. The bill would have required pay based on job titles, not on the worker's performance, tasks, duties, or risks. In other words, it would have meant equal pay for unequal work. I didn't think it was fair to women or to their employers.

After I was diagnosed with breast cancer, I lobbied and proposed legislation to promote the early detection of breast cancer and for more money for breast cancer research. I succeeded in my request for additional funding for breast and cervical cancer prevention. I also was able to secure passage of the Mammography Quality Standards Act and legislation requiring Medicare to pay for annual mammograms for women aged sixty-five and older.

One of my most successful efforts for Nevada was the repeal of the 55-miles-per-hour speed limit federal law, a victory especially appreciated by those Nevadans who travel any distance in the rural counties. Another successful effort was the passage of the Truckee River Negotiated Water Settlement. Northern Nevadans benefited when I was able to convince Speaker Tom Foley and California Democrat George Miller to bring the Negotiated Water Settlement bill to the floor in the final minutes of that session. The bill would have died in the House without my help.

Finally, many new residents to Nevada were thrilled with the passage of my Source Income Tax Bill because they had been forced to pay state income taxes to California or other states where they no longer lived. The source income tax legislation provided that no state could impose an income tax on any retirement income of an individual who didn't live in that state. I worked on the issue for several years before it was adopted as law. The bill finally passed the House on December 18, 1994, and the Senate on December 22, 1994. President Clinton signed it into law on January 10, 1995.

I am also most proud of the help I was able to provide to Nevada and to the nation's military because of my seat on the Appropriations Committee and my chairmanship of its Military Construction subcommittee. The Fallon Naval Air Station and Nellis Air Force Base both received important new funding, and I was also able to affect military bases across the country, such as Fort Benning, Georgia, which I visited with Georgia congressman Mac Collins to assess its needs.

Even though federal "pork" is always criticized, I do not apologize for obtaining federal funds to improve Nevada. Every member of the House wants "to bring home the bacon," and I was no different. The fact is, if the federal dollars available to Nevada are not spent in Nevada, they will be spent somewhere else. So if a Nevada military base had a worthwhile project for which it needed funding, it was likely to get a favorable hearing from me. It was good for the military, and it was good for the Nevada economy. One of my priorities was improved housing for military personnel and their families. As an "army brat," I knew the needs firsthand. I was able to help with funding a long list of new construction projects and improvements, including living quarters for families at the Fallon Naval Air Station and new quarters for visiting airmen at Nellis Air Force Base.

Because of my work, installations in Nevada have better facilities to assist in our nation's military preparedness, ranging from an aircraft maintenance hangar at Fallon to new runway aprons at Nellis. My impact continued even after I left Congress. During my last year on the Appropriations Committee, I was able to secure more than $44 million for construction at Fallon and $22 million for Nellis that was included in the 1997 budget year. Other appropriations helped improve the Nevada Air National Guard at the Reno airport, the Indian Springs Air Force Base, the Army National Guard's Clark County Armory, and more.

The best parts about being in the House are finding out that your state is important and making friends with colleagues and those you meet over the years. For westerners, the worst part was the long commute practically every weekend. Having little or no control over your schedule was also tough. I do not have any legislative or congressional regrets. The only regrets I do have are about the few times when I was not able to be with my family on some special or important occasion.

The biggest change in the House I saw over the years was the lack of comradeship and friendliness as the makeup of the Congress changed. Before that, it was always partisan but never personal or unpleasant. The biggest improvement that could be made is a decrease in partisan fighting.

America is a huge country of people with diverse backgrounds and points of view. The process would be better if all sides of an issue were respected, heard, and considered. There are good people serving their districts, but the emphasis seems to be growing more political. The political philosophy in the country is divided. All viewpoints should be heard in the debates on public policy before reaching a consensus decision.

I sometimes think I could describe my fourteen years in Congress on a weekly basis by saying, "I flew to Reno. Then I flew to Elko, Ely, Yerington, Fallon, Hawthorne, Las Vegas, Winnemucca, Battle Mountain, Eureka, Tonopah, Panaca, Lovelock, and/or Pahrump, and then I flew to Washington, D.C. And between flights I attended meetings, hearings, lunches, dinners, and other events seven days a week, in Nevada and in Washington." When people ask me if I miss my life in Congress, I just smile in relief and say, "I miss my friends."

After we settled back into Reno, for the next two years George and I enjoyed the time we had left together. He died on December 19, 1998. George was always my rock, in both public and private life. Like any other widowed spouse, I had to learn to do the things George had always done, such as our accounting, investing, and preparing taxes. While I had paid the household bills during our married life, he had taken care of the rest of our finances. Around the house, if repairs needed to be done, he either did it himself or arranged for someone to do it. I had to learn to do that myself, too.

But it was the companionship and sharing of activities that I missed the most. During my entire fourteen years in Congress, George was at my side, supportive and helpful and always a positive influence. Away from work, George and I shared the kids and grandkids, golfed together, and went to sporting events. We traveled together in our motor home and went camping. None of that is fun alone, so I don't do it anymore, unless my children invite me to join them. Six years after his death, I still miss George tremendously.

As I mentioned before, it was the second time that I had been widowed. George's death affected me in a different way than my husband Ken Dillon's death did. Ken's death was unexpected and was more of a jolt. I was left with three young children, and I had to maintain, as much as possible, a normal life for them. I might cry after Kenny and Tommy went off to school for the day, but not in front of Susie, who was only three and a half years old and still home. There were tears when George died, of course, often months after he had died, at unexpected times when I thought of him.

George had been ill for some time and had required more and more chemotherapy and increasing doses of medications, so his death was not unexpected. We had been forewarned of his declining health, and he became progressively weaker and could no longer do the things he enjoyed, such as travel and golf. Like anyone confronted with the terminal illness of a family member, I knew his time was short, but part of me also expected him to recover. Even though I expected his death, it wasn't any easier to accept. It was still a shock when he died.

Before George's death we bought ourselves a Christmas present, a Maltese dog named Charlie. He keeps me active and is good company. While I miss George terribly, I'm not lonely. I'm fulfilled with kids and grandchildren and great-grandchildren that I see all the time, and I have reasons to get up every day. I can't envision another relationship with a man (even though I've had an offer or two). While some parts of my life are coming to an end, I'm lucky that I still have good health.

After George's death, I returned to a normal daily life of maintaining the house, shopping for groceries, running errands. Of course, I am involved in politics and the community. I served as Republican national committeewoman for Nevada from 1996 to 2000. The highlight of that experience was attending the Republican National Convention in Philadelphia in 2000 and voting to nominate George W. Bush for president.

I have occasionally participated in "Congress to Campus" visits sponsored by the Association of Former Members, in conjunction with the John C. Stennis Center for Public Service and the Center for Democracy and Citizenship. I've visited campuses in Florida, Missouri, and Utah. These programs usually include a Republican and a Democrat. I also attended a three-day conference at the Carl Albert Center for Congressional Research and Studies in Oklahoma.

I have given a few speeches across the state, such as to the Nevada Cattlemen's Association in Winnemucca and the Women in Mining group

Charlie is my friend and housemate. In September 2004 he had his sixth birthday.
George and I bought him as a Christmas present for each other in 1998,
shortly before George died. Collection of Barbara F. Vucanovich

in Battle Mountain. And I have spoken to a few Republican groups and to some breast cancer organizations. I have not ridden in a parade, however, nor have I even watched one.

I enjoy my free time for leisure activities, but still make time for community activities. I have been active on the board of trustees of the St. Mary's Health Network, on the Casa de Vida board, and as ambassador for the Congressional Award Program. Since I was active in Congress on health care issues, the St. Mary's Health Network board is a natural extension of my interest.

The best part of retirement is having control over my schedule. I have not had to participate in any compulsory travel. The trips I've taken have been by choice and for pleasure. With Patty, Kenny, and Sandra, I toured Rome and Florence with the Former Members of Congress group, at our own expense. The group arranged for a tour of the American Embassy and the Vatican, where we met with high-ranking priests and bishops on the

Catholic Church's charitable and social justice activities in the world. We attended a reception at the embassy to the Vatican hosted by Ambassador Lindy Boggs, a former Democrat member of Congress with whom I served.

One of the highlights of my retirement was being appointed by President Bush in 2002 to serve on the President's Commission on White House Fellowships. The nonpartisan program was founded in 1964 by President Johnson and provides firsthand experience at the highest levels of government for exceptional young men and women. Fellows also participate in educational roundtable discussions with leaders from the private and public sectors and in domestic and international trips to study U.S. policy in action.

Selection as a White House Fellow is highly competitive and based on a record of real professional achievement early in one's career, plus evidence of leadership potential and a proven commitment to public service. Following their fellowship year, participants are expected to repay the privilege by applying what they have learned as leaders in their communities, in their professions, and in public service.

There is a regional selection process, after which about thirty people are named national finalists. The President's Commission on White House Fellowships interviews the finalists and recommends between eleven and nineteen candidates to the president for a one-year appointment as White House Fellows. I was disappointed last year because only one of the finalists was a woman.

The commission received 13 percent more applications this year than last. The number of women applicants rose more than 28 percent over last year. The gender breakdown, however, is 63 percent male to 37 percent female. I know of only two Nevadans who have been appointed White House Fellows: Karen Galatz and Dennis Cobb, both from Las Vegas. I look forward to the White House Fellows program activities because I see such great promise for the future of our country. The fellows are among the best of America's young people.

It has been an interesting journey from my birth at Camp Dix, New Jersey, to Reno, Nevada, and Washington, D.C. After a trip of fourscore years, my biggest hope is that I have been able to pass on the lessons I learned from my parents to my own children, grandchildren, and great-grandchildren.

My expectation for them has always been that they will have well-rounded lives, as I believe mine has been, and that they will contribute to society and to their families. The contributions should not be just volunteer service, but a true giving of themselves, setting an unselfish example for others. I have always expected my children to be good citizens, and to do so not because they will get something in return but because they care about their families and where they live.

I'm proud of being the first woman elected to federal office from the State of Nevada. I am a traditional woman, but I never felt unequal because I was a woman. I thought that I could do what I needed and wanted to do. I have never felt limited by my gender.

I represented the state fairly and honorably for fourteen years. I considered it high praise when one man told Patty that he could sleep well knowing I was in Washington protecting Nevada's interests. Another man told me, "Barbara, you did it with dignity and class."

The measure of my life, I believe, and the most satisfaction I have as I look back, is that I raised a good and loving family, sometimes under difficult circumstances. I had setbacks, of course, but I was never defeated, and I always felt I was blessed. My own mother was a wonderful role model; I hope I've been the same.

COMMITTEE ASSIGNMENTS

1983–84
INTERIOR AND INSULAR AFFAIRS
Subcommittees
Energy and Environment
Mining, Forest Management, and Bonneville Power Administration
Oversight and Investigations

SELECT COMMITTEE ON CHILDREN, YOUTH, AND FAMILIES

1985–86
HOUSE ADMINISTRATION
Subcommittees
Accounts
Elections
Services

INTERIOR AND INSULAR AFFAIRS
Subcommittees
Energy and Environment
Mining and Natural Resources
Public Lands

SELECT COMMITTEE ON CHILDREN, YOUTH, AND FAMILIES

1987–88

House Administration
Subcommittees
Accounts
Elections

Interior and Insular Affairs
Subcommittees
Energy and Environment
Mining and Natural Resources
National Parks and Public Lands

Select Committee on Children, Youth, and Families

1989–90

House Administration
Subcommittee
Accounts

Interior and Insular Affairs
Subcommittees
Energy and Environment
General Oversight and Investigations
Mining and Natural Resources

Select Committee on Aging

Select Committee on Children, Youth, and Families

1991–92

Appropriations
Subcommittees
Legislative
Rural Development
Agriculture and Related Agencies

Interior and Insular Affairs
Subcommittees
Mining and Natural Resources
National Parks and Public Lands

1992–93

APPROPRIATIONS

Subcommittees

Agriculture, Rural Development, Food and Drug Administration
and Related Agencies
Military Construction, Ranking Minority Member

NATURAL RESOURCES

Subcommittees

Energy and Mineral Resources
Insular and International Affairs
Oversight and Investigations

1994–95

REPUBLICAN CONFERENCE SECRETARY

APPROPRIATIONS

Subcommittees

Interior
Military Construction, Committee Chair
VA, HUD, and Independent Agencies

INDEX

Italic page numbers refer to illustrations

Kenneth "Kenny" Price, Jr.; Dillon, Michael "Mike" Francis; Dillon, Susan "Susie" Brown; Dillon, Thomas "Tommy" Brown

China, 12, 263–66

Churchill County (Nev.), 57, 87, 115

Clark, William, 243

Clark County (Nev.), 51, 57, 63, 65, 75–76, 92, 115, 129, 134, 145–46, 148, 151

Clinton, Bill, 29, 95, 103, 105, 118, 150, 170, 173, 181, 188, 215, 224, 235, 244–45, 248–49, 251, 272, 289

Clinton, Hillary (Mrs. Bill), 173, 188, 193, 250–51

Coats, Dan (R-IN), 156

Cobb, Dennis, 294

Collins, Mac (R-GA), 290

Colorado River, 204

comparable worth (employee-compensation basis), 188, 190–91, 289

Condit, Bill, 147

Congressional Award Program, 293

"Congress to Campus," 292

Conservative Opportunity Society (COS), 120, 155–56, 238

Contract with America, 153–55, 169–73, 228

Cox, Chris (R-CA), 165

Craig, Larry (R-ID), 142, 217

Crane, Phil (R-IL), 155

Cranmer, Amelia (great-granddaughter), 186, 285

Cranmer, Madelein (great-granddaughter), 186, 285

Cranmer, Maggie. See Dillon, Maggie

Cranmer, Patrick (great-grandson), 285

Cranmer, Toby (grandson-in-law), 285

Crapo, Mike (R-ID), 161

Crouch, Jordan, 41

C-Span, 156–57

Culver, John (D-IA), 252

Czechoslovakia, 267, 281

Dannemeyer, Bill (R-CA), 155

Davis, Janaya (step-granddaughter), 186

debates, 88, 91, 143–44, 150, 245; Presidential Debate Commission, 251–53

DeFazio, Pete (D-OR), 218

defense, 211. See also military

DeLay, Tom (R-TX), 156, 159, 161, 163, 261

Derwinski, Ed (R-IL), 155

Desert Shield. See military

Desert Storm. See military

De Wine, Mike (R-OH), 95, 96

Dibitonto, Sam, 67

Dillon, Casey (granddaughter), 44, 88, 108, 177, 186

Dillon, Cathy DeTar (Mrs. Thomas; daughter-in-law), 33, 75, 108, 251

Dillon, Heather (granddaughter), 44, 88, 108, 177, 186

Dillon, Jennifer (granddaughter), 44, 108, 186, 274

Dillon, Katie (granddaughter), 75, 108

Dillon, Kenneth "Kenny" Price, Jr. (son), 18, 20, 24, 25, 30, 31, 32–33, 44, 60, 88, 94, 108, 110, 177, 216, 274, 292–93

Dillon, Kenneth Price (second husband), 18–19, 23–24, 25, 30, 33–34, 35, 40–41, 46–51, 61; death of, 24–26, 43, 60, 292; education of, 23; law practice of, 23; marriage of, 23, 50; public administrator campaign of, 44–45;

Dillon, Maggie (Mrs. Toby Cranmer; granddaugher), 75, 108, 186, 285

Dillon, Michael "Mike" Francis (son), 18, 20–21, 23, 24, 25, 30, 31, 32, 36, 51, 60, 94, 108, 110, 150, 188, 216, 286

Dillon, "Mike Jr." (grandson), 108, 110, 145, 153, 216, 235, 274

Dillon, Nora (Mrs. Chris Golden; granddaughter), 75, 108, 186, 274, 285

Dillon, Patricia "Patty" Anne. See Cafferata, Patricia "Patty" Dillon

Dillon, Patrick (grandson), 75, 108, 216, 235

Dillon, Sandra Ward (Mrs. Kenneth; daughter-in-law), 33, 44, 108, 251, 293

Frenzel, Bill (R-MN), 192
Fulstone, Richard, 63
fund-raising, 63, 78, 82, 85–87, 90–91,
    138–40

Galatz, Karen, 294
gaming, 120, 200–201, 207–9, 287
Gardella, Hazel, 46, 59, 61–62, 64–67
Gardella, Louis, 46
Gardnerville (Nev.), 82
Garn, Jake, 71
Gaylord, Joe, 78
Gejdenson, Sam (D-CT), 218
Genoa (Nev.), 81
George, Dennis, 83
Gephardt, Dick (D-MO), 162, 196
Getto, Virgil, 57
Gibbons, Jim, 32, 214, 286
Gingrich, Marianne (Mrs. Newt), 191
Gingrich, Newt (R-GA), 78, 120, 153–59,
    161–62, 165–66, 168, 170–73, 191,
    193–94, 197–98, 229–30, 238
Gojack, John, 85, 89
Gojack, Mary, 70, 79, 81, 83, 85–87,
    89–92, 135, 185
Golden, Chris (grandson-in-law), 285
Golden, Elizabeth (great-granddaughter),
    186, 285
Golden, Nora. See Dillon, Nora
Golden, Philomena (great-granddaughter),
    186, 285
Goldfield (Nev.), 209
Goldwater, Barry (R-AZ), 64–65, 68, 249
Gore, Al, 249
Gorman, Harold, 41
Gorrell, Bob, 89
Gragson, Oran, 61
Gramm, Phil (R-TX), *212*
Grassley, Charles (R-IA), 263
Graves, Dick, 28
Gray, Les and Aleta, 45
grazing. See ranching
Great Basin National Park, 204
Greenspun, Hank, 61

Gregg, Judd (R-NH), 156
Guam, 257
Guild, Clark, 23–24, 50
Guinn, Kenny and Dema, 56
Guisti, Marshall and Marvel, 45
Gustavson, Don, 85

Hale, Norma and Preston, 25
Hall, Linn, 41
Hammersmith, Vivan, 41
Hansen, Jim (R-UT), *212*, 217
Harriman, Pamela, 252
Hastert, Denny (R-IL), 161
Hawkins, Gus (D-CA), 191
Hawthorne (Nev.), 32, 49, 80, 82, 122,
    151, 291
Havel, Vaclav, 267
Haycock, Claire, 184
Hecht, "Chic," 52–53, 59, 90–91, 153, 202,
    209, *212*, 220, *221*, 222–24, 250
Heck, Linden, 142
Heckler, Margaret (R-MA), 77
Hefner, Bill (D-NC), 164, 167
Henderson (Nev.), 76
Herger, Wally (R-CA), 169
Heston, Charlton, 151
Hicks, Larry, 214–15
Hill, Olive (Mrs. Rex Shroder), 42
Hinckley, Ward, 183
Hobson, David (R-OH), 161
Hodel, Don, 142, 217–18
Holbrook, Richard, 267
Hollings, Ernest "Fritz" (D-SC), 263
Holt, Marjorie (R-MD), 77, 189, 192
Hoover, Herbert, 4
Hoover Dam, 5
Horton, Bob, 47–48, 63, 71
Horton, Dick, 26, 47–48, 61, 63, 80,
    145, 214
Huckabee, Jerry (D-LA), 218
Humboldt County (Nev.), 81, 87, 115
Humphrey, Marvin and Lucy, 45
Hungary, 266, 271, 281
Hunter, Duncan (R-CA), 156

Redd, Si, 28

Regula, Ralph (R-OH), 112, 218

Reid, Harry (D-NV), 53, 59, 67–69, 91, 95, 112, 128–29, 131, 145, 184, 202–4, 206, 214, 220, 221, 222–28, 261

Reno (Nev.), 21, 23–24, 32–33, 35, 39–43, 46, 49, 61, 65, 68, 71, 77, 83, 87–88, 90, 97, 100, 114, 121, 123–24, 134, 138, 142, 149–51, 210, 214, 236–37, 276, 286, 290, 294

Republican, 23, 46, 59, 65, 67, 94–96, 99, 109, 111, 114, 118–19, 121–22, 129–31, 134, 136, 145, 147, 150–52, 153–73, 187, 192–93, 197–98, 236–38, 254, 293; committees, 77–78, 82, 99–101, 109, 115, 147, 153, 178, 190 (*see also* National Republican Congressional Committee [NRCC]); Conference, 97, 109, 116–17, 121, 165, 190; Leadership, 99, 116, 120–21, 153–73; National Committee, 67, 71, 178, 242; majority in the House of Representatives, 153–73; National Committeewoman, 31, 45, 292; National Convention, 48, 67, 236, 240, 245, 292; Party, 31, 44–47, 51, 59, 67–68, 128, 146, 148, 158, 163, 173, 187, 194, 197, 223; Policy Committee, 116, 160, 165; Women's Club, 45, 49, 61, 82; women's group, 192–93

Rhoads, Dean, 85–88

Richardson, Bill, 95

Ride, Sally, 119. *See also* space program

Ridge, Tom (R-PA), 94, *96*

Riggs, Roger, 132

Roberts, James, 151

Robinson, Pam, 256, *259*

Rodino, Peter (D-NJ), 191

Rogich, Sig, 65

Roosevelt, Franklin D., 4, 19, 44, 235–36, 237

Ros-Lehtinen, Ileana (R-FL), 100, 189, 192

Rostenkowski, Dan (D-IL), 240

Roukema, Marge (R-NJ), 189

Round Mountain (Nev.), 28

Ruby Marshes (Nev.), 120

Russell, Charles, Marge, Clark and David, 50

Russia, 258, 274–82

Sagebrush Rebellion, 207, 248

Saiki, Pat (R-HI), 194–95

Saipan, 257

Santini, Jim, 52–53, 67, 128–29, 131, *221,* 240, 247

Saudi Arabia, 269, *270,* 271

Sawyer, Grant, 61, 66

Schwarzkopf, Norman, *270,* 271

Second Congressional District, 75–76, 79, 85, 124, 135–36, 145, 200

Seiberling, John (D-OH), 205–6, 218

Seraphine, Sister, 43

Serbian, 28–29, 113, 194, 267

Sferrazza, Pete, 132–36, 141, 145, 148–50

Shamir, Yitzhak, 269

Sharp, Phil (D-IN), 217

Shroder, Olive. *See* Hill, Olive

Shumway, Norn (R-CA), 229

Silver Springs (Nev.), 122

Sinnott, Bill, 65

Smith, Alfred E., 4

Smith, Bob (R-OR), 156, 219

Smith, Chris (R-NJ), 100, 199

Smith, Denny (R-OR), 217

Smith, Lee, 110

Smith, "Tank," 45

Smith, Virginia (R-NE), 147, 189, 192–93

Snowe, Olympia (R-ME), 181

Social Security, 143–44, 149–50, 211–12

Solomon, Gerald (R-NY), 161, 165, 264

Soroptomists, 82

Source Income Tax. *See* taxes

Sourwine, Jay, 214

space program, 119

Sparks (Nev.), 83

Sparks Nugget. *See* John Ascuaga's Nugget

Spoo, Jim, 141–44

Stallings, Richard (D-ID), *212*

State of the Union addresses, 113–115

Sterns, Cliff (R-FL), 160
St. Mary's Hospital, 29, 42, 88, 177, 293
Storey County (Nev.), 115, 136
Struve, Larry, 25
Sundquist, Don (R-TN), 94, *96*
Susich, Johnny, (brother-in-law), 28
Sweden, *259*
Symms, Steven (R-ID), *212*

Taiwan, 263
Tallon, Robin, Jr., 261
Tarrance & Associates, 92, 133
Tavernia, George, 63
taxes, 87, 121, 134, 209–10, 289
Taylor, Reese, 71
Teresa, Mother, 188, 261, *262*
Thomas, Clarence, 191
Toiyabe National Forest, 206
Tonopah (Nev.), 28, 49, 82, 122, 206, 286
Topol, Nate, 82
"Tough Grandmother." *See* Vucanovich, Barbara F.
tourism, 200, 209
Towell, David, 67, 80
Traficant, James, Jr. (D-OH), 97
Trounday, Roger, 63
Troy, Jackie, 102, 177
Truckee River, 19, 22, 29, 81, 151, 203–4, 289
Truman, Harry, 44, 235

Udall, Mo (D-AZ), 191, 201, 208, 217, 257
Ukraine, 258
Ulrey, Bill, 142
University of Nevada, 28–29, 51, 57–59, 66, 91, 95, 120, 151
U.S. Association of Former Members of Congress, 286, 292–93
U.S. Atomic Energy Commission, 201
U.S. Bureau of Land Management (BLM), 111, 205, 207
U.S. Department of Interior, 256, 272–73
U.S. Forest Service, 205, 207, 272

U.S. Military Academy at West Point. *See* West Point
U.S. National Park Service, 206, 272–73
USS Nevada, 212–13

Vargas, George, 23
Vento, Bruce (D-MN), 218
vice presidents. *See* Bush, George H. W.; Gore, Al; Quayle, Dan; Nixon, Richard
Volcker, Paul, 113
Volkmer, Harold (D-MO), 100
Vucanovich, Anna (mother-in-law), 113
Vucanovich, Barbara F., *7, 17, 24, 27, 31, 56, 58, 62, 96, 98, 101, 105, 108, 130, 132, 182, 212, 218, 221, 244, 246, 258–59, 262, 270, 276;* Advisory Board of Higher Education, 66; Cardinals (Appropriations Committee), 166–69; caucus, 40, 99–100, 171, 189, 228–29; Central Intelligence Agency briefing attendance, 117; child care center, 191–92; children of, *31, 108;* committees, 97–102, 109–10, 115, 117, 120, 147, 151, 158, 163–69, 172; 181, 189, 191–92, 200, 208, 211, 217–18, 229, 257, 260, 272, 289–90, 297–99; community activities, 40–44 (*see also* St. Mary's Hospital); conference secretary, 159–61; Corrections Day Committee, 165–66; Department of Agriculture meeting attendance, 117; early life of, 3–8, 16–18; education of, 3–4, 6, 119; employment history of, 35–39, 60–66, 69–70, 280; family heritage of, 8–16; Federal Aviation Administration, struggles by, 122; issues, 87, 90, 121, 134, 142–43, 147, 150–51, 153–54, 180 (*see also* abortion, breast cancer, Colorado River, comparable worth, Contract with America, defense, 55-miles-per-hour speed-limit law, gaming, Great Basin National Park, judges, mining, North American Free